Live Like You Mean It

Live Like You Mean It

Discovering the life you were made for

ERIC DELVE

HODDER &
STOUGHTON

First published in Great Britain in 2010 by Hodder & Stoughton
An Hachette UK company

1

Copyright © Eric Delve 2010

A CIP catalogue record for this title is available from the British Library

ISBN 978 0 340 99503 7

Typeset in Plantin Light by Ellipsis Books Limited, Glasgow

Printed and bound in the UK by CPI Mackays, Chatham ME5 8TD

Hodder & Stoughton policy is to use papers that are natural, renewable and recyclable products and made from wood grown in sustainable forests. The logging and manufacturing processes are expected to conform to the environmental regulations of the country of origin.

Hodder & Stoughton Ltd
338 Euston Road
London NW1 3BH

www.hodderfaith.com

Contents

To Pat, my co-adventurer since 1962, and to the children who joined us:

Sarah, Glenn, Joanne, Rebekah, Andrew and Grace

With love and gratitude

YOU ARE UNIQUE

You are UNREPEATABLE

At the moment of your conception, approximately
300 million sperm fought for the privilege of fertilising one
of about 350 thousand eggs stored in your mother's ovaries.
Calculate the odds!

You are literally unrepeatable. Even if it were possible to
repeat the act that conceived you from now until the end of
time, the same combination could never be reproduced.

Remember this – the sperm that made it beat
incredible odds!

The possibilities in YOU are literally incalculable.

Prologue

BEGIN BEFORE THE BEGINNING

Potential. You are full of it! What is more, that is true of every single human being. The tragedy is that the vast majority of our potential may be unrealised. The difference between those whose potential is realised and the rest of us is leadership – not so much the leadership of others, but self-leadership. My phrase for that is Intentional Living. It releases inspiration. It energises us. It is the theme of this book.

Because self-leadership is all about character, we can learn most from the literature that has helped to shape the character of some of the greatest men and women over the centuries. Of these, no writings have been more influential than the ancient writings that form the basis of our Judeo-Christian value system. Stripped of religious jargon, they are the most comprehensive guide to personal development the world has ever seen.

Our task in the next twelve chapters is to liberate a life-transforming message from centuries-old encrustations of religious jargon and prejudice. The vitality and dynamic of these powerful stories have provided inspiration and a sense of personal destiny for some of the greatest people in history. Sir Francis Drake, Horatio Lord Nelson, Sir Winston Churchill, Abraham Lincoln, Daniel Webster, Thomas Jefferson, Ben Franklin, George Washington, Tolstoy, J. S. Bach, Mary Slessor, Gladys Aylward, Mother Teresa, Gordon of Khartoum, Elizabeth Fry, Edith Cavell, Brigadier Orde Wingate, Field Marshal Lord Montgomery of Alamein and William Shakespeare are just a few names, chosen almost at random, from the huge number of movers and shakers who were inspired by these writings to become the shapers of their worlds.

What about us? How do we emulate them? How do we become men and women of lasting influence; people like them, so that our significance outlives us? Part of the answer must be that we allow ourselves to be shaped, and our character to be sculpted, by the same influences that made them amazing.

It is extraordinary that the person of greatest influence in the history of the last 2000 years has been Jesus of Nazareth. Think of it: a Middle-Eastern peasant from a backwater of the Roman Empire took a small group of farmers, fishermen and office workers (not to mention at least one violent revolutionary) and welded them into a force that was powerful enough to penetrate to every corner of the Roman Empire and eventually to dominate the history of Europe for 1700 years. More people now belong to the Christian faith than to any other religion on the globe, and the Church worldwide is growing faster than ever before.

Today, Jesus Christ has greater influence on this world than ever. How did he do it? What principles of self-leadership can we discern in his story and how can we apply them today? That is the purpose of this book – to uncover and apply the lessons of the life of Jesus for today, so that we can move beyond survival to success, and beyond success to significance. This is the greatest adventure the world has ever known. I am inviting you to join me on the journey into the heart of your destiny.

At this point, I am reminded of the classic old joke in which a tourist in Ireland asks a local inhabitant the way to Dublin from some backwoods location, only to be told, 'Well now, sir, to be sure, if I were going there, I wouldn't be starting from here.'

You might think, 'This doesn't apply to me.' But you could ask, 'Where would I start?' Or even, 'Given the situation I'm facing, how could I get to the starting line?' But the point is that anyone can make this journey – and you can start from exactly where you are today.

GETTING TO THE STARTING LINE

How do you?

A man's wife committed suicide just a few months ago, leaving him with two children to bring up on his own.

A couple watched two of their children die over the course of ten years from a genetic degenerative disease.

A husband's young wife has been unfaithful, but pledged never to do it again.

A man is so bludgeoned by what life has thrown at him that he can barely look his loved ones in the eyes in the morning.

A young soldier blown up by a roadside bomb in Kabul is left 'dead from the waist down'.

A couple's first-born daughter, sparkling blue-eyed and wonderfully bright, catches measles encephalitis, and grows up with the mental age of a ten-year-old.

A husband walks out on his wife and children after twenty years to 'find himself' with a younger woman. The wife and children he abandoned are left alone.

Sister Mary Francis at Helen Hospice comforts young children day after day until they die.

A weary man of faith wants to finish well.

A woman with no faith wonders if there is hope.

How do they LIVE LIKE THEY MEAN IT?

Whatever *your* situation:

How do you?

How do I?

I only know one way – because, as far as I can see, nothing else works . . .

First, believing there is a Creator who has a purpose, who has *not* finished with me yet – or I would be dead!

Secondly, applying that belief – and forging it into five tools:

1. Honesty – Face the reality of the situation head on. State it brutally, without evasion.
2. Courage – No matter how bad this is, I can and I will get through it. I *will* overcome.
3. Trust – Believing there is a Creator who knows what he is doing. I commit myself into the hands of the Creator and surrender my circumstances to his control.
4. Passion – I am going to give it all I've got and when I run out, I will reach out and receive more.
5. Perseverance – No matter how I feel, whenever I want to give up, I am going to get up and get going. I will not let the circumstances defeat me.

So that's the way I would like you to approach this book – with honesty, courage, trust, passion and perseverance.

That's the only way I know to get through.

So let's get going.

Part 1

Being Yourself – and Much More

The greatest gift we have, the most valuable contribution we can make, is who we are. By our choices and relationships we can develop that to the full – one relationship in particular will bring everything into balance.

Chapter 1

Start from Who You Are

OUT IN THE WILD

Judean Wilderness, 1030 BC

Winter had definitely come early, and harshly too. Even as the boy thought it, a fresh gust of wind drove new flurries of snow across the valley, almost obscuring his view of the flock. The tops of the mountains to the west were white with snow. He knew that the mountain of Lebanon to the north was always crusted with snow during the winter. But for the mountains of Judea to have snow was unusual. It did not seem to be settling – yet. He worried that once darkness began to fall it would then settle. It would not be good to have to spend a night out in such conditions. But the prospect of leading the sheep out of the relative shelter of the valley into a snowstorm was even less appealing.

He clutched the old sheepskin coat around him, seeking to stop the snow seeping down into his woollen jerkin. As he moved, his hand involuntarily went to the bruise on his left cheek. Eliab might not be very quick on his feet, but his hand was heavy. He had made a mental note that next time he wound up his brothers, he would keep a good eye open. He smiled. Winding them up was so easy, and his quickness with words was his only real defence in a house where, since his mother's death, he no longer felt he belonged. Usually he could make the other brothers laugh. But David could not remember a time when Eliab had not resented him.

He knew that his mother, young and beautiful, coming into a household where the other boys were already in place, had not been welcomed by their mother or respected by them. He even wondered whether his father, Jesse, regretted his impulsive decision to take a younger wife. Unthinkingly, he sighed. He could hardly remember his mother's face now. But the smell of her, the feel of her skin and the assurance of her love he would always miss.

Some agitation among the flock alerted him. Only last week a lion driven out of the mountains by the unseasonal snow had tried to take off a straggler. A stone from his sling had crushed its eye socket, rendering the lion unconscious. His shepherd's knife had done the rest. He hoped it would not be another lion. They were hard enough to hit when the weather was clear, much harder in the snow.

Then he saw it, moving with the awkward grace of a heavy but powerful animal. His heart sank. It wasn't a lion – it was a bear. They were worse. The smooth stone was out of his pouch and into the sling before he had a chance to think. The bear was scrambling down the side of the valley. It would take one of the youngest and most vulnerable lambs. David was not prepared to let even the youngest one go – especially the youngest. He muttered, 'My father's flock, and the sheep of his pasture – not one do you get.'

The fear had gone as he moved quietly, the snow cushioning his footsteps. He knew the bear's eyesight was not particularly good, but his sense of smell would soon alert him to David's presence. He watched carefully. Bears were unpredictable; their movements more impulsive than a lion's. Then the right moment came. There was a moment's pause, almost as if time had stopped. Then the stone left the sling and caught the bear perfectly between the eyes. Even from where he stood the boy could hear the crack of the animal's skull as it dropped to the ground. Suddenly he was trembling, but grinning like a maniac too. Dancing.

He looked around him. The snow was letting up. Thank God! He moved down towards the gap that would take them out of the valley, with the sheep following. He would make it home before nightfall.

'IT IS YOUR DESTINY, LUKE!'

The story of the shepherd boy who was one day to become king, the lonely misfit who would draw thousands to follow him, the dreamer who became a man of action, has become iconic. It turns up in all sorts of places, in literature and in films. One of my favourites is Luke Skywalker in the first *Star Wars* trilogy. He faces all kinds of difficulty as well as his own conflicts. But finally he wins through. His greatest temptation comes at the moment when the evil emperor seeks to seduce him into changing sides with those words, 'It is your destiny, Luke! Join me and together we will rule the galaxy.' What about that word – Destiny? Is the concept nothing but a manipulative tool used to bring people into line? Or is there perhaps a real destiny, waiting for each one of us? For most people in the twenty-first century it is a concept that seems 'out there somewhere' – misfiled between Alpha Centauri and the Gas Bill. Too many confuse it with Fate – mysterious, inscrutable and random. Too many just think, 'Nothing I can do about it.' But it is the very heart of living.

CUSTOM-BUILT

You are unique. There has never been anyone like you on the face of the earth. There never will be, ever again. You are the only one there is – a unique expression of the imaginative genius of the creator. A work of art, equipped with all you need to become a human being such as the world has never seen before. You have the capacity to access the power that made and sustains all things. The difference between such people and those who never fulfil their potential is quite simply intentional living – living like you mean it: grabbing the creator's purpose and running with it.

Believing in a creator is relatively simple. It makes a lot of sense. Believing in no God is logically harder to sustain. Believing in God believing in me – *that* is the tough one. It is where the rubber hits the road: where the gearbox of faith transfers the raw power of God's engine to the wheels of our lives, and we begin to move – to get somewhere – becoming what we are meant to be: as someone wrote, 'in flesh-walking, breathing, speaking, laughing, weeping, dancing demonstrations of God's glory'. It is his purpose, his destiny for us. But it is not inevitable, an automatic consequence of existence or even of faith. It is, however, an always-available option. It can never be taken away from you. The new birth offered by Jesus makes us citizens of God's own country, brings us across the border and plants our feet on the road from here to eternity, but it is the following journey that counts.

At that point, too many look helplessly at their leaders, asking 'What now?' A wise leader says, 'Go on walking in the adventure of faith, in the power of the Spirit and friendship with Jesus.' But it doesn't need a leader to tell you: you can do it anyway, decide to get going – that is self-leadership.

What halts us? Fear: we could get it wrong. But that is not the worst thing that could happen. God's purpose for human beings is that we should take the initiative in our lives, taking responsibility in the home, workplace, community and church. He already knows we will get things wrong. We are not perfect. That is not a reason to hold back. His dream for us requires our active participation. The film most often voted 'best ever' by the British is *The Shawshank Redemption*. In a famous scene, Red, played by Morgan Freeman, stands in a hotel room looking at the beam from which 'Brooks' has hanged himself. 'Get busy livin', or get busy dyin' – that's goddamn right.' He's choosing to live. Most people live incidental lives; they do not live intentionally. Their lives lead them; they do not lead their lives. If we are not going to mindlessly follow the crowd, we have to *decide*. And the decision has to be reinforced daily so that it becomes a settled intention.

Intentional living is about choosing to believe in the God who is himself intentional and purposeful. Made in God's image, we are only truly alive when we live intentionally and purposefully. If we are resigned and fatalistic, we are running away from reality – escaping the call to initiative and responsibility. We are in fact abandoning our true humanity. Now that really is the worst thing that could happen! Because life is precious, wonderful, amazing. It is a one-shot deal. Truly too short to waste.

THE ART OF INTENTIONAL LIVING

We don't live in isolation. People who skilfully manipulate others can achieve short-term gains. But in the great game of life, users wind up being losers. Intentional living hugely influences the way we relate to others. It starts when we recognise that if we are going to get somewhere, we must change. If we are to become effective, significant in our lifetime – and maybe for generations to come – then we must begin *right now* to move from who we are to who we are meant to be. I am inviting you to consider Jesus as the key to that essential life change.

THE JESUS FACTOR – LIFE LESSONS FROM A FIRST-CENTURY GALILEAN

It has become fashionable in some circles to look at Jesus of Nazareth as a model of man-management, or a moral guide, or even a political visionary, but without reference to either his message or the part played in his life by the God he knew as Father. To consider his masterly management of relationships, his teaching or his vision without looking at the foundational relationship of his whole life is to discount the most important ingredient in his life. It is ridiculous, like trying to understand Mozart as a composer without reference to the fact that he was a musician! It can be done, but only by completely distorting him, reducing the whole study to nonsense. Jesus as a man makes sense only in the context of the all-pervading presence of the creator-sustainer whom he called Father. To get the maximum benefit from looking at Jesus, we must understand what it was that inspired him, fired him – and sent him into orbit.

'STAR TREK' AND THE PRIME DIRECTIVE

In the original *Star Trek* TV series the captain and crew of the starship *Enterprise* repeatedly had an opportunity to bring a great benefit to, and even save the lives of, some alien species, but only at the cost of violating the Prime Directive. So what was this Prime Directive? The United Federation of Planets, before it sent the *Enterprise* out on its voyage of discovery, had forbidden the crew to use their superior technology or scientific understanding, even to bring about a desirable end, if their action trampled on the freedom and understanding of those they were helping. They were to seek change by invitation, not by force. This put them in some pretty tricky dilemmas and enabled the scriptwriters to pose some interesting moral problems.

However, the creator of the universe apparently has an even more powerful and ambitious Prime Directive. 'Let us make humans in our image and to be like us,' says the book of Genesis. That is why the *Star Trek* approach is so appealing. It's God's original idea. Not to force us into what is best but to win us into relationship, partnership and friendship. This was a prime value for Jesus. To learn from it we must ask, 'What does the word "image" mean in this context?'

Like most children, I asked my mother, 'Where is God?' She replied, 'God is everywhere.' I asked why I could not see him. She told me he was invisible. I asked whether he was on other planets as well. She told me the whole universe, in fact everything that exists, was in God. Early in my childhood I found this Bible sound-bite, 'Let us make humans in our image.' I thought it meant that God was my shape. So now I had a huge – no – a simply ginormous invisible jelly, shaped like a human being, in which the whole universe was floating! OK, so that is ridiculous, but I was only a child.

These days I know that the word 'image', when used in that context, has a rather more technical and non-literal meaning. It's not about Versace suits and custom shades, either. In fact, applied to our relationship to our creator, 'image' goes right to the heart of what it means to be human. I want to outline eight facets of God's image to illustrate the awesome possibilities of being human.

1. Creative and Bold

When the creator made you in his image he made a *creator*, someone who would work together with him to shape their own destiny, to fulfil the possibilities he designed into them. You have a unique capacity to create, and to appreciate what others create.

The greatest artists have always been marked by a sense of humility and gratitude for the gift they have received. Every artist has known moments of pure inspiration: Paul McCartney writing 'Yesterday', one of the most beautiful songs of a whole generation, in just a few minutes; George Frederick Handel, composing *Messiah* over a few days. Poets, sculptors, painters, authors and dramatists have all known the moment when the spirit of creation grips them. Often they are humbled by their own abilities, even puzzled by the spark that inspires them. The problem is, most of us think creativity belongs exclusively to those kinds of people. But every one of us has been made to create. We will never find the fulfilment we seek if we do not release the creative impulse within us to give birth to something new and fresh. Don't let life or other people crush your creative gifts.

From the dreaming heart of the artist that is the creator God, you have come to live out his dream. No matter who you are, you have been equipped with a unique creativity. What could be more exciting – though it may be scary too. It will take courage, patience and self-discipline to hone that creative talent, but it will be worth it, and those around you will be grateful you did.

2. Personal

You are a once-only combination of genetic factors. Each human body is composed of hundreds of trillions of cells. In each cell are forty-six microscopic chromosomes. The main constituent of a chromosome is a nucleic acid, known as DNA. Each DNA molecule in your body is made up of two polynucleotide chains in the form of a double helix. Each one of those polynucleotides is made up of about three billion nucleotides. Each chain contains the code for approximately thirty thousand genes . . .

I wish I understood all that I've just written! The bottom line is: there will never be another person like you.

So, for a moment, hold before you the combination of genetic factors, socio-economic and cultural-emotional elements that have gone to make up the incredible, once-only event that is you. Imagine that into that mix the creator puts a tiny unique piece of himself, something never to be given to anyone else. In all creation, you are the only person equipped to receive, understand and express that part of the creator. If you can get a sense of that, then I guarantee it will be a 'Wow!' moment for you. You are amazing!

3. Rational

In spite of anything your school teachers may have told you, you do have a brain! And the brain you have is not appreciably smaller than anyone else's. It weighs about 1.5 kg (3.3 lbs) and it contains about one hundred thousand million nerve cells, or 'neurons'. If your brain cells were people, they would populate about twenty-five planets like the Earth. Even more amazing, the real action takes place along communication pathways running between the neurons, called axons. All the axons in your brain, if stretched out straight (not to be recommended), would stretch three times as far as to the moon and back.

The strange thing about it is that you probably use this awesomely powerful piece of equipment to about the same extent as everybody else. It has been calculated that our conscious minds use about 4 per cent of the brain's capacity (or perhaps 5 per cent if you are a genius of Einsteinian proportions). Oddly, in spite of all this brain capacity being available to us, quite a lot of stupid people believe they're really clever. Many more people limit their ability to use their minds by repeating to themselves that they are stupid. You are almost certainly brighter than you reckon. Rejection, ridicule and old scripts replaying in our heads create emotional baggage and cripple our ability to use the intellect we've been given. We have to face the reality of the primary part played by our emotions.

4. Emotional

Emotions – who needs them? And yet, who would want to live without them: love, joy, laughter, sadness, disappointment, longing, even fear, anger, agony and ecstasy take our lives, which would otherwise be lived in black and white, and give them colour. But how do we balance them? There are negative emotions and positive ones – and yet the negative ones can be the most valuable. Without anger, for example, slavery in the Western world would never have been abolished. Children would still be working down the mines and crawling up chimneys.

Emotions drive us in our best and worst moments. Without them, nothing would ever get done. Yet, because we don't know how to understand or control them, our emotions are so often a problem to us.

Wherever we go, we take our emotional baggage with us. We have no choice. It is a part of us. And our busy schedules allow little time to deal with feelings. Yet our emotions are there nonetheless, and they affect our judgement day after day. When I see a perfectly sane, wise human being do something completely stupid, I know they just tripped over another piece of baggage. Difficult as they are to manage, our emotions are invaluable, indispensable parts of who we are.

Most profoundly – the big one! We learn to love. More on that later.

5. Social/Relational

People are made for each other, made for relationship. Sadly, we live in an increasingly splintered society. The loss of community in our cities and towns is well documented, and often lamented. Increasing individualisation means not only families becoming isolated from other families, but members of those families drifting from their own family roots.

It is not surprising that, amid our growing affluence and the apparent near-perfection of our technologies, we find human beings, with all their tedious faults and failings, increasingly irritating. Wishing to cut out the hassle from our lives, we cut down our interactions with people who keep on getting things wrong and annoy us so much. But, of course, we are actually removing ourselves from the matrix of life that sustains us. We were made to relate to each other – and to our maker.

After all, the ultimate relationship must be with the one who invented personality, who is PERSON itself – God. We will not be emotionally healthy unless we begin to make the emotional connection, the spiritual journey into the heart of the maker. Like the gigantic robot, V'ger, in *Star Trek: The Motion Picture*, we are programmed to be united with the creator. This is not about becoming terribly religious and sentimental. It is about daring to set out on a spiritual journey.

6. Spiritual

The past three hundred years have seen the increasing prevalence of secular rationalism. What we cannot yet see is that these centuries have been an historical aberration in which we have tried to deny the spiritual factors that continue to drive us, whether we recognise them or not. However, towards the end of the twentieth century, spirituality suddenly became cool once more. High-powered executives were spending weekends in Trappist monasteries. Groups of department heads were taken away for bonding exercises. Designers were looking at the Chinese art of Feng Shui. Zen Buddhism became in vogue again. After the unrestrained materialism and monetarism of the 1980s, people longed to reassert the unseen spiritual side of their nature. 'Spirituality' became the latest buzz word. This trend became even more marked after the destruction of the World Trade Center in September 2001. Across the whole world millions who had lived as biological robots came alive to the reality of their spiritual emptiness. The financial crash of 2008–9 had the same kind of impact. Horrific events can wake us up to our spiritual hunger. This is inevitable. We're spiritual beings, and we are made for The spiritual being to interact with us so that, joined in union with the eternal spirit, we could give our souls wings and begin to fly.

7. Volitional/Moral

If you have read this far – thank you. I realise it is because you chose to. The maker and sustainer of all things made you in his image so you could exercise the power of choice on his behalf. He made you free to make choices.

One more thing – your choices may be free, but they are not without consequences. It is a moral universe reflecting the goodness of its creator. Choose right and it energises and revitalises you. Choose wrong and it depletes you, kills off your spirit. He offers guidance, but you *have* been given the power to choose.

It was a Jewish psychiatrist caught up in the most horrendous events of the twentieth century who effectively gave the lie to the philosophical blight of 'determinism'. Viktor Frankl wrote *Man's Search for Meaning* in 1946 as a result of his experiences during three years in Auschwitz and other Nazi death camps. Being a number, not a person, where every right and power to choose was stripped away from him, he discovered the power of choice. At any point he could be picked out of a line and beaten up or shot. But in the midst of it all he hit a glorious moment of understanding: 'The Nazi guards around me can make choices that determine everything that happens to me in the physical realm. They can determine my environment, they can rob me of my wife, my family and my life but they cannot take away the power I have to be me, nor my power of choice. I can choose how I respond to them.' Though his guards were outwardly free, they were prisoners of the system in which they worked. They had freedom of movement but he had true liberty of spirit. He was freer than his guards. When he left the camps and discovered that his wife and family had all been annihilated, he was undeterred. He founded a new school of psychology in Vienna based on what he discovered in the camps. Though unknown to many, to me he is one of the greatest heroes of the twentieth century.

His story gives the lie to the view that says your circumstances govern you, render you powerless. You have the power to choose but have to take authority to do so.

8. Regal

Whatever you conceive the maker of the universe to be, it is beyond dispute that the one who created it and keeps it going is sovereign over it. This means having effective say over its existence, development and completion. To be made in the image of that one who is sovereign is to be called 'to reign'. That is our calling.

For English people the word 'reign' is somewhat confused by the fact that our Queen is a constitutional monarch. Her power to govern – her ability to have an effective say – is severely constricted by the authority of Parliament and the superimposed power of the European Community.

For Americans and many nations who get to vote in *and* vote out their head of state, it is even more confusing. It is strange to find that absolute truth and ultimate authority in the universe are not subject to the vagaries of democracy. I don't get to vote God in or out! (The fight to dislodge him is exhausting and totally futile.) But once I accept God's sovereignty, his authority flows through me. I am released to be, like him, sovereign in my sphere of action, powerful and free to create something new and fresh. However, if I am to make an impact for good on others' lives, I have to begin with my own. Unless I take authority over my own behaviour, I will not ultimately be effective in the world around me. But I know I need help to change. I alone can make the vital decision to shout for help – and who better to ask than the maker? Once I give him the right to reign over me, he will be sovereign over my life. Only when I ask will he come in, and even then I can block his action. My transformation depends entirely on the creator having freedom of access to me. Therefore, that initial decision requires my continued agreement on a moment-by-moment basis. Paradoxically, yielding to him on that continuing basis sets me free to be myself and to reign in life. It sets me up for the adventure.

THE AWESOME VISION – AND A PROBLEM

This multifaceted vision of humanity is huge. Think about it: creative and bold, personal, rational, emotional, social/relational, spiritual, volitional/moral, and regal to boot. I would like to be like that, but things get in the way. In fact, my biggest problem in becoming what I should be is – ME.

I have a confession. It may not be a surprise. I have an anger issue. Driving on the motorway I get angry, even furious with other drivers. To myself or to a passenger I will observe irascibly, 'That kind of driving makes me so angry!' The most powerful word in that sentence is 'makes'. At that moment I'm ceasing to take responsibility for my own attitudes, words and actions. Why did I have a row with my partner? He/she makes me so angry. Why do I want to undermine that colleague? He/she makes me so furious.

In every single one of those sentences, the word 'makes' is the word of power. Yet it is not true. I'm using the word as an excuse to justify behaviour that I do not wish to change. Whatever they have said or done, no matter how terrible, **my response remains my responsibility**. If I am to reign in life I have to start by recognising that my thoughts, words and deeds are my responsibility.

The most powerful thing I can do today is recognise that in each facet of life I have been given the power to choose, and authority to take control and reign. Each such decision will help me grow in wisdom and authority. That will be evident to everybody in my life: family, friends and colleagues. But they will need to see that my decisions are coming from understanding and wisdom, rather than being knee-jerk responses produced by weakness, insecurity, fear and anger.

In the end our ability to extend effective influence over different areas of life will depend entirely upon our trustworthiness. Mastery of the outside world must be preceded by mastery of our inner world. We all need to be affirmed and approved, to be loved – and to know who we are. These are the most basic needs of any child, and just as much so of the adult the child becomes. Yet many of us grow up without these things. It is not surprising if there is deep-seated anger like a hard knot, a ball of tension and rage, right at the heart of wounded people. We have rarely been taught, or had modelled to us, how to deal with anger in an appropriate and constructive way. Consequently, it rears its head in unexpected ways: it can tear us apart, wreck relationships and destroy our careers. Worse, even if apparently brought under control, the seething mass of rage within us may go cold and become deadly malice, which results years later in clinical depression. As a doctor friend of mine puts it, 'Big boys don't cry – they just get heart attacks.'

Or they can change, and discover a new dynamic.

Malcolm Muggeridge was one of Britain's most prominent atheists and sceptics. But in 1982, after completing his book *Chronicles of Wasted Time*, he converted to Christ, becoming a Roman Catholic. Like another prominent intellectual atheist, C.S. Lewis, who converted to Christ after a long struggle, Muggeridge was surprised by the joy he felt. He said, 'Joy is the most characteristic and uplifting of the manifestations of conversion. It's rapture, an inexpressible joy which suffuses our whole being, making our fears dissolve into nothing and our expectations all rise heavenwards.'

Joy and anger are totally opposed and completely incompatible. Selfish anger, bitterness, un-forgiveness and revenge – sing the bass line in hell's song. We can never be happy as long as we allow their song to echo through us. That is why we have to learn to take authority over our anger. It cannot be allowed to govern our lives or it will ruin them.

So, we need to look for and maximise every occasion of joy in our lives. The beauty of a sunset, autumn leaves blowing in the breeze, the moonlight on the waves of the sea, the fierce energy of a waterfall, seeing the ball hit the back of the net, the triumph of crossing the line for a try or a touchdown, hitting a home run, the joy of a good bottle of wine shared with friends, seeing my children marry, the sheer fun of being with people to whom I owe nothing and from whom I seek nothing, with whom I'm simply able to be.

I can make sure I build that joy into myself by gratefully accepting it as a gift from the creator, and I can help myself remember it by journalling. Keeping a journal, especially to record some of the great events of my life, can ensure that, on days when it seems as though the rain will never stop, the cloud cover is about three feet above my head, and everybody hates me (including me), I'll be able to remind myself that there have been good days before. And that gives me every reason to believe that there will be good days again.

We all carry baggage from the past – old wounds, insecurities, fears – and may well find ourselves programmed to respond destructively to certain stimuli. One of my problems is technology. I get angry when it does not respond as I think it should. I suspect I am not alone in wanting to take an axe to my computer! Up to now I've taken the attitude that if I am angry with an inanimate object, no one else is being harmed and it is my right to shout and scream as much as I like.

However, I am becoming aware that even when totally alone, as I might be on the motorway, giving way to rage damages me and depletes my self-respect. In other words, I am recognising that nothing in my life is more important than self-control. It's the key to everything.

Great! So that's that sorted. Just one problem – it's the most difficult thing of all to achieve. In fact (the apostle) Paul put it like this:

> What I don't understand about myself is that I decide one way
> but then I act another doing things I absolutely despise . . . I
> realise that I don't have what it takes. I can will it but I can't *do*
> it. I decide to do good but then I don't *really* do it. I decide not
> to do bad but then I do it anyway.
>
> I've tried everything and nothing helps. I'm at the end of my
> rope. Is there no one who can do anything for me?
>
> Romans 7:15, 18, 24a (*The Message*)

I can understand his desperation. I often feel like an actor who keeps on screwing up his entrances, missing his cues, getting his lines wrong, and falling over the furniture!

As William Shakespeare observed in *As You Like It*, 'All the world's a stage and all the men and women merely players.' If that's so, maybe I need help from the playwright! After all, he apparently wrote into the script the freedom for me to wander off the plot. Suppose the author of the human drama saw his creations heading down a disastrously wrong track, what would he choose to do? Stand by and let the whole world go to hell in a handcart? Shut down the whole experiment? Walk out of the theatre, leaving the errant actors to burn it down, destroying themselves in the process? Or would he intervene? Something says he would. But how? The actors have been given freedom. My character needs a rewrite – or rather a new nature. I need the playwright's help. However, the only way for the author to intervene without violating his creation is to step on stage himself, to join us as a member of the cast. He might send messengers. Eventually, though, he would have to enter the drama himself.

And the entrance of such a figure would have to be announced.

Nazareth, Kingdom of Herod the Great, 4 BC

Gabriel was commanded to go and visit a young girl in a town many of the humans regarded as 'godforsaken'. A smile passed through him at the thought. How funny they were: did they not know that God could never forsake anything he had made?

He stood inside the mud hut, waiting for the girl to turn round. She stood in the doorway, the sun shining on her hair and the broom in her hand, still busy with the dust that constantly drifted in from the street outside. The song of praise on her lips was more than just words: the Archangel recognised the note of authentic worship. She turned, concerned about why the mud hut behind her had suddenly become brighter than the sun-drenched hills beyond the village. Wonder and curiosity marked her face as she stepped into the room. At that moment, Gabriel almost thought himself back in Eden, such was the serenity and beauty that faced him. But even in her he could see the marks of sin. Dark worms of doubt and selfishness wriggled through even her soul.

'Greetings,' he said, 'you are highly favoured; God is with you.' Now doubts came clamouring round her thoughts, obscuring her faith. Gabriel sighed. It would have been nice, just once, appearing to a human, not to have to say 'Do not be afraid!' He went on: 'Mary . . .'

As the great pronouncement of the coming king unfolded, Mary realised with astonishment that the prayers of God's people had at last been answered, and the dream of every Jewish girl had become reality for her. She was to give birth to the Messiah, but – she blurted out the question – 'How can this happen? I have never had intercourse with a man.' The warmth of an affection deeper than she had ever known wrapped itself around her as the angel answered, 'The Holy Spirit will come upon you.' For a moment the words reminded her irresistibly of the headlong plunge of a falcon coming on its prey. Gabriel continued, taking up her image, changing it: 'The power of the Most High will overshadow you like a great bird. He will shelter you and follow you wherever you go.' With a sudden pang she realised, 'This child will not be Joseph's child.' The angel answered her thoughts: 'This child will be called the Son of God.'

'Then not even he will understand. I shall be utterly alone,' she thought. She knew what happened to girls who became pregnant before marriage. It was rare these days for such a girl to be stoned, but the looks would follow her down the street, along with the sniggers and constant innuendoes. She wondered what they would say about her. The village gossip, Adah from next door, would revel in this. She could imagine her now: 'Of course, it's always the religious ones who are worst. Really, I've always said that myself. You can't tell what they are like. They put on a great show but they are worse than the rest of us.' And Joseph was absent, buying scarce timber. Who would they claim was the father? She suddenly recognised that she prized her reputation more than anything else. She feared what they would say about her.

But then she realised with astonishment, 'He's waiting for me to answer. I can still say no.' For a moment she longed to deny him, to walk back into the world of normality, to live like all the others, with a comfortable God who made no demands, who could be kept at arm's length. But she knew herself. Life without the awareness of the presence of God would be no life at all. She would be so alone. She lifted her eyes again to the face of the angel. Knowing her thoughts, he said, 'You will not be alone. Elizabeth, your cousin, will understand.'

'Elizabeth?' said Mary, 'How could . . . ?'

'After being called barren for many years', said the angel, 'she is pregnant. God is the God who turns emptiness into fullness. Nothing is impossible for him. Where he is, things happen.' 'Then God has not left me alone,' she thought. The joy rose up within her, it bubbled and fountained, becoming certainty in worship richer than she had ever known before.

'I am God's servant,' she said. 'Let it happen just as you have said.'

Gabriel was conscious of a gladness that filled heaven from end to end, uncountable angels swept up into a dance of celebration. There was nothing more to be said. He lowered his head to her, recognising that in the moment of her 'Yes' the Word, God himself, the Son of the living and almighty God had entered her womb. At this very moment he could see the brightness of that single cell, soon to become man, at last as the creator had intended man to be.

THE FETUS BECAME THE BABY, THE BOY AND AT LAST THE MAN

No cheating – real humanity.

How did this unique human being grow into the wisdom that characterised his teaching, the inner confidence that enabled him to calmly confront the leaders of the nation and the power of the Roman Empire?

The stories told by his mother must have played a part. And for a boy growing up in Israel under the heel of the Romans, no story would have been as powerful as that of David. Israel's Warrior King.

Chapter 2

Be a Human among Humans

THE ANOINTING – DAVID

Bethlehem, 1028 BC

At the crest of the hill the old man stopped, looking down over the village. The heifer plodding beside him was glad of the rest. The sun-baked hillside shimmered in the heat. He took a deep breath. He had lived with danger all his life but this was a moment of peril greater than anything he had known before. If the king should hear! His thoughts darkened.

Never God's idea that, a king. God had wanted Israel to be governed by his judges, people set apart by the touch of God's Spirit and their evident gifts and talents, recognised by the consent of all the tribes, a Spirit-driven meritocracy. But, as so often in the past, Israel had turned against God's preferred way of doing things. Now they demanded a king 'like all the other nations'. Even now he could hear God's voice speaking to him: 'It's not you they have rejected, Samuel, it's me. I will give them what they want.'

Imagine that. God had given them what they asked for, even though he knew it was Plan B, substandard. Saul had been what everyone wanted, head and shoulders above any other man in the nation; and, once he got going, a good leader, a warlord of talent, courage and ability. But success had ruined him. Every victory became *his* victory, not the nation's, not God's. He forgot who had made him king. He was running from God. His outwardly growing self-confidence hid a gnawing self-doubt. Fear had led him to disobey the direct commands of God once too often. Now, God had sent Samuel to find another king. Once, Saul had loved Samuel as much as he loved Saul. But now Saul loved nobody and nothing so much as his own reputation and power. He had become very dangerous.

Samuel shook himself. Grieving for the past would do no good. Fear Saul's anger as he might, he trembled even more at the authority of the God of all the earth.

He was not far down the road into the village before the word began to spread. The children spotted him first. Then he saw the men assembling in the centre of the village. Sweaty-palmed, breathing nervously, their voices shook when they greeted him. Their smiles were broad – but false. He could smell the fear, and he knew why. The prophet of God, Israel's last judge, had come to their tiny village. He knew they would have their squalid secrets – the mistresses hidden away, the adulterous affairs, the dodgy deals. He had been resisting the corruption that so often went along with power since he was six years old. 'Nothing to worry about,' he assured them. 'I've just come to sacrifice and celebrate.' He saw their sighs of relief and smiled. He had been right about the dodgy deals.

His eyes sought out one man. 'Ah, Jesse. Make sure you bring all your sons to the feast; all of them, mind.' By late afternoon, the smell of roasting ox filled the village. Ceremonial presentations began. One by one the sons of Jesse stood before him; the eldest, tall, broad-shouldered, noble-looking. His father, obviously an ambitious man, had named him Eliab – God is my father. 'Yes!' he thought. 'This is the one.'

'No,' said the voice of God. 'Just because he looks good doesn't mean he's right. You look at the outside, I look at what's going on inside. He's not the one.'

The same thing happened with the next two, Abinadab – noble father – and Shammah – renowned. Jesse really was ambitious, he thought. There were four more after that whose names he didn't even bother to register and to each one of them God said, 'Not the one.'

'Are these all your sons?'

Jesse looked embarrassed. 'There is another one. He's only little; he's looking after the sheep.'

'Then you had better send for him, and we will wait to start the feast until he arrives.'

A few enquiries and he knew the story. Jesse's second marriage had not been a popular one. The young widow had brought with her two other children who had slotted in well enough with the others but David, the product of their union, was the family reject, the butt of his brothers' jokes and the object of their mockery. He was hardly ever at home, always out in the hills looking after the sheep and making up songs on the lyre that he carried with him at all times. But he had a reputation as a dead shot with his sling. Now the boy stood before him. Slim and wiry, he came dancing on the balls of his feet, like a born fighter. His eyes were bright and his face open, except for the cloud that crossed it when he spotted his father or his brothers. The old man's sharp eyes saw it all – a reject, but brighter than the rest of them put together. 'This is the one. Anoint him.'

He gathered the brothers around him and made them watch while he anointed the boy. The oil flowed down over his hair and his forehead, but Samuel recognised what no one else saw, the shock in those wide-open eyes when the Spirit of God hit the young man. It would be years before anyone else knew what Samuel knew: Israel had a new king.

CROSSING THE LINE AT TAPLOW

Thursday 25 September 2008

An otherwise unremarkable Thursday in a sequence of autumn days as people in the UK and all over the world became more and more accustomed to hearing that something that had once seemed quirky, the 'Credit Crunch', was rapidly assuming the dimensions of a financial tsunami, heading towards us at increasing speed.

One of the few people in the UK who truly understood what was coming, millionaire banker Kirk Stephenson, was having breakfast with his wife, Corrina, and his son, Lucas. At 7.45 a.m. he said goodbye to them perfectly normally, drove from his £3.5-million Chelsea townhouse to Taplow Station in Berkshire, left his car in the car park, and crossed a footbridge over the main

First Great Western Plymouth to Paddington line. Out of view of passengers on the platform, he leapt onto a railway line in front of a high-speed train. The driver reportedly said that Mr Stephenson appeared to stand and face him. The driver sounded his horn and slammed on the brakes, but at 100 miles per hour it took him a mile to bring the train to a standstill. Mr Stephenson died instantly.

Everybody who knew him was astounded at his actions. Some feared that the financier had succumbed to the stress of his taxing role at a leading company in the financial sector. People knew he was tense. Three days before, he had mentioned to his wife that he had thought of suicide but could not do it because of love for her and his son. Everybody agreed that Mr Stephenson was a devoted husband and father. Yet somehow, in the bleakness and loneliness of his hugely successful position, he presumably persuaded himself that ending his life in this way would be for their good. But we don't really know, because he did not talk to anyone about what he was contemplating. Maybe he felt he could not inflict the burden of these things upon his beautiful and perceptive wife. In spite of his vibrant social life and loving family background, he clearly felt completely isolated, alone with his troubles.

It was a pleasant enough autumn morning, the warmth of the sun beginning to be felt with a light breeze from the north-east, as he strode resolutely to his death; a walking demonstration of the fact that isolation kills. A man with a glittering career, a bon viveur, expert in fine wines and gourmet food, magnificent company to his many friends, yet no friend whom he could trust with the secrets of his heart.

Others have also taken their own lives as the 'Credit Crunch' and recession have unfolded. But for me the abiding image is of this man going to his lonely end on a railway line, watching a train coming towards him. It is almost like a metaphor for our entire society.

Kirk Stephenson told his wife that religion was a load of rubbish – and yet he envied her faith. The desperately sad thing about it is that you really can have it all and yet have nothing. Isolation kills.

OUR HUMAN STORY

We were made for relationship. We were made to live in the warmth of a network of interdependent relationships and friendships in which there are at least some people who know our hearts – who, knowing our deepest anguish and the worst things about us, continue to love us. Such friendship nurtures the human spirit and keeps us alive in times of emotional famine.

What a difference between those two stories. It's not just a matter of different centuries, countries, cultures or technologies. There is a different atmosphere. David's beginning is as a rejected child of a dysfunctional family, reaching out to God who knows him and chooses him. Kirk's story is very much a twenty-first-century morality tale of cosmic loneliness, massive ability, scintillating success, fantastic rewards, and yet disillusion.

David's story, with all its pain and struggle, is shot through with rays of glory, shining heaven's hope into our reality.

Kirk Stephenson's world is bleaker, colder, limited: the lid is shut. No hope, no ultimate purpose from another dimension can penetrate. This life is all there is, limited and ultimately joyless.

I do understand why people come to the conclusion that there is no God: the question of suffering, massive injustices, the refusal of God to prove himself, can all combine to make *not* believing apparently logical. And yet I find that choice too glib, too simplistic; it begs too many questions:

What initiated the existence of the universe?
Why does the arrow of time only go in one direction?
What ultimately drives the evolutionary process?
How do we account for the reality and variety of personality?
How does the concept of beauty fit in?

There are many questions to which atheism provides no satisfactory answer. Above all, it leaves unanswered the question of personhood and the linked issue of relationship.

I was once an invited guest on a TV programme featuring the

great atheist philosopher A.J. Ayer as a panellist. At one point I confronted him with the question, 'I don't know whether or not you have a wife, but, if you do, when you say to her "I love you", how do you know there is somebody there?'

He was very angry and replied, 'Young man, I do have a wife and I happen to love her very much indeed, and I do not believe that when I say to her "I love you" it is meaningless.'

Hugh Montefiore, the Christian Jew who was then Bishop of Kingston and knew Ayer as a friend, challenged him and said, 'But, Freddie, you know he is right.' The truth is, the philosopher could not make a reasonable reply because he knew that if in our universe there is no ultimate relationship with an ultimate person, then no relationships have any ultimate value. They are all temporary. Their value lasts only as long as the people last. Most people know intrinsically that they cannot live like that.

What I did not know, indeed few people knew, was that at the time his much-loved wife, Vanessa, was dying of cancer. After she died he was grief-stricken. The great philosophical scheme to which he had devoted his life, Logical Positivism, was no more helpful in such an extremity than any other 'system'. At such a moment we do not need 'isms', we need friends, and particularly, I would argue, a friend who bridges the gap between us in our loss and the one who has left us. I know only one person who can do that.

All the evidence seems to show that we *need* relationship or something in us withers and dies. Indeed, even our physical health may suffer without relationship. Without the complex, and sometimes frustrating, matrix of healthy family life we grow distorted. Without the comradeship of colleagues in the workplace, work becomes driven and frantic rather than a chance to learn and thrive. Friendship and being in love are different. In *The Four Loves*, C. S. Lewis writes, 'Lovers are normally face to face, absorbed by each other; friends side by side, absorbed in some common interest.' Both are vital. Friendship may not have the intensity of being 'in love' but there is an ease about it that gives stability to our lives. Like the keel of a yacht, friendship helps us recover when the great waves of life overwhelm us. And it may be that we think we could live without the first glorious ecstasy of being in love, and the fear of descent into the pit of the blues if that love fails – yet who would really want to? Our *need* for relationship points irresistibly, for me, to the greatest relationship of all: with our maker.

It is somewhat amazing (indeed I must confess I actually find it hilarious) watching atheistic evolutionists trying to give logical evolutionary reasons why love, beauty, music, poetry and self-sacrifice exist. It seems wrong-headed to argue that a so-called 'selfish gene' would produce such elements. Enlightened self-interest is simply not a sufficient explanation for what we are being told is a mindless process.

In *The Sound of Music*, Maria famously sings, 'Nothing comes from nothing; nothing ever could.' Trite it may be, but also true. All the tiniest trace elements in our physical make-up have their origins in the universe itself. We are stardust. That is demonstrable, logical and accepted. Yet in the mind of the atheist, that logic does not extend to other elements that give meaning and purpose to our lives: love, wonder, joy. It seems nonsensical to propose that these qualities came about accidentally. Take some examples from sport – think of the glory of a touchdown, the grace of a beautifully hit six in cricket, the beauty of a baseball strike, the exultation of watching a great football team in full flow. Or what about the graceful flowing power of a galloping horse? How can we take so much delight from physical achievement? And why is so much of the created order superfluously beautiful? Consider again the amazing variety and complexity of personality and the wonder of relationship.

These non-material realities are as significant to humans as our physical existence. Some of us, indeed, think these are what define us as human. Why should these things exist in the material universe unless they are intrinsic to who we are just as much as the physical attributes we can measure? And surely their existence hints at the potential for ultimate relationship? For the God-believer, it is a no-brainer – they come from the one who made it all. And the purpose for which they were made was to point us in the direction of the maker, so that we could enter into relationship with him and each other.

Isolation kills because we are not designed to live that way. A solitary life is unhealthy because we are made to interact with each other. In four principal areas of life, romance, family, workplace and friends, we are drawn to relationship – yet we fear it. We fear it because it makes us vulnerable. It *may* be, as Barbra Streisand sings, that 'People who need people are the luckiest people in the world'. But sometimes it feels as if the opposite is true. A broken romance; a dysfunctional family; bullying in school, college or workplace; a betrayed friendship: all these can profoundly damage us.

So we pull up the drawbridge, cut the lines of communication. Self-protection rules. We cover up. We learn to pretend. In fact, some may even adopt another persona because their own history is so painful. Some people fantasise and over time the fantasy becomes more real than their true history. That really is a dangerous place to be. If the background includes violent or sexual abuse, people can blot out their family. These stratagems may mask the pain, but they compound the bondage. As long as our traumatic history is locked away in the dark, it grows in power.

THE TRUTH WILL SET YOU FREE

When it comes to our own mistakes and the hurts we have inflicted on others, the worst thing we can do is invent convenient reasons why what we did was justifiable. If we are to start from who we are, we have to unravel the untruths and unveil the fantasies. There is no other way. Honesty is the path to freedom. Gratefully accept the good. Thank God for it – no matter how small it may appear to be – and accept the bad stuff. *Whatever* was done to you, determine to be free of it. Face it, name it before God. Then ask his help to forgive what was done to you. Don't fall for the twisted notion that to forgive is to condone. The opposite is true.

Forgiveness identifies the offence and the size of the harm it has caused, and then *refuses to be controlled* by it. Forgiveness drops the chains of accusation tying the victim to the offender. Forgiveness is an act of power. When you forgive you are taking authority over what was done. The greater the offence, the greater the spiritual power of forgiveness. So: forgive. Then let go. Determine in your whole being not to be a victim. No pity parties. No languishing, hiding under a blanket, retreating from the world. *No* self-pity, ever. We have to be ruthless about it. Self-pity is a narcotic of the spirit, seductive, enjoyable and debilitating. How to be truthful in all this? Not easy. Shakespeare wrote:

> This above all
> To thine own self be true
> And it must follow as the night the day,
> Thou canst not then be false to any man.
> *Hamlet*

There is truth there. But it ignores the uncomfortable insight expressed by the prophet Jeremiah:

> The heart is deceitful above all things, and desperately wicked:
> who can know it?
> Jeremiah 17:9 *King James Version*

For me, these two passages encapsulate the paradox of my human nature. I long to be honest, but the heart so often has its own deceptive intentions and betrays me.

Deep within, I hate the lies that cloud my soul. In the end I have had to admit failure in my attempt to achieve transparency of heart unaided. I have had to return to the one who said 'I am the Truth', asking him to help me.

When that happens I have to come back to him and pray something like this: 'Jesus, living Truth, invade my soul with love. Set me free from fear. Shine your light of truth in me. Give me strength to drop sordid pretence. Let me tell the truth, because I want to be free.'

And that is always the truth: only honesty will set us free; transparency with ourselves – no more lying or pretending. True authority in living comes from honesty and integrity. Dishonesty and pretence generate fear of being exposed as a liar. And that fear is well founded: 'the truth will out!' We may be able to kid ourselves that a cover-up is necessary to protect others. But that is almost always a lie. It is ourselves we are protecting. Every lie is one more denial of my own identity. Lies chip away at our sense of self. We lose that vital sense of being integrated as a person.

So truth has to be the pathway that leads us to freedom. Confession is truly therapeutic. So why wait? Confess your failures, your sins, everything, to God immediately, stating it in blunt and clear terms, whatever you have done. Then hear his promise: 'If we admit our sins – make a clean breast of them – he won't let us down; he'll be true to himself. He'll forgive our sins and purge us of all wrongdoing.' (1 John 1:9, *The Message*). Act upon that promise.

Receive his forgiveness as it is – a beautifully crafted gift.

To live intentionally we must learn continually to be real before our maker and other people, who, like us, are made in his image. That has to include those over whom we may have authority. Stepping down off the pedestal is a real release. That first step is a toughie, though! However, true authority does not come from acting out a role but from letting others know 'me' as a real human being. Strangely, doing that will not strip us of authority. Instead, it will invest us with integrity, an inner strength that draws others towards us so they want to follow our lead.

I suppose it is time for a confession. That is, if you haven't already picked up the fact that I am not just an interested observer of the life of Jesus, not just somebody who finds him a fascinating and inspiring example. No, I am a passionate follower of the man, a devotee, committed to spending my life walking in his presence. So it is to him that I must return in order to find a way of expressing what it means to be a human among humans. We turn to look at him and the way he did it, because, quite simply, he is the best.

Consider this extraordinary person. Think about Jesus – the man, the leader – the most complete man the world has ever known. For me, belief in Jesus as the Son of God is not just an article of faith. It is the passion at the very heart of my being. Here is God, coming from the unknowable heart of his own being, marching out to meet us, expressing everything that he is and setting on one side everything that makes him God, becoming a mere human being. So, because he is exactly what he designed, he is perfect but not invulnerable; possessing immense power, but genuinely tired.

There are moments in his story when that is so clear – sitting on the side of a well because he is too tired to go on, sending off all twelve of his disciples to buy lunch – just how many men does it take to buy lunch for thirteen? There is little doubt that, in sending them off, he was giving himself some space. And he also listened to that inner voice that told him what to do so that when a lonely, rejected and scandalous husband-stealing woman came to the well he was there for her – tired but not callous.

DON'T BLAME THEM – TRAIN THEM

As a rabbi, his passionate concern is to impart to his disciples not just his wisdom but the powers that had been given to him for healing, for quelling the storms of life, and he spends hours with them, teaching, training, raising them up so that their performance can mirror his. Then he releases them to go and do what he has taught them. He goes away and leaves them to get on with it. But anybody who has ever done any training of others knows what happens next! Faced with praying for a child who is in the grip of constant epileptic fits, they fail utterly.

Whether or not you believe in the possibility of healing is irrelevant at this point. The evidence says that Jesus had that gift and imparted it to his disciples – but they were completely ineffective at using it. I love this moment in his story. He has done something unprecedented with these men. He has told them they are not just disciples – though in Jewish culture at that time that was the highest honour any man could have from a rabbi. He has told them, 'You are my friends.' Now he looks at them, with a look of failure in their eyes and abject misery written across their faces. 'What a generation! How many times do I have to go over these things?' How much longer do I have to put up with this?

I think he was as close to giving up at this moment as he ever was in his whole life. And he really lets the disciples see how much their performance means to him. He makes himself so vulnerable to them. His weakness was his total commitment to them, and he let them see that. This was actually (and intentionally) the area of his greatest weakness. It was what would lead him to the cross. One of these men, whom he trusted with his life, whom he called friend, would betray him to torture and death. And he knew the man would do it. But he did not give up on him; he carried on training him and drawing him into relationship. This is at the heart of our humanity: if we give up on relationship, we give up on being human ourselves.

In the light of all this, it is all the more remarkable that Jesus continued to work with this team of friends. It would certainly have been easier at that moment for him to withdraw from them and buy into a myth of his own indispensability – something we've probably all done at times. But he had come to do more than just be amazing himself. He had come to invest himself in others so that they could break out of the boredom of mediocrity and predictability; so to participate in what it means to be human that they would become as amazing as him. He built a flat team with widening circles of influence. He had an inner circle of three with whom he met regularly. These were his closest friends: brothers James and John, and a cousin of theirs, Simon. They were not the most promising candidates. There must have been many more suitable people. But he saw beneath the weakness and believed in them when they didn't believe in themselves. Friendship does that.

Of the three, Simon, renamed Peter by Jesus, is the most famous, but by far the least impressive at the start – big and blustering, emotional, often over the top, given to outbursts of anger – and apparently highly susceptible to the smiles of young barmaids.

Full of overblown courage one minute, running like a coward the next. His name, Simon, meant 'a reed'. When Jesus met him, he took one look at him and said, 'So, you are Simon, are you? I have heard about you. I have decided to give you a new name. I am going to call you "the rock".' At that point, no one could have seemed less rock-like than this big, winsome but highly unstable character. Yet friendship with Jesus transformed him. He became a 'rock' indeed, one of the building blocks of the Church that within a generation had turned the Mediterranean Sea into an ocean of Christian faith. He became a hero – and it was friendship with Jesus that did it.

John was rather different. John was a poet, a mystic, melancholic by temperament, capable of heights of exultation and deep lows of lamentation. Like most poets he seems to have been a man of extremes. He was also very much a younger brother. His older brother, James, was confident and strong in a way that Simon Peter was not. He was a natural organiser and seems to have been a good businessman. That is why whenever John is mentioned in the Gospels he is always mentioned as the brother of James.

In his own story, written some years after the other Gospels, John famously describes himself as 'the disciple whom Jesus loved'. But, fascinatingly, he does not give himself this title until they reach the Last Supper. I think this shy, insecure man really did not believe he had anything of value to offer to the friends of Jesus. I think he believed that he was only along for the ride because James, his brother, had somehow or other pulled strings and got him in. Or maybe Jesus felt sorry for him. Whatever it was, it seems he believed that Jesus actually loved him only at the Last Supper.

Special arrangements had been made for them to eat the most significant meal of all to Jewish people, the Passover, together, a day early. Jesus told them he had a special reason for wanting to eat it with them on this day. Passwords had been arranged and when they got to the room they found it ready except for one vital component – no servant was present to wash their feet. Since at this time people ate their food from a long, low table while they reclined on cushions on the ground, leaning on their left elbows and eating with their right hand, the lack of cleansing for the feet was rather crucial. Lying as they did, each man's feet wound up just behind the head of the neighbour on his right. Those feet had walked many miles in open sandals on country roads, through busy city streets used by horses, cows and wild dogs. Washing your feet before you entered the house was a matter not just of politeness but almost of self-preservation!

THE SERVANT KING

When they arrived for the meal, nobody was there to wash their feet. No lowly servant was available. Though the friends of Jesus were mostly working-class, they had their standards! There was no way one of them was going to get down and wash the feet of the others, particularly since on their way to that meal they had been arguing about who among them would be most important in the coming kingdom of Jesus. Naked ambition does not make for comfortable friendships and it is not difficult to imagine the tension present as each one took his place around the table, and as servants came in to serve the food – and still nobody moved to wash the feet of the others.

Then, Jesus moved. He rose from his place, took off his robe, stood there for a moment in his loincloth, then walked across the room to the door, picked up the bowl of water and the cloth with which to wash their feet, and the towel with which to dry them. He began to move from one disciple to another. Nobody said a word. What could they say? They had been shamed by their leader, their friend and their Master. He had shown them what true friendship was about, and the nature of real leadership.

It was Simon Peter – of course – who broke the silence, when Jesus got to him. He looked at the towel tied around Jesus' waist and the bowl of water filmy with mud from the feet of others. 'Master, *you* will wash my feet?' Jesus replied, 'You don't under-stand now what I am doing, but it will be clear later.' I think Simon was ashamed. He knew he should have had the guts to do what

Jesus was doing, but he just could not humble himself before these others who clearly thought they were better than he was. No way! He was not going to do that. Yet now the master was kneeling in front of him. 'You're not going to wash my feet – ever!' Patiently, gently, Jesus replied, 'If I don't wash your feet, you cannot be part of what I am doing.'

Jesus knew his friend. He knew that, for all his bluster and masculine pride, once Simon understood he would never refuse to humble himself to him. Peter's reply demonstrated that Jesus' confidence was not misplaced. 'Master, then not just my feet, wash my hands, wash my head, wash everything!' You cannot read this story without knowing that Jesus must have grinned at this moment when he said, 'I know you had a bath this morning. You don't need all that, just your feet will do.'

John was watching all this. Of course he heard as Jesus explained, 'This is the way it has to be in the friendship circle that I am setting up, not only when I am present with you, but when I have left you. If I, as your master and friend, have done this, then you must do it for each other, and if you can learn this lesson then you'll discover it is the secret of true happiness.'

At that moment, it seems to me that something changed in the heart of young John. Maybe it was when Jesus actually took John's filthy feet in his own hands and washed them, then dried them with the towel tied round his waist. Maybe this shy young man at that moment for the first time found the courage to look Jesus full in the face and realised that Jesus saw him as no one else saw him – loved him for who he really was. What we know is that when Jesus, a few minutes later, talks about someone betraying him, John is on the right-hand side of Jesus, ideally positioned to ask him a question about who the traitor would be. And it is then, for the first time in his narrative, that John describes himself as the disciple that Jesus loved.

I think most of us can relate to that. How long does it take for us to get it? To recognise that we might be lovable, might even be loved, that it might be possible for us to be secure in the know-ledge of that. Jesus gave that to his friends. The leader, the most complete man the world has ever known, was unafraid to be vulnerable, extraordinary to them because he was sustained by the invisible presence of his Father whose love burned within him and by the Spirit of God that surrounded him.

As leaders, husbands, wives, mothers or fathers, we may labour under often unrealistic expectations. Our insecurity may make us reluctant to take risks. If we, or those in our care, do so, we could make mistakes – and if that happens we will gloss over it rather than admit and face it. But all that kind of stuff comes out of desperate insecurity. If we admit mistakes then we are free to ask the question 'How can we all do it better next time?' The truth is that the person who never made a mistake never made anything, let alone anything worthwhile. The stakes could not have been higher for Jesus at that moment. Three days before, he had been guest of honour at a dinner party, knowing that within a week he would face the most painful death the ancient world could devise. Yet he still played his part as guest of honour at a party.

His special Passover meal was less than twenty-four hours before the crucifixion. Yet he could still take time to love these men and offer the model of relationship that would sustain them for the rest of their lives. He was well aware that delegation causes more trouble than doing the job yourself. Ask any woman who has ever had 'help' from her children in the kitchen or any man who has ever had the same kind of assistance in the workshop (or vice versa, of course!). The point is, our children cause trouble when they help us; it would be easier if we put them out of the room. They create mess, they make mistakes, they get things wrong that we have to put right. But it is the only way they are going to learn. It is an indispensable part of loving parenting.

HONESTY PAYS

Think about the king from whom Jesus derived so much inspiration – David. It is noticeable that right at the end of his life – a long and successful life in which he has become a truly renaissance figure, skilled in the arts, in war and in government – he writes a poem in which he celebrates notable companions who walked with him and helped him achieve his goals. And when after that he blows it yet again by making another huge mistake, he acknowledges his blunder to the entire nation. Walking in honesty and integrity had taken this insecure boy from a dysfunctional family and turned him not just into a great leader, but into a man at ease with himself. He was able to die at peace because he had seen his son Solomon enthroned as king, and entrusted his dream – the building of the temple – to him.

We can be so selfish. We want to be whole but I wonder how much is achieved in this world by people who are consciously whole. Isn't it possible that actually God needs broken people? That he can work best with people who are aware of their own brokenness? I don't think anyone would deny that it is not just society in Britain that is broken, as the tabloids tell us. Our world is broken, as is increasingly obvious. I can't help feeling that when God looks at it, his heart must be broken. What he wants is for us to walk in companionship with him, vulnerable to the pain that is in his heart and in his world. The fact is that strong people become increasingly inaccessible and alienated from those around them. By now it will be obvious that I feel passionately about the person of Jesus and regard him as an infallible guide to the nature and character of the heart of God. If you are not quite there yet, then I hope we can continue to walk on this journey together.

The awesome purpose of the creator is for each of us to develop as Jesus did, to be an amazing original, a demonstration of his life and glory – as we saw in Chapter 1:

Original and Bold (Creative)
               Personal
                    Rational
                        Emotional
                        Relational
                            Spiritual
                             Volitional
                                 Regal (Sovereign)

That is your future. Now resolve that, no longer predetermined by your past, you will stand on your history and use it as a springboard into *that* future.

Like the young David.

Chapter 3

Live in Balance with the Rhythm of Life

A SHEPHERD BOY IN THE CORRIDORS OF POWER

Saul's Palace, Gibeah, 1026 BC

The boy stirred. Since he was seven he had slept out in the fields with the flocks, and even in the deepest sleep his ears were attuned for the slightest sound of danger. It was a good couple of years now since the great prophet Samuel had found a ten-year-old boy and anointed him to be king of Israel. He knew something had happened at that moment. The Spirit of God like a flame burning inside him had suddenly illuminated so many experiences, and they had come out of him in poetry and song. For years his brothers had jeered at him and his dreaming among the flocks, and now they also joked about his weeping like a woman as he sang songs about the Lord.

But then the call had come. Over two years after Samuel's visit, a messenger arrived from the King's court. They needed an expert on the lyre, who could play and sing to bring joy to the miserable and peace to the disturbed. Because the King was afflicted, ill, some said oppressed by a demon. There was a madness in his eyes at times that nothing could quiet except music, the healing power of the songwriter. Someone at court had suggested Jesse's youngest son.

He lay awake now, listening intently. He knew what had roused him. It was Saul's first deep groaning as he began to stir. Either he would quieten down and go back to sleep – or else the howling would start. Even as David thought it, it echoed through the palace, the terrifying sound of the torment of the King. Leaping from his bed, grabbing his lyre, no time even to find his shoes let alone put them on. He ran, the flagstones cold under his bare feet, the howling getting louder. The madness gripped his royal master. He burst into the King's bedchamber. The servants and the guards huddled outside, frightened lest the demon that visited the King should come after them also. But the boy had no fear.

He stopped inside the door, allowing quietness to wash over him even while the howling increased in intensity. Then he began to play. At first, it was as if the two sounds were vying with each other for dominance, the music at war with the screaming. But then the music began to win. As he heard some of the terror go out of his master's voice, David began to sing, 'The Lord is my Shepherd, I shall not be in want . . .' When he came to the words 'even though I walk through the valley of deep darkness, I will fear no evil. Your sceptre and your staff, they strengthen me', the howling died and the sobbing started.

Even as David sang, and peace came to his master, he reflected and resolved, 'I never want to be like that – never. No matter how long I must wait, I will not become king without the presence of God beside me.' He looked across the room to where his master's royal robes were displayed and where the crown rested. To him it was clear: to have power without the presence of God was meaningless. The crown was empty, a symbol without substance, if the soul of the man who wore it was empty. 'Is that you, my boy? Young David, my son? Thank you. You have restored my mind. Go back to your bed, lad. I will rest now.'

The next morning, Saul was off to war. David protested at being left behind but Saul said, 'Come, now, I made you an armour-bearer, lad, because I enjoy your presence. But that was for processions and the royal court. We are going to war. It is time for you to go back to Bethlehem.' His brothers would laugh and sneer when he returned, of course, and make sure he got the filthiest jobs. But then he smiled. He would soon be back with the sheep.

The road from Saul's base at Gibeah down to Bethlehem led past the pagan enclave of Jebus. Set on a mountain, the fortress dominated the road. The sentries looked down and laughed at the lone boy wending his way south. David gritted his teeth. 'One day,' he thought, 'I will conquer that city and it shall be mine. When I am king I will rule from there. I will give it its old name, Jerusalem – the abode of peace.'

There was a new bounce in his step as he resumed his journey on the road south.

SEASONS OF LIFE

April. The sun is shining. It is spring. In England the seasons have a definite progression to them. I have a friend who lives in Los Angeles. He sends me emails, especially when bad weather here has hit the news in California. He lets me know, just in case I was worried, that the sun is still shining, that he is sitting on his balcony or out in his backyard (this name seems odd to us in England, just as the word 'garden' no doubt seems quaint to many Americans), sipping a Mexican beer and wondering whether to have a swim. I tell him there is a certain delicious joy to coming home through horrible cold weather, when the snow and sleet is coming down, into a house where a log fire is burning. He tells me he too can have a log fire, and the air-conditioning makes up for my experience of trudging through the snow and the slush.

But the fact is, I do love the winter (even though I loathe being cold!). Then when spring comes, I decide I love the spring too. I am looking out of the window now at tiny green leaves on the tree in front of our house, at blossom on the trees denoting that spring is definitely here. Then I think about summer – those long, hot days, especially days remembered from childhood holidays on a farm in Devon, participating in the wheat harvest, riding on a farm wagon or even on the side of a tractor (no 'health and safety' in those days to spoil such fun!), those glorious moments lying back looking at the blue sky, listening to the insects and the bees, watching the birds. But summer eventually runs its course. The leaves on the trees lose their freshness; the ground may be parched and cracked underfoot. Then those days immortalised as 'season of mists and mellow fruitfulness' – autumn. I love it; I love the rhythm of the year. I love the rhythm of the day.

Like so many people I know, I married someone temperamentally the opposite to me. I am a night person. My wife is a morning person. Often she gets up at five o'clock in the morning, but this does mean that she needs to get to bed by 9:30 p.m. – which is the time when I am just coming alive.

In his book *The Power of Positive Thinking*, Norman Vincent Peale says, 'When you wake in the morning; don't just crawl out of bed. Leap out of bed! Stride across to the window. Fling wide the drapes [curtains]. Open the window fully, breathe in God's fresh air and say "Man, it's good to be alive!"' I once heard Billy Graham quote this, speaking in his most authoritative and inspirational voice. Along with others in the audience I sat there looking at him and thinking, 'I bet he does it every morning.' He waited *just* long enough (the secret of all good comedy is timing!). Then he said, 'I can't do that – I have to have a cup of coffee first!'

I am with Billy. There is nothing quite like that first cup of coffee in the morning and, whenever possible, with that first cup of coffee I read the extracts for the day from The Bible in One Year. This helps to orientate my mind to the reality of God's presence. Whether I have lots of time or not I take our dogs for a walk in a park with good views of the surrounding countryside. As I walk I do the crossword and engage in conversation with God. I am not looking merely for a download of all my concerns but for a moment of genuine stillness when I can be in the presence of God, when the reality of his love and generosity can just wash over me.

C.S. Lewis called his autobiography *Surprised by Joy*. The church where I grew up was like many churches – a conflicted place. We believed in and we preached the generosity and forgiveness of a loving God. But at the same time we practised a life of rigidity bound by rules and regulations where sometimes the words of the Bible could be analysed so minutely that the passage ended up like a corpse ready for a funeral, embalmed and dressed but devoid of life. The first time I ever truly experienced the grace of God I was overwhelmed by a sense of being in a waterfall of cleansing and love and *no blame*. My aim on my walks is to come to a place of rest and joy in contact with God.

The great statesman and politician Nehemiah knew about this. In fact, looking at a group of people he felt were far too miserable because they had realised how much they had failed God by not keeping his laws and by allowing the walls of Jerusalem to be ruined, he said, 'The Joy of the Lord is your strength.' And since the joy of God is inexhaustible, those who access it tap into a source of energy that is limitless. But here is the thing – the joy comes from direct contact with God. It flows from him. When I break the contact, the energy of his joy starts to drain away. Frustration and impatience too often rob me of access to the presence of God. Instead of elation, I am marked by jadedness and very quickly become stale.

I have to confess that even at my age, with long years of experience, I struggle with the issue of time-keeping. After I have taken the dogs for their walk, it is usually off to a meeting – at which I may well arrive a few minutes late! There is so much to put into every day and I am not good at organising it. From there, other meetings will often take me through into the afternoon, so I grab a snack for lunch. I eat an early evening meal with my wife and then typically have an evening meeting, followed by sitting down with correspondence or writing. This is the rhythm of my day. I do get tired but rarely ever exhausted, provided I hold on to the reality of the joy of the Lord.

When I told my colleagues at work that I was struggling with a chapter called 'Live in Balance with the Rhythm of Life', they laughed and said, 'Wonder why!'

PREPARED IN OBSCURITY

It truly is extraordinary to think that the most influential person in the culture and history of the last 2000 years was a peasant prophet from a remote province of the Roman Empire. The reason, at least partly, is that Jesus did not just teach wonderful things. He lived them! His life exhibited balance. His self-leadership and his leadership of others demonstrated a perfect sense of timing. Timing is not just the secret of good comedy. It is the secret of living. He was a man of action, yet never once was he betrayed into unwise action by impatience.

The genius of Jesus' life was that, though his days were often immensely full, there was never a sense of rush. He had learned how to wait, with glad patience, as well as to act decisively. The most remarkable thing about him was not just his timing but that he clearly recognised the need for a God-given rhythm of life.

There was a rhythm to his life and ministry that meant he stayed fresh not stale, energised instead of jaded. The pattern of worship, work, play and rest meant that he made space to interact with God in the company of others. He moved from that to intense, purposeful activity, carrying out the mission that he had been given. This was followed by times of play, celebrations, meals and dancing and then moments of rest and quiet.

The problem with so many of us, especially the idealists, is that we want the good stuff to happen and we want it NOW! Often the impatience with which we want what may well be manifestly for the good of humanity precipitates us into action that betrays the very cause for which we are fighting. I have done it. Every leader I know has been guilty of that failure. Yet Jesus never fell into that trap. There was a purity about his judgement that sprang from the fact that it was never all about him. He was there to serve a cause – the kingdom of heaven. In his mind and heart he had already acknowledged that he would lay down his life for the sake of this cause. Therefore, all the other things that worry us so much – reputation, emotional rewards, physical desires – were secondary to the purpose for which he came. He had settled the priorities of his life from a very early age and this gave his decision-making a glorious simplicity.

I love the story of his visit to Jerusalem at the age of twelve. He had gone in a huge party from the local village, one of a number of young men who were to profess their adult commitment to the Jewish faith at the age of twelve. In their culture, it marked the moment when he stepped from childhood into manhood. From that moment on he was responsible for his own spiritual life. His walk with God was now his life priority. When the time came for the whole party to leave Jerusalem and make the ninety-mile journey back to Nazareth, Jesus stayed behind. He was in his element, debating with the greatest thinkers in the nation. What astounded them was not just the accuracy of his answers to their questions, but the penetrating wisdom of his questions to them.

For three days he stayed in the temple. Maybe he stayed in one of the study houses with other students. We are not told. All we know is that on the fourth day his parents finally found him. They had discovered his absence after a day's journey towards home and returned to Jerusalem. No doubt, like all parents in such a situation, they assumed the worst. After all, Jerusalem was a big city with criminal gangs, political factions, violent revolutionaries, oppressive troops. Their minds would be filled with horrific pictures of what could happen to a young boy in the big city. They must have searched every hell-hole in Jerusalem. Had they remembered how he came to them and who he really was, they would have looked in the right place straight away. But they didn't, because they had forgotten what they knew. Too frequently, that is the case with us. We forget what we know, and allow fear of the worst to take over our thinking.

When they finally found him in the temple, I love to imagine Joseph standing there with a rueful smile on his face, full of pride that 'his boy' was holding his own in this distinguished company. All his mother could do was vent her anxiety, and maybe release some of the sense of foolishness she must have known when she realised, 'I should have known he would be here all along.' So she reproached Jesus and did what many husbands and fathers will be familiar with: she drew her husband into the reproach. 'Your father and I have been very worried about you.' I can imagine her nudging Joseph, 'Haven't we?' and him of course agreeing, 'Oh yes, absolutely, yes, very worried.' But if I had been that dad I would have winked at my son. The words would have said, 'You have been very inconsiderate,' but my face would have said, 'Well done, son, I am proud of you.'

Jesus' response to their worries is so simple. It reminds me of occasions when I perhaps unjustly reproached my own children as they were growing up, and they would look back at me and ask just this sort of question. 'Why were you looking for me?

Didn't you know that I would be in my Father's house?' Ouch! What a question. Didn't you know? Had you really forgotten? Had you put who I really am so far out of your mind?

Mary never forgot this incident. She stored it up as she had other memories, which became a precious resource for her in the years ahead. Jesus went home with them and the Bible simply says he submitted himself to their authority. He had made his point. He had reminded them of who he was.

Eighteen years go by of which we know nothing except that he became, like his father, a builder. A carpenter in Judea wasn't just a maker of fine furniture; he would construct anything that was needed. The hands of Jesus were the hands of a workman – calloused, rough-skinned, strong, skilled and yet careful. His mind was agile, wise, focused and skilled at what we call lateral thinking. So he spent thirty years preparing for just three years of public service, hidden away until the right moment. Preparation matters.

Freddie Mercury was a prophetic voice for a whole generation when he sang, 'I want it all and I want it now!' The truth is, you can't have anything worthwhile without patience. In our day of mass production and instant fixes, it is perhaps harder for us than for any previous generation to recognise that it takes time, and lots of it, for the supreme work of art that is a beautiful human life to be crafted. Preparation matters.

Hundreds of years before Jesus, the prophet Isaiah put in the mouth of the Messiah who was to come a poetic declaration in which he likens his life to that of a polished arrow. The production of an arrow was a work of skilled craftsmanship and artistry. Most archers would never entrust the production of their arrows to any other person. They would make them themselves, selecting the right wood, splitting it, laminating it, selecting the feathers for the flights and finely crafting the head for its purpose. Finally, the shaft of the arrow would be polished to ensure that the arrow would fly swift and true.

The prophet imagines the frustration of the arrow, having been so painstakingly prepared, then hidden in the quiver of the archer with absolutely no control over when it is to take flight; longing to be taken at last from its hiding place, set against the drawstring of the bow and sent streaking straight to its target. Hiddenness of that kind, in a person, creates longing and even tension. But Jesus was willing to live with the tension and hold it in trust. When we do that, the process trains us in patience.

So he waited until he knew the right moment had come.

RELEASED INTO ACTION

Then Jesus once again made the long journey from Nazareth to a place on the Jordan River, near the village of Bethany outside Jerusalem. Here his encounter with John the Baptist happened. We look at that moment in the next chapter. As a result of John's public endorsement, two young men decided to follow Jesus. One was Andrew, the brother of Simon Peter; the other almost certainly was the idealistic young fisherman, John, younger brother of the able administrator James. But it was not only John's endorsement that was ringing in his ears as he began the journey back. It was the voice from heaven that sounded like thunder and yet was discerned by others as a voice that said, 'This is my Son, whom I love. I am so proud of him.'

Accompanied by John and Andrew on the long walk back to Nazareth, Jesus must have reflected on these things. As they drew near the area of Galilee, they met Philip, who responded instantly to Jesus' call, 'Come and be my disciple.' Philip immediately drew in the wise, statesmanlike Nathaniel. Now there were these four named disciples, and probably others too, walking, talking together, before arriving back in Nazareth.

Then the invitation came to a wedding at Cana, a village about ten miles away in the hills. The invitation was to Mary. She invited Jesus and of course he had to bring his friends. That's the thing about Jesus; he keeps inviting all the most unsuitable people to join him. Those of us who recognise that we are pretty unsuitable should be very grateful!

When they arrived, things were going extremely well – too well, in fact. They ran out of wine. In those days, a wedding feast could

last as long as a week and the provision of wine was the responsibility of the bridegroom. To run out was to be known for the
rest of your life as 'the man whose wine ran out' at his own
wedding! It was unthinkable. But the unthinkable had happened.
Cana was not on a major trade route and a wedding of this size
would have involved the whole village, so no doubt all available
supplies of wine had been used up. If there was a local wine store,
it had been drained.

Mary took one look at this bunch of men, who knew they were
in desperate trouble, and said to Jesus, 'They have run out of
wine.' Jesus' response is not necessarily what you would expect:
'Is that any of our business, Mother – yours or mine? This isn't
my time. Don't push me!' (John 2:4 *The Message*) Why did he
speak like this? Was he saying to Mary, 'There are no special
favours for family members'? Or perhaps, 'Mother, you are speaking
so loud that I cannot actually hear what my Father is saying to
me'? After all, his own rule of life he summed up later as 'I do
only what I see my Father doing'.

It was a crucial moment and a forerunner of the time when his
brothers would say to him, 'Why don't you go into Jerusalem for
the big feast? No one who wants to be involved in public affairs
hides himself away.' Their concern was for what we might call his
'career'. His concern was, what does my Father want me to do,
and how does he want me to do it? He was not going to be driven
by their agenda. Neither was he prepared to be driven even by
Mary's passionate concern for her neighbours. Wisdom for Jesus
meant just one thing – what does my Father want me to do?

Mary could have decided to be offended. I can hear her, like
any other wounded mum, speaking to her best friend and saying,
'Did you hear how he talked to me in front of all those people?
And I'm his mother!' But God had chosen well. With wisdom and
maturity she quietly said to the waiters, 'Whatever he tells you –
do it.' She must have been there in some position of authority,
because they now came and stood in front of Jesus, looking as
helpless as only men can: 'What are we going to do, boss?' It is
remarkable how swiftly the whole thing turned. Jesus now knew

exactly what to do, because he had seen what his Father wanted. Those few minutes' delay were crucial. He waited for his Father's direction, and then obeyed immediately.

'See the six water jars over there?' See them! They could not miss them! Six jars holding twenty-five gallons of water apiece, there for the washing of the filthy feet of those who had come along the dusty roads, through fields used by cattle, sheep and wild animals. 'Empty those. Fill them with fresh water from the well.' One hundred and fifty gallons to be dragged out of the ground from a deep well, by rope, on a bucket. But these men were so desperate they did it. They would have done anything. They came back and stood in front of Jesus. 'OK, we did that, now what do we do?' Jesus must have grinned. 'Do you have your boss's cup? The one he uses for tasting the next vintage.' Of course they had their boss's cup. 'Fill it and serve it up.' They had their orders. But I have no doubt that nobody employed on that team wanted the job of serving *this* vintage to the man in charge of the feast. It would have been passed down the line to the youngest apprentice. 'You, boy, go and serve it up.' 'Why me?' 'Because you're smallest and if you don't we'll belt you!' So he went.

Picture him, standing by the high seat of the man in charge of the feast. He looks down. 'What've you got there, lad? Is that the next vintage? You've been a long time. Been making it yourself?' A nervous giggle from the boy. 'Well, give it here then. It'll be rubbish! It always is. They serve the good stuff and when they think people can't tell the difference any more, they serve the rubbish.' A sip. A pause. Another sip, then a long draft and a sound of appreciation. 'That's beautiful! In fact it's the best I have ever tasted.' Imagine the surprise of the boy! 'Where'd you get it from?' Wisely, if that question was asked, the boy never answered. After all, what could he say? It would be unthinkable to respond, 'Out of the foot-washing jars.'

The man in charge of the feast called the bridegroom to him and utterly confused him by congratulating him on waiting till the end to serve up the very best wine. Imagine the bridegroom standing there, covering his confusion as best he could and saying,

'Thank you so much, sir, I am glad you enjoyed it', not having the slightest idea what has been going on. The servants knew. The common people knew. The ordinary people understood something phenomenal had just happened.

What an amazing few days – the baptism in the Jordan, the ringing endorsement of John the Baptist, the voice from heaven, the first disciples, miracles of healing. Now a sign that told anybody who wanted to know that God was on the move in Galilee. Rumour spread fast: 'Messiah has come!'

A FEW DAYS' R & R

The longing for a deliverer meant that within a few days Galilee would be flooded with those seeking God's Messiah. The momentum was with Jesus. Whether he wanted it or not, he was about to become the biggest celebrity in Judea. At a moment when every normal impulse would say 'This is the moment, go for it', Jesus drew back to take time out with his disciples, his brothers and his mother. I have no doubt this was his way of preparing for what was to come. He knew his brothers would come under pressure and regard him as a danger to the entire family. In the bubbling ferment of Middle-Eastern politics, it was a dangerous thing to be prominent and Jesus was coming into prominence. This threatened to bring exclusion, arrest or even death for his family members. Later they would think him mad, but how could they understand if they were not called by God, or not yet anyway?

So Jesus took them away to his base of operations at Capernaum, where they would be surrounded by those who supported him. A few days watching the sun dancing on the Sea of Galilee, or the wind off the Syrian hills creating patterns across the surface of the lake. Like hundreds of thousands of others who have visited Galilee, I know there is nowhere quite like it.

What fascinates me is the importance Jesus placed on this visit at this crucial moment in his life. He has received the clear affirmation of John the Baptist, already seen his first healings, drawn his first disciples to him and done a spectacular miraculous sign.

Everything is going his way. Yet he steps back from it all to be with his mother, brothers and friends.

I do not think it too fanciful to imagine that this was in order to reassure his mother of his deep love for her. And also to get her to move towards accepting the fact that she no longer owned him. Mary believed, as every mother does, that her child was special. But, of course, she had unique reasons for believing that, things that she had held in her heart for years. In a sense Jesus as God's messenger had been in her stewardship. She had watched over him and guided him. But this was the moment when he had to step away from all that. And he did it with firm gentleness. He took time out at a high point of his early ministry to be with her and to establish with his disciples that though they were excited about the public ministry, he was even more committed to his relationship with them. It would take them years to understand, but he was determined that they would get it.

It seems that what brought this time of rest and recreation to an end was a visit to the synagogue. When Jesus sat in the teacher's seat, people had no idea what to expect. What they heard amazed them. All rabbis taught on the basis of the teachings of the rabbis whom they themselves had followed. Like modern lawyers, who present arguments based entirely on established precedent, what they did was predictable and always derivative. Jesus, though, taught as one who had his own authority. An authority not derived from another rabbi, but from his God-given commission.

In the middle of that electric atmosphere suddenly a man erupted, screaming, with rage and terror in his voice: 'What do you want with us, Jesus of Nazareth? Have you come to destroy us? I know who you are – the Holy one of God!' The last sentence oozed mockery. Jesus refused to turn this into some kind of show. He did not want a spiritual three-ring circus. He spoke firmly, briefly and sternly, addressing not the man but the evil spirit that he could see within him. You may not believe in such things. The people of Jesus' day did and it is worth remembering that our understanding of the world may be blinkered by what we think we know, even in the midst of our pride in our modern scientific rationalism. Jesus with his special wisdom and understanding certainly believed in the reality of spirits of evil. 'Quiet! Get out of him!' The man was shaken by a spasm and with a shriek the evil presence left him whole and at peace. People were amazed – religious teaching that genuinely had God's healing power at the heart of it! It was amazing and unique. The news spread like wildfire.

Jesus and his disciples went back to the home of Simon Peter for a meal. By the time the evening came, in the cool of the day, people were arriving in crowds from all the surrounding area. He prayed for them all, laying hands on the sick, setting free the oppressed, and when unholy voices began to shout, he shut them up. He was up very late. But before the dawn he was up, slipping quietly out of the house and away into the hills to be alone with his Father and pray.

When they awoke, Simon and the disciples were astonished to discover Jesus gone. They fanned out searching for him, calling his name. Imagine the sinking feeling in Jesus' mind and heart as he heard their voices and realised his time of peace and reflection was over. Across the centuries, you can still hear the astonishment in Simon Peter's voice: 'Everybody is looking for you – what are you doing here?' I can really understand Simon. Jesus had just become the hottest property in town. Simon and the other disciples wanted to go back to the scene of yesterday's triumph and bathe in the reflected glory of Jesus, the miracle-working prophet. Jesus' response was quiet and a little disappointing. 'Let's go somewhere else. There are lots of other villages. Let's go and proclaim Good News to them. That's why I came.' They set off on a tour of the whole of the area of Galilee. After his triumph it would have been easy to bask in celebrity. But Jesus opted for solitude, for long enough to come to a place of genuine stillness and real prayer, and then renewed intense action. It was a pattern he was to follow throughout his entire ministry – solitude, prayer, action, reflection. He certainly got the balance right.

GETTING THE BALANCE RIGHT

And if we are to get the balance of *our* lives right, we have to learn when to go and when to stop. Impatience can make us so intense that others will avoid us, and we spoil what we are trying to achieve. People who have the assurance that God has something special for them are released from anxiety. They are free to apply themselves wholly to what needs to be done.

Abraham Lincoln is said to have declared, 'I will study and get ready and someday my chance will come.' Certainly he was a man who made a difference. He had the assurance, as we should, that in the hand of God's providence my purpose awaits me; I will get myself ready. And he did. As Jesus did. He put first things first.

If we are going to live in balance with the rhythm of life then clearly we need to learn to step back and take stock of our lives. We need to look at our emotional health, our mental fitness, our soul and spiritual health, our physical fitness. All these things working in harmony will release us to be so much more effective. Jonathan Aitken, the high-flying Conservative politician who went to prison on corruption charges, later confessed that he had lost contact with his foundations – family, friends, faith and fellowship. All these were neglected, and ironically it took imprisonment for him to be able to readjust his life and put first things first.

Jesus was applying himself at this point to make sure that the emotional connections in his life were sound. He knew strain on the family would come. He was preparing, using the time wisely to celebrate, relax and make memories. He intentionally made room for love and laughter.

I try to draw from him principles to direct my own life. Here they are:

Recognise your need for the God-given rhythms of life – worship, play, rest and work.

There need to be seasons of rest and intense activity. Live in balance.

Let there be room for love and laughter.

Finally – I am a lover of classic movies. And for me one of the classics is definitely *Dead Poets Society*. In it the character played by Robin Williams exhorts the young men in the school at which he teaches not to waste their lives or let them float by in a fog of conformity or dull, soul-destroying habit. His mantra is *Carpe diem* – seize the day.

At first sight it might seem as though that phrase is in opposition to the title of this chapter, 'Live in Balance with the Rhythm of Life'. Yet I think the two are actually complementary to each other. If we are living in balance then every day has its special character, each day is special and every day therefore must be seized for its purpose, its place, its meaning in our lives. This is the heart of what drives me to do what I do.

I see too many people inside the church and outside it spending their lives observing others. Television, DVDs and even computers encourage us to be watchers rather than to actually participate in life. Relationships that we form via websites are not a substitute for face-to-face encounters. We risk becoming observers rather than active participants.

Sometimes it seems to me that through the rage of the predatory groups of young people from the underclass that stalk our city streets and the drunken gangs that bring fear into the nightlife of our town centres an almost incoherent cry is coming from the souls of human beings robbed of their significance – 'I want to live!'

Life is not a dress rehearsal. Too many of us are sitting waiting for the performance to begin, not realising that we are already on stage. All too often we have failed to make our entrance when we were called upon. We are missing our cues. Our lines are not being spoken and the world is the poorer because we are not playing our part; we are not expressing those unique flashes of the divine purpose for which we each were made.

We have been told that 'for evil to triumph, all that is required is for good men to do nothing'. Yet we are passive rather than active, waiting to be told what to do, not realising that the director is God himself and if we will but listen we will hear him directing us.

The lights are on, the cameras are rolling. It is time for us to answer the call of 'Action!'

　After all, that is what David did.

Part 2

Becoming God-Energised

Our effectiveness in life depends on our being fuelled by the one who made us. Accepting his purpose and developing connection with him to its full potential is the secret of true success. His limitless energy is freely available to sustain us in all we have to do.

Chapter 4

Feed Your Soul

THE VALLEY OF DEATH

Judea, 1025 BC

When the war actually started, life became more comfortable. His three eldest brothers, Eliab, Abinadab and Shammah, joined up. And the three brothers who had stayed at home were not threatened by him as Eliab had been. Yet he felt no more secure here than he had before, for a different reason. He was no longer at home in Bethlehem. Even out on the hills with the sheep he felt restless. It was not helped by being sent regularly by his father as a messenger to his brothers in the army.

The front line was about eighteen miles from Bethlehem. He grew familiar with that journey not only because of visiting his brothers but also because when the King was troubled by his inner darkness, his aides would send for David to come and sing until the darkness lifted. But he did not really belong at court either. In fact, the boy who had grown up feeling an outsider in his own home now felt stretched uncomfortably between two identities – son of Jesse and minstrel to the king – and at home in neither.

Then came a day that was to change everything. His father sent for him: 'Go and visit your brothers, here are supplies for them, and take these special cuts of cheese for the senior officers.' He arrived at the camp just as the army was setting out for the battlefield, and walked out with his brothers. Then he saw him: a massive figure dominating the valley between the armies. Goliath. Nine feet tall. They said his iron spearhead weighed fifteen pounds. When the giant roared his challenge of man-to-man combat, David was amazed that nobody responded, even more so when he heard that the person who killed the giant had been promised marriage to the King's daughter and exemption from taxes for his whole family. David looked around him. How was it possible for someone serving the occult powers of a heathen god to defy the armies of the Living God?

It was Eliab who squashed him. 'What are you doing here anyway? You should be looking after those sheep at home. I know what you're up to. Just wandering round looking at the battle, causing trouble.' But it was already too late. David's questions and his confidence that Goliath could be defeated had already been reported. The King sent for him. 'Let not the King be concerned about anything. I will fight this Philistine.' The senior officers chuckled and Saul responded, 'Don't be so stupid! You can't go and fight this man. He is a professional soldier; you are just a boy.' David burned at being called *just a boy*. He had seen fourteen summers. How could he be a boy?

'Your Majesty, I am a shepherd. I have killed lions and bears when they came to attack the flock. The God who helped me then will help me destroy this pagan Philistine.' Saul smiled. The men with him grinned. The boy's faith was impressive – but foolhardy.

Saul intended to show the boy he was not yet the man he claimed to be. 'You can wear my helmet and armour, and take my sword.' David was not yet fully grown and Saul was head and shoulders taller than every other man in Israel. The coat of mail hung down, ridiculously loose, and the helmet came down over his eyes. The generals around Saul chuckled quietly. They could all see what the boy could surely now see – that for all his enthusiasm, he would be no match for the Philistine. But they had reckoned without the faith that burned within him. His mind was clear. After a few trial steps, David turned and said, 'I can't wear these. I am not used to them at all. My God is my armour.' He knew what he had to do.

Agile as always, moving lightly on the balls of his feet, he stepped out of Saul's palatial tent and went to a stream, where he carefully weighed pebbles until he had five that felt right. The others were frightened of Goliath but David looked at him with glee – the lumbering giant was a target too big to miss. He felt the texture of the pebbles in his hands. They were dry now. He put them into his pouch, mentally selecting the best to go into the sling. Shepherd's crook in one hand, sling in the other, David moved down into the valley towards the giant.

READY FOR THE MOMENT

David's moment of destiny came about in the middle of routine. He simply went in obedience to the command of his father. He was doing what he was told.

I wonder about that moment when Jesus made the journey from Galilee down to Bethany at the lower end of the Jordan to be baptised. I do not think it was routine. There is no indication that this was a regular trip. On the other hand, did he actually know this was the moment when he was moving into the fullness of his destiny? Or was he simply doing what David did – going in obedience to *his* father? There is so much we do not know about the life of Jesus. We do not know when Joseph died. This man fathered Jesus so unselfishly that, as a young man, he found nothing in the memory of that relationship with his earthly father to prevent his relationship with his heavenly Father being all it was meant to be. Joseph was a good dad, but long gone. Somehow Jesus knew this was the moment to move out of that place of hiddenness and begin the ministry to which he had always been called.

THE ANOINTING – JESUS

Bethabara, Jordan Valley, AD 30

John was weary. He stood upright and eased his back. It had been a long day and his muscles were aching. It went with the job – when you were dipping hundreds of people a day in the Jordan. That's why they called him John the Dipper. He chuckled. It sounded rather more dignified in Greek – the Baptiser. He looked across at Andrew; a good lad, great at bringing people. A friend to the unlovely. He turned to the next one in line.

The evening sun shone into his face. He realised with surprise that it would soon be dark. The long line of people whom he had been baptising had now been reduced to a small group. He looked at the priests standing on the ridge looking down over the Jordan Valley, watching, like vultures circling in the desert, waiting for their moment. Of course vultures would be circling something dead, but here, though the vultures did not recognise it, they were circling new life.

None but his inmost circle knew that alongside his call from heaven to draw the people of Israel back to their God was a greater dream; God had promised him, 'One day, as you are baptising, I will send you the Messiah.' He wondered: would this be the day?

He looked at the next in line and asked his name and, as he always did, spoke the familiar words, 'I baptise you for the forgiveness of sins.' The crowd shifted and his eyes caught the face of the man at the end of the line. In his time in the wilderness, John had seen plenty of lightning strikes but had never been hit by one. Until now. He was electrified, immobilised. It was Him. Deep in his soul, he knew it was Him. The promised one had come at last. It was quite automatic, the rest of the line. He did not really remember any of them. He just kept seeing that face.

Finally, the One stood before him. John felt the tears standing in his eyes; his own insecurities and inadequacies, his own sins rose up before him. 'Why have you come to me? I need you to baptise me. I don't understand. Why have you come?' As he looked into the man's eyes, John realised that, at that moment, he was known as he had never been known before. The eyes of the One stared into him: 'You are just going to have to let it be. It's the right thing. I have to fulfil everything that is right. And this is right, for all Israel.'

Trembling, hardly able to believe what he was doing, John adopted the position so familiar to him, standing next to God's Messiah; he held his shoulders, one arm around him, his assistant on the other side, steadying. He found the words coming quite naturally: 'I baptise you for the forgiveness of sins.' At that moment, he saw it. He was baptising the Messiah for the forgiveness of sins. Not his own, but the sins of the whole world. Somehow this man was God's sacrifice. He would be God's own lamb.

As Jesus emerged out of the water, there was a thunderous sound from heaven and in the vibrant tones John heard the words: 'You are my son, marked by my love. I am so proud of you.' Then something he had never seen before; it wasn't an actual dove but it looked like one and it flew almost like an arrow straight to the head of the man and sat there. At that moment what he already knew was confirmed: he had seen the Spirit of God come and, for the first time in human history, that Spirit had come to stay. Not just to visit, but to live in and on a human being.

From this moment on, something that had been hidden until now would become obvious. Jesus of Nazareth was the Messiah, the Christ. John realised that this was bigger than he had ever understood before. Not just Israel would be delivered, but the whole world.

TRULY HUMAN?

How did Jesus know he was the Son of God? Along with all Christians I am convinced that Jesus really was God in human form. I am also convinced that, in becoming human, he set aside and left behind everything in his divinity that was incompatible with being human, including his awareness of himself. He became genuinely human. He was not cheating. He was not wearing a disguise. Unlike Superman, he did not wear a superhero costume under his robe! In becoming human he became what he, as God, had designed human beings to be. As a man, he walked in relationship with his heavenly Father. He learnt to hear his voice and obey him, just as he expects us to do, by faith.

How and when did he first become aware of his extraordinary destiny? At the age of twelve he was in the temple in Jerusalem conversing with the leading scholars of the land, answering their questions and constructing questions of his own. At some point, he became aware that he was uniquely the Son of God, and he determined that he would walk with his Father, in trust and obedience, for the rest of his life.

As far as we know, there were no extraordinary direct communications from heaven to Jesus in the eighteen years that followed. When he made the journey to Bethany to be baptised in the Jordan, he did so in obedience to the will of his Father. How did he know? Just the same as you and I would. He had to do it by faith. It is an amazing record. At the time when his body was pulsating with adolescent hormones he was learning stillness, waiting. Not trying to push events forward, nor trying to force God into an open affirmation.

Finally, after eighteen years, he was released to set out on the pathway of destiny. That word is much overused, but obedience and trust of that magnitude are simply awesome. And since we are told that he was tempted in the same way that we are, I have to ask: did he feel at least a twinge of uncertainty? Was there a small voice whispering, 'Maybe this is the wrong time'?

As the line moved slowly towards where John the Baptist stood in the water, was he wondering, 'Have I got it right?' If he was truly human, surely something of that was going on? So the words from heaven must have come with enormous power: 'You *are* my Son. I love you. I am so pleased with you.' What did that mean to him? Joy! Joy rising up within him as he sensed his Father beaming at him and saying, 'You got it right, Son.'

In Psalm 45 we are told that the Messiah was covered with gladness more than any other human being. I believe it. Jesus lived like that – in the constant glow of his Father's approval. No wonder the Bible says he was the happiest man on the face of the planet. He did not just know the secret of happiness. He lived it. And that is what still makes him so gloriously magnetic. This rugged man with the strong, work-hardened hands of a carpenter comes up out of the Jordan shaking his head, droplets of water going everywhere, sparkling in the evening sun. The smile on his face reveals a river of gladness inside him big enough to engulf all creation. It is the same joy that will sustain him through the hell of the cross, wait for him in the tomb, then empower him to rise from the dead and walk out of his tomb.

So, Jesus spent eighteen years learning how to nurture his soul in relationship with God. Eighteen years, not of noise and argument in a Yeshiva, a rabbinic college, but rather in stillness, listening to the voice of the Father, waiting for the command to move, waiting through years, honed by the discipline of resting in his Father's presence as he went about his normal life. It was the quiet and easy camaraderie of those who walk in friendship – a companionable silence. The walk with his Father provided him with a depth of relationship unprecedented in human history. The flowering of Israel's pain and long apprenticeship had arrived. Many hundreds of years of God's hard training of the nation had finally produced her finest son.

He was to engage with the powers of darkness that have devastated the human race and our environment. For that purpose, swift as an arrow, the dove of God's Spirit winged her way to union with his spirit. It was not momentary but permanent – staying for ever. It marked the inauguration of the true New Age. At that moment, Jesus was the turning point that marked a new humanity.

At last!

BE REAL!

Through being dipped in the River Jordan by John the Baptiser, Jesus committed himself to a pathway that would lead to enormous suffering and a horrendous sacrificial death. But he truly believed that, beyond all that, there would be resurrection, reunion with the Father. It is hard for us to understand. We have been nurtured on a fashionable diet of pessimistic storytelling and film noir in which everything goes wrong, people die and even if the hero does live, it will be without the heroine. She has been killed in the last reel of the movie, so it is all pointless and for nothing. It is of course a style, an affectation, as much a child of its time as the sugary *happy ever after* endings of many films of the 1930s and 1940s.

We believe ourselves to be far too sophisticated to expect that everything will work out. We are smart. It will inevitably go wrong. And we will all die, so everything is pointless. However, Jesus' approach was radically counter-cultural: not 'too good to be true', but 'good enough to be true!' After all, this is God's creation. We will all die – and it will be glorious.

Yet this man was no naïve optimist, but an utter realist, who knew what would happen to him. Later on he spoke about it so brutally that Simon Peter took it upon himself to rebuke him. 'God forbid, Lord, this shall never happen to you.' Jesus looked at Simon, and at the impact those words were having on the other disciples. It is almost as if Simon had been reading some modern book on self-motivation. 'Come on, Lord, you are just getting depressed. Of course that won't happen to you. There is no way God would allow that to happen.' He should never have invoked God. It is when we really get religious that Jesus has to become truly ruthless.

Across nearly 2000 years, what he said to Peter still cuts like a knife: 'Get behind me, Satan! . . . You do not have in mind the things of God, but the things of men' (Mark 8:33, NIV). There could not have been a bigger put-down. Then he called the whole crowd to him. He told them that not only was he going to die but they were being called to give up their lives too. 'If anyone would come after me, he must deny himself and take up his cross and follow me. For whoever wants to save his life will lose it, but whoever loses his life for me and for the gospel will save it' (Mark 8:34–5, NIV).

That last sentence is the key to Jesus' radical realism. He knew what lay before him. Yet he also believed in ultimate victory over the corruption of the world, the guilt of the human race and the powers of darkness. By faith he believed that he would rise from the dead. Inviting others to lose their lives for him and his good news was a call to adventure, death *and* resurrection. It still is!

This radical call of Jesus was echoed in Nazi Germany during the 1930s when a young clergyman called Dietrich Bonhoeffer famously reminded Germans that the call of Jesus was 'Come and die'. Imprisoned for opposing the rule of Adolf Hitler, he faced his execution with courage, dignity and joy because of the Christ whom he followed.

Jesus was able to face his destiny on the basis of three assurances given at the moment of his baptism. First, 'You are my Son.' This declaration gave him assurance of identity. So he did not operate from insecurity. His gifts and talents were used only for the good of others and for the extension of that kingdom he represented. *He knew who he was.*

Next, 'Chosen and marked by my love.' We yearn to be loved. Often we try to generate it from others by our actions or words – by manipulation. Jesus lived in the assurance of affection and it gave him a truly rare freedom. *He knew he was loved.*

Finally, 'You are the pride of my life.' Think of the lengths to which we are driven by our own desperate need for approval. We simply *must* find people to tell us we did all right. Coming off a stage, we can't help prompting somebody, anyone, to say, 'It was great. You were terrific.' Even though we know that approval generated like this is phoney. It is an addiction. Jesus was not driven by that sort of torment. He lived in freedom. *He knew he was approved of.*

Those pledges refreshed Jesus every moment of his life. Knowing he was made for relationship, living in acceptance, affirmation, approval and affection from his Father. Without such things, we all eventually shrivel and die. It makes sense to nurture relationship with God and with people. That should not be a surprise. When Jesus was asked for the first principle of living, he said, 'Love God with all your heart, mind, soul and strength and love your neighbour as yourself.' We know it makes sense to nurture relationships with family and friends, which in turn nourish us, even if the people concerned are not sure about God.

Sadly, we can be incredibly short-sighted. In the rush and tear of a busy life, we often say to ourselves, 'I'll deal with that tomorrow.' I'll make time to call my father tomorrow. I'll make time to visit my mother tomorrow. I'll spend time with my children tomorrow. I'll take my partner or my spouse out to dinner tomorrow.

And tomorrow never comes – because we are running not just to catch up with our schedules, but to evade the obligations that chase us. Relationships are painful, and we avoid pain. But sometimes the pain finds us.

'IT IS YOUR DESTINY, ERIC'

April 1972

In 1970, when I was twenty-eight, my life was a mess and my marriage was in trouble. I turned to the most brilliant teacher of the message of Jesus that I had ever heard. I asked if I could help by driving him to his engagements and by processing the recording of his messages. Roger Forster agreed to let me do this. I was very grateful. I am not sure how much of a help I truly was. But the fact is, I didn't just want to hear what Roger said. I wanted to be like him. There was a steely strength in him that I longed to have myself. So I adopted him as my mentor.

One particular evening in 1972, I stood in his study and started to talk about somebody who had irritated me, a young man who had become a full-time evangelist and had then given it up. I was crowing about this as if it were some personal triumph for me. Roger turned on me: 'If that young man was not meant to be an evangelist then that is fine. But if he was called by God for that task, it is just about the saddest thing that I have heard in months. For me, "evangel" is the most beautiful word in any language, and the greatest privilege anyone could ever have is to be an evangelist.' Like a scalpel, his words cut through my defences and opened up a memory I had suppressed since I was twelve.

The little back-street chapel I attended had taken a group of us to Harringay Arena to hear a wild young American preacher called Billy Graham. I stood in that building with about 10,000 people. I had never seen such a huge crowd nor ever heard so many people singing. Billy Graham was different from every preacher I had ever heard. He preached as though he meant what he said and said what he meant. There was a passion and authority

I had never seen before. It touched me to the core. As I sat there I knew that, above all else, that was what I wanted to do. And I felt God was saying to me, even at the age of twelve: '*That is what I want you to do.*'

But the response from inside me was, 'I could never do that. People that come from my kind of background never get to do stuff like that.'

Roger's words had opened up that memory. It was as if a curtain had been drawn back and I was there again. I excused myself, got into my car and drove home. My eyes were streaming with tears as I realised that, at the age of twenty-nine, God was saying to me: 'The call you received seventeen years ago is still there. I still want you to be a proclaimer of my kingdom.' I could not believe it. The very thought that God would want somebody who made such a mess of things was shocking. It was foreign to my understanding.

It still shocks me today. I had absorbed the conventional religious understanding that, in order to serve God, I had to be good enough. And I knew I was not good enough. Then I heard that it did not matter. God was willing to take me from where I was and release me into his purpose. The destiny I thought I had flushed down the toilet had been restored to me shining, pristine and unsullied despite my stupidity and rebellion. I truly could not believe it. At times I still find it hard to believe – and yet . . .

That moment transformed my life by presenting me with a purpose, my destiny, a dream from God for me. I came alive because now I had a reason to live.

A purpose – bigger than me.

A destiny – out of this world.

And a relationship – passionate, exciting, stretching from here to eternity.

My life changed with those realisations. From then on I had a direction. I knew I was going somewhere. That sense of going somewhere is what empowers us to keep going when everything around us seems to say *just give up, it's too much; it's too difficult.*

'Life is hard, then you die.' The first time I saw those words, I was a young messenger of Jesus in America. They resonated with me because at that time we were facing real difficulties in our marriage and in our family. If you communicate with integrity, people sense what is happening. Those going through tough times ask, 'How do you keep going?' The simplest answer I could find is the theme of this chapter – *'I depend on God in everything.'*

WORK

Jesus came to complete a task, walking in partnership with his Father, totally dependent on the love and power of God. He spoke of 'the work my Father gave me'. At the end of his ministry he was able to say, 'I have finished the work.' At the climax of the agony of the cross, he was able to shout, 'Finished!' The import of the word is that he had done the job he was sent to do. He had completed the task. It was a shout of exhausted exultation.

Few things in life are as satisfying as the moment when a difficult or even seemingly impossible task has been successfully completed. We are wired for that moment. Jesus points us to this reality. It is part of our humanity, not just to work, but to see work as a task from God – a vocation. Not just a means of earning one's living. Too few of us have a genuine sense of purpose in our work – even those working for 'a good cause'. Far too many of us have jobs that are just a form of drudgery. This cannot be the way the creator intended it to be.

Jesus, as our model, was able to say, 'I've got work my Father gave me to do.' Clearly, that was part of what made him the dynamic, exciting human being that he was. I am aware that some people will say, 'Well, we can't all have the luxury of doing what you do!' Trust me – it is entirely possible, indeed very easy, for those engaged in running a faith enterprise like a church to become completely divorced from the presence of God. We talk 'God' words and we look at 'God' plans. But we easily become disengaged from the God we are supposed to serve. God's truth becomes commonplace. Familiarity breeds contempt. Our lives become *religious* drudgery. There is nothing worse than that!

It is the genius of Jesus' message to take the ordinary and make it extraordinary, to take what others regard as secular and make it the stuff of a heavenly purpose. In the kingdom Jesus came to set up, there is no such thing as the profane. All is sacred. I am aware that you may still be saying, 'Yes, but my job is so boring.' From the perspective of my urbanised lifestyle, the life of a herdsman looks rather boring! But God loves to show up in the routine.

It was a day like any other. A shepherd was tending his flock in what our King James Version of the Bible quaintly describes as 'the backside of the desert'. He saw a flash fire, not uncommon in the desert heat. When he went near, a bush was burning – but not being consumed. A voice spoke and told him he was known, honoured with a great task and commissioned. Once he had dreamed of great destiny. Now, Moses was reluctant to take up the offer. He had settled for life as a shepherd and feared disturbing the even pattern of his life. Furthermore, dramatic failure forty years previously had left him convinced that if he did try, he would fail. He was literally a no-hoper. He came up with objections of every kind. Then God asked him, 'What is that in your hand?' He replied, 'A staff.' It was a shepherd's staff. The standard equipment he used every day in his work.

I wonder how often God asks us the question, 'What is that in your hand?' and we are too dumb to hear or too stupid to answer. Does it not occur to us that God could use the very thing I use every single day? He can use the ordinary implements of my occupation to do something amazing. Hebrew Scriptures later refer to Moses' staff as 'the Rod of God'. So an ordinary shepherd's staff, greasy with the lanolin of sheep's wool, became a conduit for God's power to touch the greatest empire then known, and bring an entire people out of slavery into freedom.

Maybe it is time to revise our understanding of the work we have been given or perhaps to seek that vocation God has for us instead of just settling for earning a living.

WORDS

Beyond question, Jesus gave us some of the most memorable words the world has ever heard. Sometimes people use his words or his expressions or concepts without knowing where they came from. They have become part of the culture, not just of the nations of the West, but of the whole world.

Consider the following list taken almost at random:

- Don't hide your light under a bushel
- An eye for an eye
- The sun shines on the righteous and the unrighteous
- Don't let the right hand know what the left is doing
- Don't cast your pearls before swine
- It's like feeding the five thousand
- They're like sheep among wolves
- By their fruits you will know them
- A wolf in sheep's clothing
- They're the salt of the earth
- Going the extra mile
- The straw that breaks the camel's back
- The black sheep of the family
- Suffer the little children
- It's a millstone round my neck

All these are direct quotes from or corrupted references to his teaching. But Jesus was not precious about copyright! In fact, he said, 'The Father who sent me commanded me what to say and how to say it.' Jesus was not *trying* to be original! He was listening to the creator. Because of that he was inspired to unsurpassed creativity. He was a magnificent and economical creator of haunting stories. It wasn't just what he said, it was the way he said it. He communicated with life and excitement. Words have great power. They form our inner world, and our inner world inevitably shapes our outer world.

Isn't it time we drew on his example and changed the way we speak, changed our words so that they reflect God's purposes, God's promises and God's destiny for our own lives?

Consider this excerpt from an article called 'Patient knows best', printed in the *Reader's Digest* magazine in August 1991:

> A person's answer to the question 'is your health excellent, good or fair?' is a remarkable predictor of who will live or die over the next four years according to new findings. A study of more than 2800 men and women aged 65 and older found that those who rate their health 'poor' are 4–5 times more likely to die in the next four years than those who rate their health 'excellent'. This was the case even if examinations show the respondents to be in comparable health.

This truth may only now be getting statistical back-up, but it is not new – it has been known for thousands of years. About 950 BC Solomon wrote, 'Words kill, words give life; they're either poison or fruit – you choose' (Proverbs 18:21, *The Message*).

Jesus chose. He chose to listen to his Father's words, respond to them and make them his own, then give them to others: 'These words you hear are not my own, they belong to the Father.' Instead of trite repetition of religious truths, his words invited people to a conversation, a dialogue through which his Father reached out to people, to touch them with life. No wonder that when Simon Peter was asked whether the disciples would like to join those who found it all too complicated and left, he responded, 'Master, to whom would we go? You have the words of real life, éternal life' (John 6:68, *The Message*).

So, if we walk through life in conversation with Jesus, there is at least a possibility that, like his, our words will have life in them. That seems an objective worth pursuing!

MIRACLES/WONDERS

'The impossible we do at once – miracles may take longer.'

I have seen various versions of that poster in different work-places. It expresses the understanding that we are often capable of achieving much more than we believe. Jesus said of his own life, 'The miracles are my Father's work.' So Jesus never claimed to be a miracle-worker. Yet it is clear to all except the most biased observer of his life that amazing and miraculous signs did accompany him. His attitude was full of 'possibility thinking'. He, as a man, but depending entirely upon God, truly knew all of God's power was available to him. So he was able to say, 'With God, all things are possible.' And, 'By myself, I can do nothing.'

The seeming tension between those two sentences is the paradox of an utterly dependent human being walking in partnership with his creator. There are moments when we all reach the end of our resources and abilities. Either we accept the limitation of what is reasonable – *or* we dare to reach out to the God who did amazing things through Jesus. We open ourselves to the possibility that the loving Father may want to do something wonderful through us. Why not? Wonders never cease!

THE ADVENTURE OF DEPENDENCE

Trusting humans we *can* see is hard. Trusting in the God we *cannot* see is even more difficult. But that is the adventure. The childish person demands to see, and says I won't believe unless I do see. Mature people understand that seeing is not the same as believing. I have seen many women in the world, some of them as nice-looking as my wife. But the fact is I have not *seen* any of *them*. I have seen their exterior. But the woman who has been loyal to me through forty-six years of marriage, has loved me and brought up our five children with me, is someone who can be seen only through the lens of relationship. When I see her, I see the person that she truly is. (Even then I don't know everything. She is, after all, a woman! And women remain a mystery to men.)

I love her, not just for her outward beauty, but for who she is. It is the same with knowing God. The truth of who he is is accessible to me, through the lens of relationship as I walk in companionship with him.

Nobody can deny that Jesus was a truly remarkable human being and someone who shook the world. As we observed in the last chapter, there is something about him that is never stale. He is fresh. If we are going to receive the same refreshment we need to learn from the way he depended on the inward power of the Spirit of God, the fuel for our humanity – as essential to us as petrol to a car. Most of us have managed to drive our car till 'empty' on the dashboard became reality on the road. Coasting to a halt at an intersection or roundabout, honked at by irate drivers, we become aware that, separated from fuel, even the most glamorous cars become embarrassing heaps of junk; going nowhere – like humans without God's power. Jesus was God-energised: he received the Spirit of God for his inward resourcing and outward empowering.

Here is a difficult issue – if Jesus was truly human, was he ever ill? Did he ever have a cold? Personally, I believe he experienced illness but never gave in to it. So he walked in health by faith in the covenant-keeping God who said, 'I am the LORD, who heals you' (Exodus 15:26, NIV). Did he get tired? Yes. Did he yield to that? Give in to depression? Withdraw from relationship with God? (All things I am conscious of doing.) No, he didn't. He stayed alert and in contact with his Father.

There was one more area where Jesus exhibited remarkable composure, even playfulness – money. His awareness of God's abundance in the Spirit extended to every area of his life, including finance. He was not plagued by the need to get wealthy. But he did live in biblical prosperity. Let me unpack that – true poverty is not the state of not having, but the fear of not getting. Prosperity is not the state of having loads of money, but the assurance of sufficiency; that all my needs will be met and I will have enough to give some to others. Jesus lived in prosperity. He did not allow what he scathingly called Mammon to govern his life.

After his baptism he was driven by the Spirit of God into the wilderness to face a battle with the powers of darkness. That is the sort of thing that we have relegated to the fantasy world of horror movies. This is convenient, because it stops us having to think seriously about the possibility that spirits of evil really do exist. As far as Jesus was concerned, he was under no illusion about the reality of the one who rules the kingdom of evil – Satan. As always, I defer to his wisdom. In that battle in the wilderness he discovered first the power of temptation, something with which we are all familiar. Second, the weakness of humanity, with which, again, we are all familiar. Third, the availability of the power of his Father, to defeat temptation in us: *not* something with which most of us are so familiar! In short, he learnt what it costs human beings to obey God in a screwed-up, messed-up, fallen world. He won the battle, partly because he knew he had a purpose. More significant than his own comfort, more rewarding than any merely personal desire, and more fun than the pursuit of any pleasure that this world could offer.

Having a purpose is at the heart of intentional living. The weird thing is that some people take for their purpose the task of telling others that there is no purpose. So we see Richard Dawkins, amazingly charismatic and brilliantly talented, dedicated to telling people there is no God. Yet he finds himself talking and writing incessantly about God. It is ironic that this has become his purpose. It is what he lives for. This militates against the argument he presents. He says he can find no purpose in the universe. Yet he himself is clearly driven by a sense of purpose. It is not just para-doxical; it is illogical. Unless he finally discovers that he was actually created within the universe to reflect the sense of purpose at the heart of the universe, placed there by the one from whom it comes.

Human personality is complex, made of many different elements. It reflects the infinite variety of the creator. So it needs interaction with him for its full potential to be realised. Even if you are an atheist it's worth the experiment of making contact. You never know, you might get a reply!

You are what you eat

'You are what you eat.' Physical health and well-being depend on taking in the food that gives our bodies the right vitamins, minerals and trace elements to keep us at the peak of fitness – well, at least somewhere halfway up the mountain!

Soul fitness is even more important. We all have a soul – a unique amalgam of invisible characteristics and traits, our true identity – our personality. No soul comes fully formed. It develops through things that happen to us and most powerfully through our own choices.

Our souls become fat, blubbery and shapeless if we spend our lives watching nothing but soaps, chat shows and quizzes on TV. Junk food of the soul – though not the worst we could consume.

Some things will do us real harm. They are poison for the soul. Pornography is one of the most profitable industries in the world. Like drug barons, pornographer chiefs live in huge mansions, surrounded by the trappings of wealth and opulent bad taste. They are parasites, living off the exploitation of the most vulnerable.

The first hit of a drug usually produces the best high. Pornography is the same. It draws a man (usually) to look continually for more of the stimulus he craves. His taste becomes increasingly jaded. His perversion gets worse, involving the kind of thing he thought he would never even look at. It poisons the soul, sinks deep, stains the core of his being and robs him of real joy. The ordinary beauties of nature no longer stir him.

Maybe you are addicted, and are saying, 'You think I don't know that? I just wish I could stop.' Well, here's a suggestion. Enter an agreement with someone you trust to call them *before* you press the key to enter that site. And decide to feed your soul on good stuff, not the filth vomited out of the depraved soul of a pornographer. Watch classic movies. Read great books. Listen to the music of great composers. Feed your soul on the art of those who were plugged into 'the big picture' – the Great Story.

The best art comes out of the struggle to make sense of what seems a crazy world. But if there is no creator there is no reason we should expect the universe to make sense. Even the words 'I love you' depend on a wider context. If there is no God, the whole universe is nothing but an accident. And the words 'I love you' should be retranslated, *'I, as an accidental conglomeration of proto-plasmic globules from some antediluvian swamp, happen to feel a completely arbitrary attraction towards you, another accidental conglomeration of said globules. Let's get together and have an accident.'* I don't think any of us wants to be hearing that from the most significant person in our life. 'I love you' demands a grander vision than the idea of humanity as a cosmic accident.

After all, without a personal creator, nothing in our universe actually means anything, apart from any meaning we arbitrarily assign to it. Post-modernism, the dominating philosophy at the end of the twentieth century, makes a huge leap. It says that we cannot prove 'scientifically' the existence of a personal creator, so we have to operate as if that person does not exist. The universe is just one big cosmic accident, we ourselves minor accidents. There is no big picture, only our own individual narratives. There is no 'meta-narrative', no overarching theme providing meaning for our exist-ence or that of the whole creation. But all great art denies this.

Epic literature, the plays of William Shakespeare, the novels of Tolstoy, the vast mythical landscape of *The Lord of the Rings*, the 'Harry Potter' series, all depend on the characters playing out their lives against a wider backdrop in which evil is finally punished, and good is not only its own reward but also rewarding.

Tolstoy's epic, *Anna Karenina*, demonstrates that when we strike out selfishly for the fulfilment of our own desires, we court disaster. In *Superman – The Movie* Superman stands in Loïs Lane's apart-ment and says to her, 'Loïs, I never lie.' It's a shame that the only man on planet Earth who can say 'I never lie' is an alien.

Liar, Liar with Jim Carrey makes a powerful plea for integrity in relationships. Meanwhile, in *Groundhog Day* the character played by Bill Murray is condemned to live the same day over and over again until he learns how to genuinely care for someone else. Until we can learn to care we will never grow. We will never move on. We will always live the same boring, pointless life as the day before.

These are only a few examples, but almost all great art acknowledges a universal moral framework – that allows no escape, no matter how we wriggle and squirm.

The great music of the classical masters has a standard pattern. Two themes in conflict make different statements, but they're woven into a harmony and reach resolution. Whether it's the operas of Wagner or the symphonies of Beethoven, Bruckner and Mozart, the same musical journey happens over and over. It depicts our yearning for the day when there will be a resolution of all the conflicting elements, incorporating true justice and the triumph of all that is good and most beautiful. In one of Beethoven's greatest works, his Ninth Symphony, the 'Ode to Joy' contains the line from Schiller, 'Above the starry tent, there must live a loving Father.'

I love the arts, but I have found nothing more effective for feeding my soul than the ancient wisdom and amazing stories contained in what we today call the Bible.

There are many editions of this amazing book, some of which have been split up into daily readings, taking you through the whole Bible in one single year. On average the readings take about fifteen minutes a day. It's possible to get them on CD, or listen to them on your iPod. Even if you don't have religious faith, the stories in this book can still give you confidence to face the world day by day. Certainly they help me face my world and its special pressures, and the issues we deal with in church culture are the same for people in all spheres, including the military, political, scientific and economic.

Human beings remain innately religious/spiritual. Ninety per cent of people still believe there is a God. Seventy-five per cent of people pray. Even in secularised Europe forty per cent of people attend some kind of service at Christmas. Whatever their attitude to church, most people still admit they need God. So the ultimate food for the soul is not just the great works of art that have provided inspiration and healing for the wounded spirit throughout centuries. The ultimate food for the soul is a relationship with the creator himself.

One of the glories of Renaissance art is Michelangelo's statue simply entitled *David*, and this is fitting. Long before the Renaissance, David was a Renaissance man. A consummate leader and military genius, he was also one of the finest poets the world has ever known and a musician of great skill. The poetry he left us demonstrates the extent to which he was dependent on his relationship with God. Passionate and strong-willed, there were times when David strongly disagreed with God. There were also times when he adored and worshipped him, as he adored no one else. If that sounds rather familiar, like a love affair, it's because, well, it *was* a love affair. David knew God loved him, and he loved God with a passion that released energy into every other part of his life. From an early age Jesus must have picked up from the Psalms that sense of David's total dependency on the God who constantly inspired, refreshed and sometimes infuriated him. It was this relationship that defined him.

So when Jesus said, 'I do always those things that please the Father,' he was giving us a window into understanding why and how he was the person that he was. He was always moving within the pleasure of his heavenly dad. There was never a moment when he did not know the smile of God. This gave him enormous resources. If it is true that 'the joy of the Lord is your strength', then Jesus had access to unlimited energy. The joy of his Father shone down on him always. Walking in that way produced a human being remarkable by any standards.

That is what will sustain and enable us to reach beyond the ordinary to become extra ordinary – something David was to demonstrate early in his life.

Chapter 5

Remember, You Are Invaluable

FROM A BOY TO A MAN

Valley of Elah, Judea, 1025 BC

Goliath was tired and bored. For six weeks now he had been standing in front of these wretched Israelites. Each day he issued the same challenge: 'Why should whole armies bleed to death? Send your champion to fight with me! Whoever wins will have the victory for his whole nation. If I win (cue roars of approval from behind him), you will be our slaves. If the God of Israel is as powerful as we hear and your champion wins (shouts of derision and mocking laughter), then we will be your slaves. Is there not a single man in all Israel that will fight me?'

Day after day for six weeks, standing in the hot sun in the Valley of Elah, the sweat trickling from under his helmet, puddling in the hollow of his muscular shoulders, running down under the armour, the best that Philistia could provide. At the beginning it had been fun. The five warlords of Philistia had chosen their ground well on one side of the Valley of Elah, but the Israelites had also chosen well, arrayed on a steep escarpment. It would be a costly thing to storm their positions. The warlords had not wanted to risk the massive casualties that would be involved and so they had turned to Goliath, as he knew they would. He surveyed the serried ranks of Israelites facing him on the other side of the valley. There was only one among them who looked as though he would give him even half a fight. The circlet of gold upon his head proclaimed him their king. No doubt the politicians had advised him against taking up the challenge. Even so, you would have thought that he would be prepared to stand up as the champion of his people.

Suddenly Goliath's attention was taken. A young boy, skinny but muscular, was leaping lithely down the rocks into the Valley of Elah. Goliath could not believe it. It was a joke, surely?

He watched as the lad bent over to check some pebbles . . . pebbles! . . . from the stream in the valley. Did he really think that pebbles were going to penetrate the armour of Goliath? It was ludicrous. The boy picked up some pebbles. Maybe he wasn't very confident about his aim? Actually David knew exactly what he was doing. He was making sure he had the perfect stone for Goliath and wanted to be ready for Goliath's brothers. He would need no more than one stone for Goliath, this lumbering ox in front of him who was ready for slaughter.

It had to be a joke, but the boy – what was he, thirteen, fourteen? – probably with the first fine fuzz of beard on his chin – took up the position of challenge. Suddenly he realised the boy was serious. Anger rose within him. Never in all his years as champion of Philistia had he been so insulted. Red-hot rage boiled within him and burst out.

'What am I, a dog to be chased off with a stick? Did you send a boy after me? Is there no man in Israel who's willing to face me?' Unbelievably the boy spoke. His voice was strong, stronger than his years.

'You come against me with a spear and a shield and a sword and I know your reputation, but you have forgotten to take into account something stronger than yourself. You serve a god who is a mere idol. In your insults you have insulted the Living God, the God of all the earth. He is Israel's God. If you have prayers to say, say them now. Prepare to die, Philistine.'

The red rage was in his eyes now. He could see, think and hear nothing else. This pipsqueak, this piece of dog turd on legs dared to challenge *him*?

'Boy, you'll be sorry. I'm gonna kill you. You little piece of crap – I'm gonna toss your body so high in the air, it'll be half eaten by the birds before it comes down.'

But David had been brought up in a house full of bigger brothers, slow and stupid just like the one in front of him, and he had learned fast how to survive the bullies and best them. Winding Goliath up to a state of almost helpless rage had been child's play for the boy David, who had been doing it to his own brothers since he was old enough to speak. What Goliath could not know was that from the moment he picked up his spear and prepared to throw it, he was doomed.

Not only were shepherd boys of David's age expert with a sling, in this particular shepherd boy Goliath had come up against a once-in-a-generation phenomenon – a Michael Jordan, a Babe Ruth, a Donald Bradman, a Cristiano Ronaldo. Mind and body flowing flawlessly, hand/eye co-ordination perfect, once in a generation. Goliath was dead; he just didn't know it. He was walking around. But dead. As he saw the boy lift his sling he still didn't know that he had only seconds to live. His brain did not have time to process the information that the stone had left the sling before five hundred foot-pounds of energy smashed into his frontal lobe, just beneath the lip of his helmet. Bereft of instructions, his knees buckled, his greaves smashing into the rocky floor. The rest of his body, dragged downwards by sixty kilos (or one hundred and twenty-six pounds) of bronze armour, smashed forward and slid down the hillside. The sound of his fall echoed round the valley. In that moment of paralysis, David was the only man who moved. Jumping lightly across the rocks in the brook, he moved towards Goliath's body. Everyone expected Goliath to get up. Only David knew that he was dead. The deadly intent that blazed from David's eyes was enough for the armour-bearer, who dropped the enormous shield and ran.

Incredibly, unbelievably, David now stood astride Goliath's body. Taking the huge sword from his dead hand, he raised it high and brought it slashing down across the back of the neck. The head rolled free, the helmet clattering among the stones. Now David, with the unerring sense of showmanship that would never abandon him, lifted high the head of Goliath, dangling by its long hair. Suddenly all Israel broke into a triumphant roar and the Philistines began to run. David smiled. He knew that from this moment on his brothers would be junior to him. Never again would they sneer at little David. From today he would always be the man who killed Goliath. David was made.

DIFFERENT GIANTS

We face different giants today: global warming; disastrous world-wide diseases; religious fanaticism and global terrorism; catastrophic economic imbalance; the rich growing richer on the backs of the ever poorer poor. Our giants are not so swiftly slain as Goliath. But the same battle needs to be won in our minds as it was in David's. Alone among the hosts of Israel, he truly believed the giant could be slain. He had already seen Goliath's death before it occurred. He knew it could be done.

Our biggest battle is the same. We have to begin to believe that the giants can be defeated. If that is to happen, we have to become activists. But that alone will not bring about the radical changes we all want to see. A juster, fairer, greener world will not come about at a single stroke or because of one gifted individual. It can come if lots of us will believe, like David, that our gifts, at the disposal and direction of God who made everything, really are able to achieve what is otherwise impossible.

There is enough food to feed the hungry, enough resources to house the homeless and clothe the naked. There is enough dispos-able income in the affluent nations to ensure that every single child in the developing world is sponsored, through one of the many programmes available. But we hold back. We refuse to believe that our tiny contribution could make a difference. We are oblivious to the fact that a gigantic flood is made up of individual drops. It is time for those of us who live in the developed world to get up off our often over-broad backsides, and do something. Yet all too often we are convinced by the spin of our enemies: the problems are too big; it can't be done. Beset by guilt and fear, paralysed by anxiety, we find ourselves stuck fast in the mire of our own indecision.

In the darkest days of the Second World War, Franklin D. Roosevelt famously told the American people, 'We have nothing to fear but fear itself.' Fear is extraordinarily irrational. In our society, my guess would be that no fear is greater than the fear of what John Wayne called 'The Big C'. Even today there are people who refuse to use the word 'cancer'. As if naming it would give it power over us. My own father-in-law lay dying in hospital and my mother-in-law steadfastly refused to believe that it was cancer that was killing him. After he died she acknowledged he was dead, but she still could not bring herself to mention the 'C' word. Her fear of that word was greater than the fear of death itself.

In some parts of the world, cancer has been dethroned as King of the Phobias by AIDS. But in Jesus' time, the most feared affliction was one that would make you an outcast from your own family and community – leprosy.

Galilean Foothills, AD 30

In the half-light of dawn, the drunk staggering unsteadily on his way home stared blearily at the bundle of rags at the side of the road. It had been a good night – too good! And now he was feeling the effects of mixing good Judean wine with Roman beer. He felt like kicking the bundle just for the heck of it. Then it moved. A clawed hand on the end of a scrawny arm waved a bell. A voice said, 'Unclean.' Instantly sobered, he leapt back in disgust.

'Filthy scum! What are you doing here? You shouldn't be among decent folk. Back to your hole!' Now he really wanted to kick it. But you never knew. And if you touched a leper you were ritually unclean. If his wife found out he had kicked a leper he would not only be expelled from the synagogue – not that he minded that too much – he would be subjected to the whiplash of her tongue for weeks. Still mouthing curses, he edged past the leper and continued his somewhat unsteady path home.

The leper tucked himself further into a dark corner, waiting. For so many years he had been alone, with only other lepers for company. It was years since he had been able to hold his wife and hug her. Such moments of beautiful intimacy, now nothing but a fading memory. Always from a distance, he had watched his beloved elder daughter grow up and change from a pretty little girl into a lovely young woman, now betrothed to a young man of the village. He would not be able to hold her, to play a father's part on her wedding day. His own son grew up without the apprenticeship a father should provide. When they could afford it, they left him food. They could give to him, but he could give nothing to them. He had no trade now; no one wanted leather goods made by a leper.

Not even as valuable as a child or a woman, he was not a man. He was nothing. Yet, the rabbis taught that Messiah would be known by miraculous signs: raising the dead; restoring the sight of someone born blind; *cleansing a leper*. Some were saying the young rabbi from Nazareth who had moved to Capernaum was Messiah, not just another false messiah. They said this one was *the* Messiah.

None of the other lepers from the little colony where he lived had come with him. They would not risk the hatred and abuse they would receive from the people. Even more, they feared the disappointment of yet another healing that failed. Leprosy was unconquerable. Better not to hope.

He thought again of his older daughter and his son, and the baby girl, now ten years old, whom he had never held. He saw again the lines of care etched into his wife's face and he knew it was worth trying. Even at the cost of disappointment. Besides, if the prophecies were true, Messiah had to come one day. Who knows? This could just be that day.

He settled down to wait. He was good at waiting. The sun rose. Heat built up till the hillsides shimmered in the haze. He gnawed on a piece of dry bread and drank water from a leather bottle, one of the last he had managed to make before he finally lost the use of his hands. He knew where Jesus was. The word had gone out the day before that he was going to what they called 'the Mount'. It was a bit of a Galilean joke. The Mount was not in any sense a mountain. It was a small rounded rise that commanded a natural amphitheatre.

He had been wise to come early. Thousands came, chattering happily as they passed him in his hiding place. The banter of good neighbours and the occasional sour tongue of a village dragon: a carnival atmosphere. But he knew all that would disappear with just one move on his part. Emerge from his hole and that easy, happy atmosphere would vanish. People would fall back in horror at the very idea of coming near, let alone touching the leper. He didn't blame them. How could he? He had been just the same.

The afternoon wore on. He decided to risk moving. He needed to be closer to the track that led down from the Mount into Capernaum. He tucked himself into the shade of a bush. Now he could hear the voice of Jesus as he came toward the end of his teaching. He had heard him before. Jesus was different. Other rabbis made God austere, distant, judgemental, pernickety, obsessed with the minutiae of life. Jesus did not describe God from the outside like a philosopher, cataloguing the attributes of a mighty mountain. He described him from the inside, like a mountaineer who had criss-crossed the peak many times until he knew it and loved it and was inviting you to join him on the same journey to the summit, like an invitation to a family party.

Jesus reached the end. He rose from the place where he had been sitting. People gathered around him, holding up babies for him to bless, withered arms for healing. Slowly, surrounded by his disciples, he moved down the slope. The sense of carnival was palpable. Children ran laughing and screaming. Mothers scolded. Men discussed what Jesus had said. There was much laughter.

He knew all that would stop when they saw him. And it did. The crowd melted away before him as people shrank from even the possibility of touching him or being touched by one of his torn rags. He was used to it. For years now, everywhere he went, he had to say 'Unclean, Unclean'. The word had sunk into him until he felt he was not just defiled but was himself a defilement. They hated and feared him, he could see that. He understood. He hated himself. Yet he had to do it. So, as Jesus made his way down the slope, the leper did the unthinkable. He moved resolutely towards him. The comments of the village dragons – 'Disgraceful!'; 'Shouldn't be allowed!'; 'People like that . . . !' – faded away as he saw Jesus continuing to walk towards him. Almost within touching distance he fell to his knees.

'What is your name?'

The leper struggled to form the syllables. It had been so long since he had been anything but a leper.

'Simeon.'

Jesus smiled and said, 'What do you want of me?'

Looking into that face with its clarity and compassion, he had never felt so literally 'unclean'. With all the courage he could muster he looked straight into the eyes of Jesus and said, 'Master, if you want to, you can make me clean.'

As he said it, he knew it was true. This was not a maybe messiah like all the others. Suddenly he became conscious of how quiet everything now was. The crowd's chatter had died. Even the children were still. There was an audible gasp as Jesus came close enough to touch him. He simply said, 'I want to. Be cleansed.'

As he said it, incredibly, unbelievably, he reached out and touched the leper. The leper had never felt such warmth. It flooded through him; his skin was glowing and becoming supple. His joints were freed, moveable. He felt like dancing.

'Thank you, Master, thank you so much.'

'Simeon?'

'Yes, Master?'

'Will you do me a favour?'

'Anything! What?'

'Keep quiet about this; don't tell anybody. I have so much to do and only limited time.'

'Of course, Master, but how? People will know.'

Suddenly Jesus grinned. 'I suppose they will.'

He embraced him in farewell and moved on down the slope towards Capernaum. Simeon wondered whether he should follow. Then he thought of his family. Smiling inwardly and outwardly, he turned to go home.

TWENTY-FIRST-CENTURY GLOBAL VILLAGE

So how much is a leper worth? Or an AIDS sufferer? Or a starving rape victim in Darfur? How much is a national hero worth, for that matter?

Given the astounding complexity of our genetic make-up and the flexibility of our stem cells, plus the astonishing effectiveness of our brain and nervous system, it is fascinating to realise that the elements of which we are made, including enough iron to make a single three-inch nail, are commonly found throughout the earth. The creation story in Genesis is remarkably accurate. We really are made of the dust of the ground. The chemical components of which our bodies are made are probably worth about 50p, or 75c in US terms. Clearly, our worth is not tied in to those kinds of statistics.

In Chapter 1 we looked at the uniqueness of our genetic make-up, the complex web of relationships into which you were born and in which you have been nurtured. This has resulted in a personality that is quite literally irreplaceable, unrepeatable. None of those things can ever be replicated. So you are impossible to value – to put it another way, valuable beyond calculation. It is the rarity of diamonds that makes them precious. The scarceness of gold makes it a valuable commodity to which people turn for stability in times of crisis. So you bring something to the table of life that is incomparable. No one else can make that contribution. The crucial question is: are you confident of that reality? For most of us, life has battered that sort of confidence out of us.

For all his insecurities and the mess of his dysfunctional family, David grasped the fact that he was special and acted on it. The leper whose story we looked at was somebody at the other end of life's battering and yet something inside him did not let him lie down under the weight of misfortune, would not allow him to accept that it was all over. It drove him to reach out towards the one person who could help. As a result everything changed, and a completely new destiny opened up before him and his family. If we are to see our lives become what they should be then we must grasp the nettle of self-leadership.

SELF-LEADERSHIP IS CRUCIAL

The wisest person in the Old Testament is David's son, Solomon. He said, 'Where there is no vision, the people perish.'

Though there are other versions of that particular proverb, this seems to me to encapsulate the pithy wisdom of Solomon himself. And it is the truth; where there is no vision, people die. They die from the inside. They die slowly. They fall apart. They become denatured, dehumanised in every sense. They perish. I use the expression about the tyres on my bike – the inner tubes perish over time. They lose their capacity to hold the air that gives them shape. The kind of vision that will keep us alive as human beings is the vision we have of ourselves, of others and our world. It is not enough merely to have the kind of vision that will enable us to be effective businessmen, great performers, writers, singers or dancers. It is possible to be a success in all those areas, yet not to have sustaining vision. We saw that in the tragic story of Kirk Stephenson in Chapter 2. But if our background is dysfunctional like David's or things have happened to us that have made us feel unclean, unfit, paralysed by guilt or anxiety, how then can we have a positive and sustaining vision of ourselves? It can only come from the one who made us.

SELF-LEADERSHIP IS FORMATIVE

Even when we make no conscious effort to choose direction for our lives, to lead ourselves anywhere, we are still exercising leadership. Admittedly, it is based on a decision not to decide, maybe even on an attitude that says life is too difficult and I will withdraw from it. But even that will form us. It will take charge of us. Decision never remains singular. It always leads to other decisions, and these in turn to others, so that a direction is set even though we had no intention of it.

If we do not exercise conscious, deliberate self-leadership, we will actually be electing to be undirected, shapeless, ineffective and in the end depressed and miserable. We ourselves will be insignificant, indiscernible except as somebody occupying space on planet Earth, breathing its air, taking in its resources, contributing nothing.

SELF-LEADERSHIP IS INEVITABLE

Whether we like it or not, our choices will turn into courses of action. They will make us into something. In other words, it is inevitable – we will exercise some form of self-leadership.

The question to be asked is this – will my self-leadership be incidental or intentional? Will it be the product of a series of accidents; things that happen *to* me, rather than conscious responses to the accidents of life? Or will I determine to fulfil the potential within me, to exercise talents and gifts, some of which I do not even know I have but which are all there within me – and somehow grasp the destiny for which the providence of God intended me?

Maggi Dawn, a songwriter, musician and Cambridge University chaplain, wisely observed, 'Someone has to lead, and even if nobody is appointed to lead, a leader will always emerge.' That is the truth. Something inside us will lead us and, if we have got any kind of sense at all, we will elect leadership from within that is positive, courageous and creative. Something with integrity, that's what we will choose.

The problem is that I know many people will not consciously take those steps. They will remain undecided, immobilised by that very indecision. Paralysed, and finally rendered incapable of becoming what the creator intended them to be. In the end, the only thing that's going to change that kind of process is an inner conviction of our true worth.

NOBODY'S PERFECT

I am a lucky man. I was brought up by parents who loved me and believed in me. Both my mum and my dad were people who believed in God and prayed for me every day. They believed their prayers made a difference. I share that belief. Of course, that did not prevent me having enormous conflicts with both of them, especially, in my teenage years, with my father, with whom I argued about everything. My father was regarded by most people as fairly good-natured. I was the one person who could reduce him to almost speechless rage. But he never stopped believing in me and never stopped loving me.

I grew up with my sense of worth shaped by their histories. My mother's father walked out on a whole family of children when she was young. She, her brothers and sister made their way down the economic chain from a comfortable middle-class existence to virtual penury, living in two rooms over what my mother assured me was 'a knocking shop'. She was tiny, feisty, vital, dark-eyed, dark-haired, attractive, full of vitality, aspirational. She was quicksilver.

Dad was completely different: tall, dark and handsome. He was outwardly calm, a deep thinker, a machine-turner by trade; an expert in mechanical engineering with an instinctive feel for metal and for what could be achieved using the technology of his day. He was also innovative when it came to working out how something produced on paper by a designer could become reality in the workshop. If my mother was quicksilver, he was slow water running deep. He was also very much a product of the still rather Edwardian age of the First World War. He knew his place and for the most part accepted that.

I became the conflicted inheritor of their backgrounds – aspirational and yet knowing my place. That was my attitude towards God. Trying through my childhood to be a 'good boy', brought up in the safe but constricted world of a back-street chapel that was part of the Plymouth Brethren movement. They spoke of freedom yet I saw bondage. They spoke of grace yet I perceived a legalistic lifestyle that left only a tiny place for inspiration. It may not be fair but that is what I felt growing up. I felt like a wild bird trapped in a cage, and I raged against my imprisonment. Yet at the same time I wanted to conform, to be that 'good boy' I had been brought up to be.

Pat and I met (collided almost!) and married quickly, much to the annoyance of my dear mum. I was her first and only son. No one would ever have been good enough for me, and Pat had a 'questionable history'. She was definitely not suitable, and of course that made her even more desirable in my eyes. We swiftly produced offspring. At one point, we had three children under three. Like many men, I thought marriage was a licence to sex 24/7. I discovered the extraordinary fact that my wife expected me to do stuff, to engage in relationship. That was all too much! I was working as a youth leader in our church and found myself attracted to some of the girls in the group. How could that be? I had been led to believe that commitment to Jesus would be instantly transformational, turning me permanently into that mythical 'good boy'.

THE DAM BREAKS

All this built up within me until there came a day when finally the whole encrusted façade of religiosity, the thing that masked me and yet imprisoned me, cracked. Rage poured out of me at God. I'd had enough. I was going to tell him the truth about the message that had been oversold to me, the frustration that I felt, the anger towards everything and everybody and especially towards him. I'd had enough of his church, this so-called new society. I was told it was full of the spirit of life. But it felt to me like a tomb. Our services were not celebrations of a risen Saviour but funeral services for a poor, noble but dead Jesus, with God remote and uncaring. Having no power to transform, legalism still commanded that I be righteous. I just knew I couldn't do it. So I poured out my rage and it carried on – words, swear-words, curses, all the four-letter words I could think of poured out of me. There seemed no end to the rage. Next day I woke up in the same state and it went on for another day at least.

But there came a point when I was exhausted and stopped. I became conscious of a very quiet voice deep within saying, 'Is that all?' It felt almost quizzical. I gathered my strength and replied, '*No!* There's more!' I gave him the rest, finishing, 'You can send me to hell if you like. At least you know how I feel.' Again the quiet voice: 'Have you finished?' I was too tired to say anything but 'Yes'. I have never forgotten the next words. They rang within me so clearly. 'Shall we get on with it, then?' I couldn't believe it. This angry God, whom I had pictured as being hungry to condemn me, turned out to be eager to enter a relationship with me in which honesty was not a sin to be punished but a quality more highly valued than almost anything else.

I realised then I had a value in myself, a value rooted in who I was, not in my conformity to religiously programmed standards of behaviour. That is such a risky thing to say. But then, that is the nature of God's grace and the distinguishing feature of the Christian faith. No other religion offers this, because at the end of the day only Christianity is truly about relationship with God. It is not a system of making myself good enough for God, but about giving God access to work in me throughout my life to finally make me what he has dreamed of me being.

My value, therefore, is in who I am and not in what I do. His love for me and even his approval are focused on what he made me to be. Even at times when my behaviour has been reprehensible, there has always been something that says, 'I am pleased with you – not pleased with your behaviour – but pleased with you.'

Jesus' followers are humans who have learnt to live in the unjustified approval of a Father who loves them for who they are, not how well they perform. Consequently, gripped by the message of grace, they respond with passionate longing to fulfil God's purposes. They *want* to live up to his standards not because the rules say they should but because God has implanted new life within them, joining his Spirit with their human spirit to produce something utterly unique – a new creation. That's the romance of faith in Jesus. The adventure is living it out. The problem is that so much of the church unthinkingly responds to the inbuilt legalism of human religiosity. As I grew up I discovered that the hidebound fussiness I thought was unique to my Brethren upbringing was common to other churches, as to other religions.

Sometimes when out walking, you can push through tangled undergrowth and dark woods and emerge suddenly at the top of an escarpment to be confronted with a wide and glorious vista.

That is how I felt on that day. It changed my (interior) landscape, beginning a process that would transform me through the years.

That moment granted me a newfound sense of worth. The revelation released me to begin what I now recognise to be the first steps on the road to self-leadership. It was almost as though I could hear the voice of God who said to Abraham: 'Walk in front of me. Be perfect.'

THE GREAT REVERSAL

My discovery of the great reversal inherent in God's value system was mirrored by the experience of Adrian Plass, now well known as a Christian writer and speaker, who remains in touch with his past failures. He has helped many to grasp the depths of God's love for even the most unlikely of us.

Early in his life he was a practising Christian employed as a social worker. It was partly the culture of that work environment and partly his own neediness that drove him, each lunchtime, not only to visit the local pub, but to drink too much. His colleagues were concerned and friends gave him little sermonettes and even sermons on why a Christian should not be a heavy drinker, and some even explained carefully to him why the Bible says Christians should never drink alcohol at all. None of it made any difference, apart from making him feel condemned for his own failure and inadequacy. (That seems to be something that religious people do for their friends very effectively.)

Nothing made any difference until one day, staggering out of the pub, he heard a gentle voice filled with a kindness and compassionate concern he had never experienced before: 'Adrian, why do you drink so much? It doesn't do you any good, you know.' The love in that voice, the simple question, was enough to set him free. He was never the same again. That single moment of revelation launched him on a journey that would uniquely unveil God's heart for the hurting.

TWO SIDES OF THE COIN

There are two facets of the life and work of Jesus uniquely balanced in him as never before among people of position and power.

First of all, there was the **authority** with which he spoke. Other rabbis appealed to senior rabbis of previous generations to give weight to their arguments. They almost never preached their own ideas. They drew on the precedents of the past. That is understandable. Rabbis were more like lawyers arguing a case than prophets or messengers of the Living God. This was a safeguard for the Jewish people, and a wise one, but it had become stultifying.

What stands out about Jesus is that the freshness and life with which he preached gave him an authority that was uniquely personal. Yet it was not the 'authority' of a ranting madman. People recognised it as prophetic because they heard through this man the voice of God. He spoke with authority, not like the other rabbis. That is understandable if he was who he claimed to be and who Christians believe him to be – the Son of God, uniquely God, but in flesh. WOW! Sorry to shout, but WOW is the word. In fact, in the Gospel that most scholars affirm as the first written, Mark says on many occasions the people were amazed. To put it quite simply, everyone could see that Jesus was amazing.

That is hard to convey to people whose vision of Jesus is defined by sunlight through beautiful stained glass and wonderful singing in cathedrals. Or filtered through sadly dreary singing of endless hymns in local churches and sermons that drag the life out of people, rather than putting life into them, as a preacher should be doing!

So what about this Jesus? What drew people was an amazing immediacy: as he spoke, they were hearing God's voice. He spoke with authority, not like other rabbis. That is not in any way to devalue their work. If Jesus was who I believe him to be, they were much-needed servants building the roadway down which he, as Messiah, would ride.

Jesus was a radical. In his preaching, he undermined the establishment in Jerusalem. He challenged their right to run the temple as a private fiefdom from which the ruling families gained huge amounts of treasure. Millions of Jews came from all over the world to worship at the temple and, as they bought their sacrifices and laid them out before God's altar, the money they paid always included a cut for the families of the high priest.

Lord Acton wrote in 1887 that 'power tends to corrupt, and absolute power corrupts absolutely'. He could have found no greater example in history than these dedicated, talented, priestly families. They finally could not resist the power and the money that was laid before them.

Jesus challenged all that. He also challenged the easy assumption that by good behaviour and regular giving people could buy their way into God's kingdom. Jesus told them, 'You can't do this. Only God can, and it's his choice, not yours, that counts. You have to lay your life before his sovereign authority.' John's Gospel says that many people turned away and left him. This kind of radical, spiritual kingdom stuff was far too demanding for them. Turning to his disciples, Jesus asked, 'Do you also want to depart?' Simon Peter, on this occasion thoughtful and perceptive, said, 'Master, to whom shall we go? You have the words of eternal life.' All they knew was that when they listened to Jesus *life* came into them. When they listened to the other rabbis they did not receive that same life.

Jesus' authority was not in the strident tones of one who shouts, but in the quiet, firm reality of the life of God present within him and his words. Even today, after nearly two millennia, his words still have unique power to bring life to those who read them.

Second in this unique combination was **love**. It oozed from every pore. I believe Jesus' evident compassion was what touched a Roman governor notorious for his brutality and insensitivity. Is it possible that, in the final analysis, it was that same quality that frightened the high priestly family as it plotted the downfall and death of Jesus? Nothing would have been more scary to them than the fact that he genuinely cared for the people – and that the people knew it. Standing alongside his integrity and his wonderful life-giving words, his compassion would have been unaccountable, strange and terribly unnerving when it was directed towards them. Perhaps in the end that was the reason he had to die.

Burning love for other people is always hugely attractive, especially to the down-trodden, the dispossessed and the powerless. They discover somebody who looks at them with approval, values them for who they are and believes in what they can become. In one of the most famous passages of the New Testament, Paul, the ex-rabbi so radically transformed by his own encounter with Jesus, wrote these words: 'Love never gives up. Love goes on believing.' That is so right.

However, love always seeks intimacy. Perhaps this was what threatened people in the love of Jesus. It may have been that very quality that drove Judas to betray him. Looking at the dynamics at the Last Supper, it is clear that Jesus was trying to let Judas admit he was the one who had already betrayed him. Judas could not bring himself to do it. It was one thing for him to know he was the traitor, but another thing entirely to admit it to someone else, even to Jesus, or perhaps *especially* to Jesus.

That's the problem, isn't it? We find the eyes of truth and love looking at us, searching us, asking, 'Will you actually enter into relationship with me?' It is scary. I think it is the reason why most of us run from the presence of God. It's not that we mind so much the idea of knowing God; it's letting God know us that is really frightening. Yet it is the heart of the Christian faith, of the message that Jesus himself came to bring. We can be known by God and, once known, we can be forgiven. It is the unique message of Grace.

INVITATION TO TRANSFORMATION

The disciples got that from Jesus. They had absorbed this amazing new message: that faith was not about gearing yourself up to keep rules and regulations and meet the impossible demands of God. Rather, it was about allowing God into your very centre so that he could change you into something new from the inside out. Looking at Jesus they saw the uniqueness of his holiness, not something that froze and repelled people, but a holiness demonstrating that Jesus knew he was special, set apart for God's purpose. And he was inviting others on that same pathway of adventure.

This was not about negativity – not doing bad stuff – it was a holiness of positivity, a life so filled with God's life, glory, laughter, joy, fun, adventure, a burning passion for people and justice, that there was no room for disobedience. Jesus had elected to commit himself utterly to the purposes of the God who had called him as his Son. He knew himself. He *was* the Son of God from eternity stepped into human form. Yet as the Son of God he had chosen to live in Sonship rather than set up his autonomous stall as 'alternative god' for the universe.

He was in full relationship with his Father all the time. That's what made him so special and drew others to him. His passion for God, his compassion for people, drew people. When the Bible says of him, 'The common people – the great multitude – heard him gladly', it was no wonder, because he spoke their language and he cared so much for them. His pastoral care for the disciples, his diffusing of their quarrels, his faithfulness to them when they failed and let him down, his love for them as his followers, guaranteed their loyalty.

The only way you and I can ever have the kind of satisfying and happy relationships we are meant to have is if we learn to love as he loved. But it is not something you can do a course on at a university. To love as Jesus loved you have to have the same spirit Jesus had. That's a challenge! Jesus did not waste energy in competition with others. He did not lose his temper or get angry at personal discourtesy or rejection. He refused to waste time trying to get even. He did not hold a grudge against those who publicly insulted him. I don't know how you feel, but that seems to me an impossible standard. Finally, he prayed for those who crucified him even as they hammered in the nails. Can't we learn from him?

Wouldn't it be wonderful if the world were filled with the same kind of behaviour? So many situations in our personal lives and international affairs would be transformed if we could learn to let go of grudges. How much energy could we discover if we did not waste it in competition with others, but aimed to excel, to exceed our own limitations? Suppose we let go of the anger we feel at discourtesy and rejection and got on with living our own lives? Would it not be a transformed world? An impossible standard it may be, but surely wisdom calls us to aim at it.

Yes, but how? Well, the only way that I can think is by using the same resources he used. Draw on the same Holy Spirit that filled Jesus. But we have to understand that this Holy Spirit is not an invader. He will not enter unless we invite him.

In refusing to waste time attacking others, Jesus was not being hopelessly idealistic. He was recognising that the real battle was against another foe – more significant, even though invisible. For him the existence of God's enemy, Satan, the accuser, was not a matter of intellectual discussion, but a constant experienced reality. He was opposed by this presence at all times and in the end he faced this enemy of human beings in the most fundamental way. That is the story at the very heart of the Christian faith.

Sometimes I ask myself what I am doing. I know that in asking the question, I've actually got three questions: Why me? Why here? Why now? And there is a fourth. What did God have in mind bringing these three elements together? For Jesus, the answer was clear. Thinking about the same questions, Jesus said, 'The Son of Man did not come to be served, but to serve, and to give his life as a ransom for many.' It is fascinating that in an age when people would claim a special status because of their special knowledge, Jesus was saying, 'I did not come for a few select people; I came for the many, for the multitude, the common mass.'

In our world, where we seem to hear almost daily of hijackings and kidnaps, his use of the word 'ransom' is astonishingly contemporary. In using such language, he paints a graphic picture of a world hijacked by powers of darkness, and individuals kidnapped and held to ransom by implacable terrorists of the spirit, who are without mercy. Jesus came to give his life to rescue the entire human race from that situation. That is his statement of intent. At the very least, it deserves our consideration.

Chapter 6

Be an Obedient (Hard-Working) Servant

SNATCHING DEFEAT FROM THE JAWS OF VICTORY

Judea, 1025–1017 BC

In the heady days following the death of Goliath, Saul should have exulted. For nearly twenty years he had battled valiantly against the armies of Moab, Ammon, Edom, Zobar and, repeatedly, the Philistines. Again and again he had faced them, pushing them relentlessly back. But now, with the death of the giant, Israel's army swept the Philistines before them, chasing them back to their cities and the coastal plain, laughing as their enemies ran inside the walls and shut the gates behind them. Then they returned to plunder the camp of the Philistines. Just a few years before there had been only two swords in the whole nation of Israel – Saul's and Jonathan's. Now, they had thousands.

In the weeks that followed, morale rose inexorably as triumph followed upon triumph. Wherever Israel's armies turned, victory ensued. Saul should have been rejoicing, filled with a sense of personal vindication. But there was a sour taste in his mouth, a knot of anger buried in his stomach that would not dissolve. Instead, it was growing in power. The fly in the ointment was David.

At first, when Goliath fell, the King had rejoiced along with all Israel. And he had loved the chase after the Philistines. But when they returned to his capital city, Gibeah, they were met by teenage girls dancing in the street, singing over and over again, 'Saul has slain his thousands, and David his tens of thousands.' The words lodged deep inside him. They would not go away. They ate at him. He saw the way the men looked when David walked among them. He had only to pass through the camp and their shoulders went back, their eyes brightened and they stood straight. He was their champion and when they were with him they felt like winners.

He knew he should rejoice. But jealousy infected every part of him. The trouble was, he recognised what was going on with David. Once, that same light of God's blessing had rested on him. He remembered. Head and shoulders taller than any other man in Israel, handsome, young, the product of a good upbringing, polite, modest, considerate, unassuming. He had been genuinely shocked when that fiercely passionate old man, Samuel, had found him on an errand for his father and the next morning anointed him king of Israel.

When the moment came for him to be recognised as king, they found him hiding among the baggage. What had frightened him most was not the task that faced him but the old man's fiery passion for God. A reluctant hero at first, he soon discovered that he was actually quite good at this business of leading men in battle. But the spiritual demands were something else. He understood it. In his world, all kings were supposed to be priests as well. They had to touch the powers of the heavens. For Israel's king that was even truer. You could not be king of God's people without being in partnership with God.

But Samuel was unreasonable. He refused to recognise that at times the absolute standards and demands of God had to be compromised. The realities of politics simply required it. Saul understood that relationship with God was important. But the idea that God claimed absolute authority over every area, including government, was just unworkable.

It was true that when he first became king he had experienced God's Spirit. It was amazing. He had been opened up to the unseen realm. He received the gift of prophecy. He knew how to access that inner voice of God. But he had stopped listening. God was a distant presence. And a rift had grown between him and Samuel that was now unbridgeable. So he instantly knew what he saw resting on David. It was the glowing presence of the anointing of God, fresh and unsullied.

In Gibeah, the words of the young women continued echoing in his mind. Saul descended once more into the pit of madness. A gift had been opened up long before. But the God who once prophesied through him was now silent. Another darker voice insinuated itself into his mind. Suspicious and vengeful, Saul raved. As always, David began to play his harp and sing. As always his voice reflected his fierce love and passionate worship towards God. Saul, in the midst of his raving, in anguish, recognised the voice he had once known so clearly for himself. But now he heard it as an outsider. The pain was unbearable. He just wanted it to stop. The picture in his mind was clear – David pinned to the wall, lifeless, blood draining from his body. The spear in his hand seemed to rise almost without his help. With a roar he hurled it. David's agility came to his aid. He avoided it, and the second spear too, which Saul seized from one of his men.

Frustratingly, David remained loyal. Made a senior commander in the army, wherever he led his men they had victory. All Israel loved him. Saul's own son, Jonathan, joined the nation in its adoration. His daughter Michal was in love with David. Saul gave him the impossible task of killing 100 Philistines, hoping the Philistines would kill him. He returned with the foreskins of 200 Philistines – irrefutable evidence of their deaths!

Jonathan pleaded with Saul, pointing out what a loyal servant David had been. Saul relented and received David back at the royal court. The crisis passed – until war broke out again. David and his troops defeated the Philistines so devastatingly that they began to flee from him whenever he turned up on the battlefield.

What ate at Saul more than anything else was the certainty that God had deserted him and placed his blessing upon David. He nurtured his rage and jealousy. However he tried, he could not bring himself to turn back from bitterness. Once again, the madness came. Urged on by Saul's officers, David began to play. The screaming in Saul's mind was unbearable. This time there was no doubt that the King was trying to kill David. He hefted the spear and drove it with such power that it stuck in the wall. David fled.

There were still moments when Saul would feel genuine affection for the young David, but these were almost against his will. They may even have helped to feed his growing paranoia, his sense of grievance. Saul was not God's enemy. He wanted God's blessing. But he wanted it on his own terms. That seemed only reasonable. What he feared in David above all was the completely *un*reasonable relationship David enjoyed with God. It was all the worse because of its unconscious freedom, the spontaneity it gave him, as he accepted relationship on God's terms alone.

The sadness of Saul's story, his descent into darkness, despair and madness, reads like a Greek tragedy. It is hard to read it without weeping. His own epitaph on his life was heartbreaking: 'I have been a fool and very, very wrong.' When he finally died about sixteen years after Goliath's death, David wept for him and for Jonathan who died with him. In one of the greatest elegies ever written, his lament begins: 'Your glory, oh Israel, lies slain on your heights. How the mighty have fallen!'

In a generosity of spirit that was beyond Saul, David wrote of Saul and Jonathan, 'In life they were loved and gracious.'

Extraordinarily, throughout their relationship, David continued to regard himself as Saul's loyal servant. On several occasions he could have taken Saul's life, but refused to do it. Others offered to kill Saul for him. He refused them permission. In their last encounter David rebukes the commander-in-chief of the army for not guarding Saul with due diligence and Saul calls out, 'Is that your voice, David, my son?' It is a poignant moment. With all the jealousy and bitterness that was in his heart, Saul could not help but feel affection for the young man whom he had tried on so many occasions to kill. David's amazing generosity exemplified lines that Andrew Marvell wrote of King Charles I in 1650:

> He nothing common did or mean
> Upon that memorable scene.

TO SERVE AND NOT TO SEEK REWARD

David was proud to call himself Saul's servant. The word 'servant' is now regarded as more of an insult than an honour. That indicates how far our culture has moved away from any kind of truly Christian understanding. Yet it was Jesus' willingness to step down to a lower status that so challenged the mindset and captivated the hearts of his early followers.

Earlier, we looked at the moment when Jesus washes the feet of the disciples. For us, it is demeaning, perhaps unpleasant. But we have no real idea of the radical nature of this action. It was astonishing. Quite simply, no free man washed the feet of others. It was regarded as so degrading, so defiling, that a Jewish slave could not even be asked to do it. Only a non-Jew could undertake it. That is why Jesus's actions were so shocking. He was taking the place of a Gentile slave. In their world, that really was the lowest of the low.

So Jesus began an entirely new kind of community, in which people would serve God by serving each other. He explained, 'The kings of the Gentiles lord it over their people, and those who are tyrants call themselves Benefactors. You are not to be like that. Instead, the greatest among you should be like the youngest, and the one who rules like the one who serves. Who is greater, the one who is at the table or the one who serves? It is the one at the table. *But I am among you as one who serves.*'

Jesus was right about the preposterous claims of tyrants. In his time the Syrian kings, at least one of the Ptolemies in Egypt, Greek rulers and the Roman Caesars all described themselves as benefactors. It almost seems that the more hideous their tyranny, the more likely they would be to describe themselves as 'the friend of the people'.

Take Joseph Stalin – pictured in propaganda shots as kindly old 'Uncle Joe' (born Iosif Vissarionovich Dzhugashvili): he is estimated to have been responsible for the deaths of 73 million Soviet citizens in purges, imprisonment, forced resettlements, manufactured famines and war. History is littered with power-abusers like Stalin.

As Carl Beech describes in *The Twelve Codes*, a story is told about Stalin and a chicken that horrifically illustrates the mindset of a tyrant. Struggling to get his team to understand the relationship between control and power, he grasped the chicken and started to pull fistfuls of feathers from it. As expected, the chicken fought back, but Stalin kept ripping the feathers out. Once it was bare of feathers, it stopped fighting and became still and, to the amazement of his team, it tried to press itself into Stalin's body.

Even when he threw grain on the floor, it followed him around the courtyard. Devoid of all protection from the cold, the chicken now needed Stalin's body heat to stay warm and was also dependent on him for food. Finally, he explained, 'This is how we lead the people: take what they need from them and they will always follow us for food.'

That's what he did. He terrorised the nation. Millions had property taken by the Communist party. The whole population lived under constant threat of torture, execution or exile. They had no choice but to peacefully submit in order to survive. Staggeringly, there are still old people in the former Soviet Union who long for the good old days of 'Uncle Joe!'

THE UPSIDE-DOWN KINGDOM

It is with some relief that I return to Jesus. His actions then over-turned the conventional picture of kingship. They still do now. Such radical challenges to this world's power systems remain almost impossible for us to grasp, let alone put into practice. So we relegate them to the theological/philosophical status of 'hopelessly idealistic'.

Yet the romance of this story gripped the young church. It was the crazy idea of an upside-down kingdom that did it. Greco-Roman myths told of gods disguising themselves as mortals to seduce humans or create mischief, but never this! That the supreme God, creator of all things, would become human out of love for human beings was never even on their horizon. That he would then sacrifice himself for the human race, *first taking the status of a slave*, was literally unthinkable.

In their sagas, a mighty hero could sacrifice himself tragically in battle to save others, as Hector did before the gates of Troy. But to demean himself by becoming a slave – never! That was the revelation that turned the world upside-down. It tore apart their limited understanding of the cosmos, the earth and above all their own destinies. Suddenly the sky was not the limit. And it came about because God had become a slave. That thought transformed them. Now the slaves walked with God – and walked tall!

When Paul wrote to a church at Colosse in what is now Turkey, he encouraged them: '*Whatever* you do or say, do it as a representative of the Lord Jesus, giving thanks through him to God the Father' (Colossians 3:17, NLT).

Later he says, '*Whatever* you do, work at it with all your heart, as *working for the Lord*, not for men . . . It is the Lord Christ you are serving' (Colossians 3:23–24, NIV).

The people Paul was writing to there were mainly slaves. He was lifting them to a totally different level. He was transforming their work and their self-understanding. Labour was given dignity by identification with the King of all things. They had become officers of the Great King. They believed Jesus would one day rule every ruler, including Caesar, and they were his servants – agents of the final revolution. Working-class people have never had a greater liberation than this. It was internal, untouchable by their oppressors. In the light of this, Paul asked them to serve their earthly masters with enthusiasm. They were to drink in the same spirit that filled Jesus, living enthusiastically, whatever they were doing. Enthusiasm literally means *filled with God*. That is the way we are all meant to live: filled with God.

Such a lifestyle has not always characterised those who run or belong to the Church of Jesus. Often our actions and behaviours have mirrored the pomp and self-importance of worldly rulers, not his joyful freedom. Even more often our self-righteousness, life-denying legalism and judgementalism have driven away those we should draw to us and alienated those who are close to us. Far from wishing they had what we have, most have thought, 'Whatever they've got, I hope I don't catch it.' It's a long way from the first century's 'Look how those Christians love one another'.

'You're far happier giving than getting.' Jesus said it. It is true. We will be happier if we give. Yet still we cling to our rights and possessions instead of seeking ways to contribute to our fellow human beings. So our jaded view of life and the selfishness of our consumerist lifestyles guarantee to us a lifetime of disappointment. Because it's all about us!

During the latter part of the twentieth century, few images were as powerful, challenging and inspiring as the smile of Mother Teresa of Calcutta. By supreme irony, this Albanian citizen was the most famous woman in the world at a time when President Hoxha, the communist dictator of Albania, was proclaiming it as the world's first completely atheist state. She said, 'When I wash the wounds of a leper it is the greatest privilege because for me they are the wounds of Christ.' The vast majority of those she served in this way were not Christians. But they were humans, and she loved them for the sake of Christ.

Jesus' call to serve is his most challenging teaching. A friend of mine said, 'I don't mind being a servant, until someone treats me like one!' I echo that. Reluctantly, I sense here an opportunity for me to identify with Christ and be more like him. Now the last thing the world needs is a bunch of people determined to serve others whether they like it or not. As I heard somebody observe, 'She simply lives for others – and you can tell the others by the hunted look!' What would be refreshing would be people who love because they are grateful. Having learned they are loved, the love they have received flows from them.

Jesus did not just teach the theory of serving others. He lived it. His washing of the disciples' feet was not tokenism. It was natural, an outflowing of love honouring them as inheritors of the kingdom of heaven, which he had come to set up. In his vision of their future he saw them ennobled by the purpose and love of God. Vision is at the heart of serving. Without our eyes being opened to see people differently, our service just becomes drudgery. Jesus gives us a different viewpoint. We see people as *he* sees them. This is tough! He calls us to be servants, putting others first. But we, in the self-indulgent, pleasure-driven consumerist societies of the West, have unthinkingly adjusted to the idea that others are there to serve us. To lay down our lives for the convenience of others feels completely alien.

But think about it! The creator made us to play our part, to make a contribution. The smart thing would be to take notice of that and work out how I can do it, not just by giving money but by personally investing myself in the lives of others. I am ashamed that too often, as a busy pastor, I find myself driven by an overloaded schedule, slave to a timetable, not the servant of my people, my church and my parish. The most haunting challenge is what Jesus taught in his parables: I alone am responsible for the gifting and the service entrusted to me. No one else is responsible. Not even God. I want to, but if I fail in this I can blame no one but *me*.

IT'S NOT MY FAULT

From the beginning, when things have gone wrong, humans have defaulted to blaming others or seeking excuses. Like the Adam and Eve story. Faced with the question, 'Have you eaten from the tree that I commanded you not to eat from?' Adam says, 'The woman made me do it.' In her turn Eve says, 'The serpent deceived me and made me eat.' We blame others. Our 'victim culture' strengthens this and gives it the endorsement of a whole society.

In *West Side Story*, the Jets tell the local police officer, 'Dear kindly Sergeant Krupke,/You gotta understand./It's just our bringing up-ke/that gets us out of hand.' The song parodies the reasons liberal do-gooders then put forward for what was called juvenile delinquency. Ironically, by unpacking the influence of people's backgrounds they have only made them more fluent in their excuses.

If we are going to grow as human beings, we have to reject the blame culture, including blaming ourselves. Instead, we have to step across into a new kind of understanding, that is *responsibility*. I take responsibility for my actions, good or bad, so that I can at last begin to deal with the reality and not try to pass it on to someone else.

In one of Jesus' most famous parables, the parable of the talents, one man loses out. He has received just a single talent, and buried it because, as he says to the master, 'I know you are a hard man and you ask much more of people than they can give. So I was afraid and I buried the talent so you could have it back untouched.' The anger of the master is directed at this man. 'You should have acted in a way that was consistent with your vision of reality. The hard master demands a return and refuses to help? Well, at the very least you could have invested my money in a bank deposit account and I would have received some interest.'

The master is not worried about the money. But he is longing to give approval, affirmation and reward to this man. He is massively disappointed, outraged at the sheer laziness of someone who refuses to take even the slightest responsibility for their own life, whose only real occupation is whingeing about everything that has gone wrong and complaining about how unfair it all is. It is difficult not to feel sympathy with the master. I have travelled in the developing world and met people who have almost nothing. Yet their outlook on life is positive. They are cheerful and friendly and often they have a faith in God that is vibrant, passionate and refreshing.

Then I return to the overindulged, consumerist members of Western society, complaining about the colour of the toilet paper in the bathroom, groaning about the doctor or pastor who did not do enough for 'me', griping about how difficult life is. There will be elements of truth. Yet the real problem is their refusal to move on. Their complaints are a justification for not contributing to the community. And they hang on to them. No wonder they are miserable. In extreme cases their grievance becomes their most treasured possession – continually poisoning their view of the world. They never give anything. Since 'it is happier to give than to receive', they have cut themselves off from any possibility of genuine happiness.

If we live like that, we are guaranteeing misery for ourselves, locked into a vicious circle. But maybe, just maybe, there is hope of escape, if we are willing to ask the right questions. Not questions about who is to blame, who screwed up. But: what went wrong? And: how can we change what we do so it doesn't happen next time? In the wonderful event that something goes right, we could ask the reasons for success and what we could improve so that it goes even better. In Luke's Gospel, Jesus says our attitude should be like this: 'When you've done everything expected of you, be matter of fact and say "The work is done; what we were told to do, we did. We were lucky to be part of it".'

THIS WILL PUT A SMILE ON YOUR FACE

So this is not about being grumpily, resentfully, reluctantly obedient. The chance to serve is a privilege and such fun. Contributing to life is much more fun than merely consuming everything we can. Not only did Jesus say 'It is happier to give than to receive', he also expressed his own purpose – 'I have told you this so that you will be filled with my joy. Yes, your joy will overflow!' – words that suggest the explosion of a cork from a champagne bottle. Life should be like this.

So, thinking about obedience to the designs of God, we need to grasp that life is a stewardship. The talents and abilities entrusted to us are subject to evaluation and assessment by the one who gave them – God. He is the only person who knows the whole truth. The end product is not intended to be fear and misery, but awe and jubilation. Jesus indicated that the master is looking for opportunities to praise us. He will greet anyone who has faithfully used their gifts to work out God's purposes and their destiny with 'Well done, good and faithful servant! You've been faithful with a few things. I will put you in charge of many things. Come and share your master's happiness!'

The point is that there is *always* something you can do to help others. We are bombarded by opportunities to contribute – sponsor a developing-world child, go on a trip to dig wells in a desert, do *something*!

We are being prepared for a life after this one marked by the happiness of God himself, bigger than the whole creation. So it makes sense, first, to ask the same Spirit that lived in Jesus to enter and empower us, and, second, to ask Jesus himself to guide us in the right direction. That way, when we have to give an account of ourselves and our lives, we will have the hope of meeting with God's delight and the roar of heaven's approval.

Whatever we do, we should do it with passion and energy. Why? Lazy people are always losers. People who put their heart and soul into a task know this will build enthusiasm and so energise them for the task itself. Too many of us are gripped by fear, especially fear of failure. That can hold us back, paralyse us. But failure can also be a stimulus, a springboard to the future. It is a choice we make.

The legendary journey of Thomas Edison in inventing the light bulb included 10,000 attempts. Each time a light bulb failed, he simply said, 'Now we know another way it won't work.' He was certain that passing an electric current through a filament would produce a lasting source of illumination, and would change the world. He was right, and it did change the world. Each time something went wrong he analysed it so that next time they would not repeat that mistake. Asked how he managed to keep going with the light bulb after so many disappointments and failures, he replied, 'I didn't fail; I invented a light bulb. It was a 10,000-step process.' As J.John frequently says, 'He didn't work harder, he worked sharper'. That is our responsibility: to get off our rear ends, take life by the scruff of the neck and say, 'I am going to live; I am going to sharpen myself until I become truly effective at what I do and who I am.'

From Yorkshire comes a famous saying: 'Where there's muck, there's brass [money].' Often the task no one else wants to do because of its muckiness is the one that yields the real reward. Not just the financial reward, either. My friend Nick had been in management in various Christian projects and in the charity sector. He realised that almost nothing he was doing was satisfying him any more. So, having finished a management contract, he enrolled at the local college to train as an electrician. Many people would regard that as a step down, but he is thrilled – very excited. 'I am loving doing some *real* work. I've realised I need to get my hands dirty! And now I'm actually working with men for whom Jesus is *news* – and I love it.'

After years of high living, a merchant banker in the City of London could not remember why he was doing what he was doing. He resigned and enrolled on a course to learn to be a plumber. When interviewed about it, he said, 'I'm enjoying working with my hands, like nothing I've done before. It's truly satisfying to be doing something that people really need.'

Healthy self-worth is inseparable from serving those around us, and the God that made us.

To serve is to stand in the place of honour.

UNLIKELY CIRCUMSTANCES

District of Samaria, Tetrarchy of Archelaus, AD 32

Midday. Blazing out of a cloudless sky, the sun made the hills shimmer in the heat. Leaving the Jordan River in the District of Judea around five o'clock in the morning, they had walked about twenty-five miles on their way to Galilee. The disciples did not understand why Jesus had to go through Samaria. The road to Galilee went straight along the Jordan Valley. It was cooler, more pleasant and easier than the road up into the hills of East Samaria.

But Jesus knew his Father was directing him. As they came close to Shechem he sensed he was in the right area. The disciples longed to stop. After all, Shechem was a large town. But Jesus passed on until he came to Sychar, a small town to the north. 'This is the right place.' He sat down on some of the stones set at the wellhead and leaned backwards, grateful for the rest. They had had days of intense activity preaching, teaching and baptising new disciples, until it had become clear that the Pharisees were trying to set up a rivalry between him and John the Baptist. So he decided to leave.

Setting out in the cool of the day had been the right decision but now he really was tired. The last few days were catching up with him. As ever, the disciples were hungry. Some of them had offered to stay with him 'to make sure you're all right'. But it had been a relief when they had finally all departed to go and buy food. He smiled to himself. Solitude was a rare gift.

At last the twelve had gone. Now as their chatter faded he was able to listen to the quietness, interrupted only by birdsong, and watch the occasional farmer making his way down from the terraces on the hillside where he clawed out his living. He was enjoying it, just being in the presence of his Father, waiting.

Then, from the direction of Shechem a mile away, he saw her coming towards the well, her water pot carried on her head with practised ease, each step graceful and the sway of her hips just a little provocative. She was taken aback when she saw him. But she came nearer, defiant of his presence. They were wrapped in silence. She was a Samaritan woman and he was a rabbi of the Jews. She knew well enough what rabbis thought of her people. They would refuse even to touch a cup touched by a Samaritan for fear of being defiled, made ritually unclean.

She stopped, swung the pot to the ground and moved the cover from the well. Neither spoke. A tense silence, almost palpable. She lowered her pot using the looped rope and pulley at the top of the well. He could hear it scraping occasionally against the walls of the well. It seemed to take for ever. He calculated it must be as deep as the height of twenty-five men. Finally there was the sound of water gurgling into the pot. Then a long pull of the rope until the pot rested on the side of the wellhead. With the ease of habit, she flicked the loop of rope off her jar.

Jesus knew. This was the one he had been waiting for. That she was coming a mile from her home to draw water in the middle of the day told him a great deal already. In that moment, he knew just what to say. 'Will you give me a drink, please?' Had he slapped her she could not have looked more surprised. In fact, she would have expected that.

Her lip curled. 'You! You are a Jew and I am a woman – of Samaria! How come you are asking *me* for a drink?'

Jesus regarded her steadily. 'If you knew God's generosity and who I am, you would ask me for a drink and I would give you fresh flowing water.'

Rejection and bitterness chased themselves across her face. Many men had spoken kindly to her to get what they wanted. Was he any different?

Her lip curled again. 'Sir, you haven't even got a bucket and the well is deep. How are you going to get this "flowing water"? Are you better than our ancestor Jacob who dug this well and drank from it?'

Jesus' eyes still searched her face. 'Everyone who drinks this water will get thirsty again and again. Anyone drinking the water I give will never thirst – not ever. It will be like a spring inside, gushing fountains of life.'

His compassion reached out to her, reminding her of her long-dead and much-missed father. It was unnerving – painful. Sarcasm was her defence. 'Oh, sir, give me this water so I won't ever get thirsty again and won't have to come back to this well!' Still he looked at her steadily with a smile on his face. She was flustered, disconcerted.

'Go, call your husband; then come back here.'

Her hands went onto her hips as she stated in bitter triumph, 'I have no husband.'

'Nicely put, that "no husband". You've had five and the one you are living with now isn't *your* husband. You spoke the truth there!'

Her sarcastic smile was replaced with shock. Involuntarily: 'Sir, you must be a prophet.' Pause. She was gathering her wits. How do you get a prophet off your back? Religion – that's it! 'You Jews say that Jerusalem is the right place to worship and our teachers insist that it's here at Mount Gerizim – right?'

The contentious nature of the question was belied by the wistfulness in her eyes. She had known many men but no man had ever looked at her as this one did – his glance tender, penetrating but not invasive. His eyes were understanding, kind.

'Lady, believe me, the time is coming when it will no longer matter whether you worship here on this mountain or in Jerusalem. It is true; salvation comes through the Jewish people. But the time has arrived. Those looking for God to give him real adoration will find that the Father is looking for them. They will find the Spirit of God joining with their spirit. Love, joy and praise will come out of their very being, their true selves in real adoration.'

She looked at him, past disappointment and longing mingled on her face. 'I know that when Messiah comes, he will explain everything.' Still he held her eyes. Now her eyes were searching his. He did not look away.

'That's me – I'm the Messiah, talking to you right now.' She got it! He could see that. Instinctively she knew, 'All my life, I have been searching in the wrong places. At last the love I've been looking for has found me, a love that's bigger than I am.' She could feel the chains of her past falling away. She knew this was the new start she had always been seeking.

In the silence, Jesus became aware the disciples had returned. Standing with their packages of food in their hands, gaping open-mouthed at Jesus talking not just to a woman but to *this* woman. She leapt up with a smile on her face, tears in her eyes, instinctively brushing her hands against her skirts. She didn't even see her water pot.

As she entered the village she bubbled irresistibly: 'You must come and meet this man. He knew all about me, told me my whole life story. He explained it all to me. Why I've hurt people. I was looking in all the wrong places. Come and meet him. Could this be the Messiah?' Given her history they would not have been impressed if she had simply said, 'I have met a man.' After all, she was notorious. But the way she spoke and her radiance set the whole town talking. They came out to meet Jesus.

Meanwhile, the disciples were impressing Jesus with the brilliance of their purchases. 'Try this one, master, you'll like this.' He looked at them and smiled.

'I have food to eat that you know nothing about.' They were puzzled – who could have brought him food? He replied, 'The food that energises me is doing my Father's work – and finishing what he has already started.' He gestured to the terraces on the hillsides. 'Take a look. What do you think? Four months till harvest? Open your eyes. It is ready right now. All you have to do is look.

See what God has already done, the task he has put before you.'
The Father's harvest is ready right now!

Jesus was receiving the energy that comes when, at the very limit
of our own resources, we discover that special task for which God
created us, and in that moment we rise up to do his will. In that
instant, not before, we discover that when he commands he also
empowers, energising us from the inside out, his River of Life
flowing and effervescent, his wind beneath our wings. All the
resources we need are right there, when we step out in faith to
do what he asks.

Two hundred years ago, a man named William Carey said,
'God's work done in God's way will never lack God's supply.' He
was right.

Part 3

Holding on to the Big Picture

In the scramble of living, the great temptation is to forget why we exist and where we are going. Too easily we get our heads down and ignore the big picture – yet it is vital if we are to triumph against adversity. The creator's enormous vision inspires enduring passion for life, and moves us from success into true significance.

Chapter 7

Follow Your Vision

THE ONLY WAY IS UP

Judean Wilderness, 1016 BC

The cave was dark. Smoke from many fires and oil lamps had covered its roof in soot. But David's eyes adjusted quickly as he stepped in from the rocky valley. The sun had dipped below the horizon; a brief dusk would be followed quickly by nightfall. The thick woven curtain was dropped back into place to mask the cave opening. Though it was unlikely there would be any travellers on the road after nightfall – unless they were Saul's spies. But they would have to get by the men on watch up and down the ravine in his other caves, about 400 men in all.

He laughed briefly. A few months ago he had been a commander of thousands. Now he had this ragtag bunch. His brothers had come to him first. That had been a miracle. Somehow his being in trouble had released them from their jealousy. They had now become his firmest allies. Along with them had come many members of his father's household. The cave was only about thirteen miles from home, less than a day's walk. His father's household supplied a steady stream of supplies. Neighbours helped.

Then others had joined. They all came: the hungry, the down-on-their-luck, the dirt poor, pledging themselves to him. Men hopelessly mired in debt also came, along with those who were discontented, convinced the nation would never be right as long as Saul was king. So he had this motley band of brigands. But, ragged as they were, they were totally committed to him, pledged to his service, David's men.

Already there were thirty leaders, each with his platoon of twelve or so. Some of those leaders were of outstanding quality. But always there were problems, problems of supply, the constant need to be on the alert for Saul's search parties. At times it was hard to remember why they were there.

Some men had brought their wives and children. Others had left them at home but still somehow had to supply the needs of the family. Then there were tribal allegiances, which could cause trouble at any time. That was why he had made every man make a personal pledge to himself. Their loyalty had to be to something greater than their clan or their family. He had discovered that these desperate men were drawn to him. In him, those down on their luck seemed to find hope for the future, the debtors began to believe that they could prosper and the discontented found not only a focus for their discontent in Saul's irrational behaviour, but in David a focus of vision for the future.

He was under no illusions about his personal appeal. He knew that, although they did not understand it, what they saw in him was the brightness of the hand of God that had rested on him since the day Samuel anointed him. For a while after that happened things had gone quiet. He had almost wondered whether that moment was of any significance at all. Yet he could not forget either the sense of God's power entering his soul or the reality of the presence of God. Then came the opportunity to play for Saul in his palace, and disappointment when he was sent home again. Months later, the encounter that changed everything – Goliath.

After that his career had blazed across the sky of Israel's communal life like a comet. Young as he was, few had questioned his rapid rise. First the platoon, then a company, then a regiment had come under his command. His marriage to Michal, Saul's daughter, had made him part of the royal family. It was no surprise when he was made Commander of the King's Bodyguard. Everybody knew David's loyalty to Saul was something beyond the normal, something mystical. It made Saul's attacks on him all the more shocking. They were still at war with the Philistines on the day when Saul made it clear he wanted David dead. In the midst of war he sent an assassination squad to kill his most talented commander. Only an intervention from Saul's own daughter

Michal saved David's life that night. Saul pursued David with a madness that was alarming.

In the meantime, there had been a bitter moment of parting for David from his closest friend, Jonathan. From the moment they met something inside them had bonded in a friendship that was deeper than brotherhood and more powerful than death. Jonathan had given him the final warning: 'My father intends to kill you.' Escape had left him without weapons or provisions. He had gone to the City of the Priests. There he received bread from the altar of God and the sword of Goliath from the old man Ahimelech. Feeling that every man in Judah was against him, he had taken refuge in the city of Gath. Ironic that Goliath came from Gath. The King had not forgotten it. Achish would have given him shelter but his own servants called David 'King of the Land' and reminded him of the song of the teenage girls, 'Saul has slain his thousands, and David his tens of thousands.' David had heard their whispered conversations and known that, as always in the politics of the Middle East, alliances shifted very quickly so that his life was now in grave danger. So he pretended to be mad, letting saliva run down his beard and scrabbling at the gate making marks with his nails. He smiled to himself now. Achish had said, 'I've got enough madmen here already. Why have you brought me another one?' So they let him go.

He had arrived at the cave of Adullam. Ironically, it meant 'Resting Place'. His grin was sardonic as he surveyed the straw pallet set on a rock ledge which was his privileged position as leader of the band. Spiced lentil stew was brought to him. As always with a group of men, there were brief arguments, laughter, the rough humour of soldiers. But they were beginning to be a unit, no longer just a group of discontented individuals. They were beginning to be a band of brothers, joined by bonds of loyalty that would hold for decades. Reviewing what had happened in the last few months had recalled him to the truth. His meteoric rise had been followed by a very public fall. Many had written him off. But David knew the God who had raised him up once would raise him up again and this time he would raise him up at the head of an army that was pledged to him and not to any other king.

His thoughts were interrupted by Josheb, his second-in-command.

'Boss?'

'What is it?'

'It's a matter of discipline, boss.'

David was irritated. 'Can't you deal with it?'

'It's Abishai, boss.'

David groaned. His nephew was not much younger than he was, but was always using his relationship with David to wind up the others. He was the bravest of the brave in battle, but a constant troublemaker in camp.

'Bring him to me.'

Abishai stood before him, looking just a little sheepish.

'What was it this time, Abishai? An insult to the family? A fight over a woman?'

'Not my fault, boss. The guy's an idiot!'

David's eyes blazed as he looked at his nephew. 'No! Abishai, you're the idiot! You're my nephew, you're a member of this family, and you set the standard. We all do! One day you're going to hold senior rank. They have to be able to *respect* you, not just because of your rank but because of who you are. The man who is going to control others must first learn to control himself!'

For the first time he looked ashamed. David looked at him, his eyes hard, his face set. 'Will you accept my punishment?'

'Yes, boss.'

'Six nights' guard duty.'

'OK, boss.'

'Any problems with that?'

'No sir, thank you, sir.'

He saluted and turned. David allowed himself a brief smile. Abishai would be all right.

And so would he. The vision implanted by Samuel all those years ago would not die. In due course it would be fulfilled. All they had to do was follow the vision.

DETAILS, DETAILS

As I thought of David and the sudden eclipse of his rising star in Israel's politics, I really felt for him. As the youngest general in the army, he must have had staff, capable young assistants delighted to run around after him and do his every bidding. Working for David was one of the most glamorous postings in the whole Israeli army. But then that powerful figure is suddenly stripped of his rank and privileges, reduced to the level of refugee, accused of being a defector, a traitor. He is a fugitive. With every man's hand against him, who then of those with their eyes on a glittering career path is going to want to become a refugee along with their vaga-bond captain? The people who came to him were not by and large the well-educated, capable and gifted. They were themselves vaga-bonds, refugees from broken lives, people who had failed in busi-ness and men who may even have had reputations as whingers, discontented with the status quo. In among that band was David going to find capable administrators, brilliant strategists? I don't think so.

The situation of his outlaw army was precarious in the extreme. Where were they going to get the food to feed 400 men, plus the growing band of women and children? Where would they find the weapons and armour, the space for training? All they had was a crazy dream founded on a prophecy from a wild-eyed prophet increasingly at odds with the King. Suppose the Bethlehem busi-ness bureau had run checks on David's men looking for people with ability and talent, those voted by past classmates as 'most likely to succeed'. I doubt they would have found many among David's raggle-taggle band. The administration of this group, always on the move, with no headquarters to speak of, would have been very much in the hands of the young David and one or two of his officers. It would have been so easy for the details of everyday living to mount up in his mind until there was no room for vision or for dreaming. But, at the end of the day, David's most valuable commodity, the thing that kept the men loyal to him, was that sense of vision that they saw in him. Their personal failures, their screwed-up backgrounds could all be put aside when they looked at David and saw in him the promise of a victory that was bigger than anything they had ever dreamed of before. They knew that if David won that victory, it would be their victory too.

At this point of his life 400 vagrants had flocked to him; the unwashed and uneducated, the underclass who had found in him a hope they would never have found in anybody else. But among that group were a few who had an educated background. Somebody, somewhere, must have had the ability to write records. How else would they have known how to allocate the prize money when they went out on raiding parties? There would have been a scribe. There was certainly a priest. He also was a refugee.

There is probably no better example of the cynical aphorism 'No good deed ever goes unpunished' than the story of Abiathar's father, Ahimelech. David had lied to the priest, telling him he was on a secret mission for Saul. Ahimelech had no idea of the danger David had placed him in. Doeg, a member of a racial group that had always hated Israel, infiltrated the circle of Saul's inner council. When Saul asked for news about David so that he could find him and kill him, Doeg was the one who said, 'I saw David go to the chief priest, Ahimelech. He asked God for advice for him and gave him food and the sword of Goliath, the Philistine.' Saul was enraged and in his jealous anger proceeded to one of the most despicable acts of his whole life. He sent for Ahimelech the priest and his father's whole family, who were priests in the City of Priests. Saul asked Ahimelech, 'Why did you help David when you knew he was a traitor against me?' Ahimelech answered, 'But who of all your servants is more loyal than David, your son-in-law and the captain of your bodyguard, most respected in your household? It wasn't the first time I've prayed for him. I know nothing of any rebellion or of any traitorous behaviour.' Saul would not hear it. He ordered his men to kill Ahimelech, his father and all the family. But none of them would dare to do it. They were afraid to become enemies of Israel's God by killing his priests. Then Saul turned to the one man he knew he could rely on to do this – the man with no love of Israel or of Israel's God. Doeg and one or two others with him killed eighty-five priests that day. Then they went to the City of Priests and killed everyone in it: men, women, children, babies and all the livestock.

One member of the family escaped – Abiathar. He came to David and told him the whole story. I think it was one of those moments of real shame in David's life, a moment when he looked at the floor and knew that his devious nature, the lies he had told Ahimelech about his reasons for going to him that day – his failure to admit that he was on the run from Saul – had caused the death of a trusting friend and his whole family. To give him his due, David apologised to the young priest and told him, 'I knew that Doeg the Edomite would be sure to tell Saul about it.' Mind you, I think David could justifiably say that it never occurred to him that Saul would be crazy enough to kill the priests and their families.

Every so often, someone like David hits a moment when they realise that no amount of charm or winning speech can atone for the damage done by their lies. David's honest apology had won Abiathar over. He stayed with David and became his loyal spiritual advisor. By then David had placed his own father and his step-mother with the King of Moab – another of Israel's enemies! He had taken his men to the Forest of Hareth. There, deep in the trees, he took refuge. Shades of Robin Hood! His position was extreme. It would have been so easy for the pressures of finding food and money to feed his growing band of men to have ground David down to the point at which he lost entirely his vision for the future. At this moment, his vision still sustained him.

DAILY GRIND

Because David's position was so extreme, it can serve as a kind of reference point for us. It is so easy for the proliferation of tasks, the endless succession of almost meaningless minutiae, the bits and pieces of daily life, to become the defining moments of our days; the mending of a washer on a tap, the handle that fell off a door, streams of emails, the puncture on the car, paying the credit-card bills, the leak in the roof or the burst pipe. When that happens there is a genuine risk that we will lose sight of who we truly are and become drudges, just getting through the day, doing the stuff, worn down to a shadow of what we once were or dreamt of one day becoming. It happens to me. I want to write a book but there is always another email to attend to, a phone call, someone ringing at the door. If you are reading this far you will know that my response to those interruptions is irascibility. Really, it does feel at times as if 'they' are out to get you. Then I discover that if I am going to write the book I am supposed to write I have to carve time out of my day and *make it* work. If I am going to do that then I must have a vision of what this is about.

I wanted to write a book that said to people the life you are living is so precious, so important, so significant that you must not allow the details of life to overwhelm its major purpose. Whatever our personal situation, somehow we must hang on to our own big picture. For that to be the case, we must believe in the big picture. We must believe in the possibility that life means something, that somebody eternal and almighty has already assigned to it a significance far greater than anything I could otherwise dream of. Whatever special thing God has given you to do and whatever special destiny he has planted within you, you have to have a vision that lifts itself above the downward pressures of daily routine. Unless we have something in us that is looking at the stars, we will find it very hard to rise above the mud in the gutter.

So, every so often we must stop and ask ourselves, why am I doing this? Why am I fixing the broken washer on the tap or clearing the snow from the driveway, or the dog poo from the grass (and we have *large* dogs!)? It's because I love my wife and I want her to live in an environment that is worthy of her. I love my children and my grandchildren. I want them to have a house to come to where they feel secure and safe, and that if Granddad cares for this house like this then he'll care for us too. In the end I am doing it because everything I have is a gift from the God who loves me. I will take care of it because he has entrusted it to me.

FROM HERE TO ETERNITY

The point of all this is that God has a dream, not just for the tasks he has given me to do, but for ME as a person. He dreams of my becoming something glorious and unique that demonstrates the wonder of his creation to anybody who cares to look at it. He promises that that process is what is driving his every interaction with me. He has covenanted that he will fulfil his purpose. So I have to understand that I am a work of art and the work of creation is still in progress. I am not yet what I am meant to be. For that I am enormously grateful. God has promised that, if I will allow him to, he will keep on working away at me every single day of my life. He sees the end from the beginning, and encourages me to do the same. If I have entrusted myself to him to walk in obedience every day, then *I will not die* until he's finished doing what he has to do. He wants to make me into something that shines out *his* glory in this life. But he also has in mind an eternal destiny, something that goes beyond death.

Some of us are very goal-orientated. People both inside and outside the great historic faiths are driven by the need to achieve, by dreams of success that are all to do with results. The problem is, the world is littered with examples of people who have achieved the pre-eminence that they set out to, only to discover it simply isn't enough. There was a moment in my own life when the young travelling evangelist had really begun to make a mark. In fact, people spoke about me as being England's Billy Graham. To anyone outside the church that might not seem like a big deal, but to anybody inside the world of evangelical Christianity it was a huge claim. In the winter of 1983–84, it seemed that at every conference I attended I was publicly referred to from the front as 'Britain's leading evangelist'. It was the oddest experience for me. I had worked towards it for years and now I had achieved it – the initial goal on a pathway to world domination! I distinctly remember sitting in one of those gatherings with a sense of anticlimax and thinking, 'So is that it?' I was disappointed. I thought there would be an immense sense of achievement. Instead – nothing. In fact, at that moment it felt as though a spring had broken inside me. Something that had been a driving force within me had gone.

Stephen Covey, the famous author of *Seven Habits of Highly Effective People*, puts it like this: you climb a tree, the tallest tree in the jungle, to find out where you are and when you get to the top you find yourself shouting down, 'Wrong jungle!' That was me. I had forgotten that I was called to be a human *being* not a human *doing*. No amount of achievement would fill the yawning gap inside me. So I would have to go and find the right jungle, or take my ladder and put it against the right wall. No matter how good and worthwhile the job is that I do, my vision must be bigger than that. Because eventually, one way or another, I will be leaving that job. Solomon, the son of King David, said, 'Where there is no vision, people perish.' It is a fact that without inner vision we lose the reason to live.

Somebody whom I look back on with a great deal of affection was a man who reminded me of my dad. Like Dad, he was called Fred. He was manager of a departmental office in the industrial conglomerate ICI. I was a relatively young follower of Jesus and, I have to say, not particularly good at it. But I knew what my aim was. Consequently, in the course of my annual review, he asked me about my priorities and I said, 'God comes first, Fred, then my family, then ICI.'

'NO, NO, NO!' he said. 'You can't do that. It's got to be ICI first.'

I said, 'While I'm here, Fred, ICI does come first. But in my life as a whole it's God who comes first and then my family.'

'NO, NO, NO!' he said. 'You can't do that; you've got to put ICI first in every area of your life.'

I said, 'I'm afraid I can't do that.' Soon after that, on Fred's recommendation, ICI decided it could manage its affairs perfectly well without my undoubtedly invaluable services. Two or three years later, Fred retired after about fifty years in the service of ICI. About eight months after his retirement and having spent hardly any of the pension for which he had served so loyally, he dropped dead in the local high street. I still can't tell that story without seeing his face in front of me and thinking how much like my dad he was and yet how different they were. It seems that once he left ICI Fred had nothing to live for. You can give your all to a company or a career, but it will never answer the need for a vision that gives meaning to who you are.

My dad, equally loyal to the company he worked for, had a bigger priority – to serve God. He ended his days in a home for the elderly where he sat every day in the entrance hall or living room with his Bible beside him and a big smile on his face, greeting everybody. The whole family came to his ninetieth birthday celebration. Soon afterwards, he died. Months later people were asking, 'What happened to the man with the Bible? I miss him.'

My vision must be bigger than a mere job or career, no matter how significant.

DWELL ON WHAT YOU DREAM OF BECOMING

There is a frightening process at work in our human psyche – we become what we worship. Of course, I understand that some people reading this may well say, 'But I don't believe in God, any god. I don't worship anything.' Those two statements don't necessarily hang together. You don't have to believe in a supernatural god to worship something. In fact, whatever you give most importance to in your life is what you worship. It might be a football club. I understand that those kinds of allegiance don't always make a lot of sense, but they can have a powerful hold over us. After the air crash in Munich in 1958, in which eight members of their team and fifteen others died, I found myself drawn to follow Manchester United. I have to face the fact that ever since then, as a South London lad, my football allegiance lies in a city in the north-west of England with a team that is at times the most hated in the country. I can't help it. It's just the way it is. But I can't *live* for that team. Frankly, it's just not big enough for me to worship.

The word 'worship' is taken from the Anglo-Saxon *Weorde-scipe* – 'worthship', now contracted to 'worship'. Worship identifies our top priority and gives it what we believe it is worth. Clearly, if I give it everything, it must be worth it, or, inevitably, I will be disappointed. If it's a career, it's not big enough. Marriage, family, my house, a great car, huge amounts of money – none of these things is big enough. Even the process of evolution is apparently regarded by some people as worthy of their life's devotion! The problem is, it's strictly a one-way relationship.

How do we identify and grasp the right vision? Part of the process must be looking back at the way my life has moved in the past, its meanderings, wrong turnings, wild and crazy downhill bits, and steady-slog-uphill bits. It is not always easy – as L.P. Hartley observed in *The Go-Between*, 'The past is a foreign country. They do things differently there.' That is true, even of our own past. That's why we sometimes look back and say, 'I can't believe I acted like that.' But, however hard it might be, I have to steel myself to this tough task, because there are conflicting parts there, stuff of which anyone would be deeply ashamed. There are regrets which I must not hide from or hoard in secret. I have to deal with all this because a conflicted and unreconciled past clogs the stream of my consciousness in the present – in other words, guilt induces paralysis.

There is only one person I know who can help: once I give the shameful bits, the regrets and the guilt of the past to God, he can set me free at last from the chains that hold me prisoner. It is Jesus who makes it possible – the same Jesus who looked compassionately at the paralysed man lying helpless before him. He saw that guilt held him prisoner so he was incapable of breaking free. His first words were, 'Your sins are forgiven.' When all that stuff is surrendered to him, I am free to consolidate the past in order to build for the future. Now and again I will be able to look back and miraculously see something that gives me a warm healthy glow of satisfaction: 'I know I did that right' – and that may become a pointer to my vision of the future. Jesus will help with that too. As I interact with him, I am set free from the bondage of the past so I *see* the present with new eyes. And I enter a place of unleashed creativity, because the outflow of a life full of vision is a new creativity.

His vision for us is always bigger than ours. He looked at Simon and said to him, 'You are Simon, son of John. You will be called Cephas.' We have already looked at that. A reed to a rock – that's a good transformation. He took all the disciples together and said, 'Come, follow me, and I will make you those who draw others after you.' He is still doing the same thing today. He offers new paradigms, new ways of thinking about ourselves, as well as new challenges. He offers new freedoms: freedom from the weight of the past and anxiety about the future, freedom from the fear of what others think, freedom from guilt. With those new freedoms come new responsibilities, because he entrusts to us tasks bigger than anything we've ever known before. So let him impart his dream to you and then dwell on that, on what you now dream of becoming. Write it down. Have it clear. Dare to speak it out.

I want this: to be like Jesus himself. For me, he is the end product that I dream of becoming. He put that vision before me so it would form me into his image as he has always dreamed.

INTO THE CRUCIBLE

Jerusalem, April AD 33

The Passover meal in Jerusalem was memorable primarily because, here, Jesus inaugurated a simple meal that would mark Christian gatherings throughout the following centuries. Looking round the table he poured the communal cup of wine which marked the beginning of Passover. He gave thanks and distributed it to them. He took thin unleavened bread, much like tortilla or a chapatti, gave thanks for it, then tore it apart, saying, 'This is my body, given for you. Do this in remembrance of me.' Nothing so strange had ever happened to the disciples. They had heard that in some barbaric places people ate the meat of human sacrifices. But for it to be offered to them even symbolically was incredible. They could hardly believe their ears. Such was their trust in the man who led them that each of them took a piece of the bread and ate it.

After he had washed their feet, he put on his clothes and returned to his place at the table. He looked at them and said, 'If you treat each other this way, you will truly be happy. But not all of you will want to do this. One who has shared friendship meals with me has already begun the journey to betrayal.' They were completely nonplussed. They looked at each other.

'I am telling you now, one of you will betray me.' Even more nonplussed, they looked at each other and back to Jesus.

'But who, Lord? Who would do that? Is it me?' They were confused. They thought perhaps that without even understanding, without even meaning it, one of them might betray him. Peter was on the other side of John, who as we saw in Chapter 2 was actually leaning on his left elbow, almost touching Jesus' right shoulder.

Peter motioned to John. 'Ask him who it is,' he whispered, his mouth close to John's ear.

John leaned back towards Jesus. 'Who is it, Lord?'

Just as discreetly Jesus said, 'It is the one to whom I will give this piece of bread.' He dipped it in the dish.

That was the way they ate. They would take a piece of bread and dip it in the stew in the centre of the table, scoop it up and eat it. In many homes in the Middle East today you would be offered food in the same way. Being offered a piece of bread by the host of the meal like this was a sign of special favour and friendship. So it was Jesus' pledge of loyalty and love. When it was accepted it would mark Judas' pledge of the same love and loyalty.

When Jesus took that bread, dipped it in the stew in the centre of the table and offered it to Judas, both of them understood the dynamic. Judas knew this was an opportunity for him to confess that he had already betrayed him – made arrangements with the Chief Priest to reveal Jesus' movements so he could be arrested quietly. Jesus' eyes searched his face. Judas was tormented. He wanted to confess. But he could not do it in front of all the others. He loved Jesus. But he could not bring himself to expose his disloyalty so publicly. Eating it was a lie but he did not know what else to do. The embarrassment! He took the bread, renewing his pledge of loyalty. Only Jesus knew it was a lie. As he ate, it was as if a darkness entered him. He felt there was no going back.

Jesus regarded him steadily. 'Whatever you're going to do, do it quickly.' It was the last chance. Jesus, the evangelist, was reaching out. But Judas was sliding away from him, down the cliff face into oblivion. He knew this was the last chance of rescue being offered. The disciples thought Jesus was saying go and get some money to buy Passover food for beggars in the streets. Jesus watched. Judas stood, his mouth working as he tried to find the words. Routine took over.

The treasurer answered. 'Right, Lord,' he said, and walked out into the night.

After the Passover meal, Jesus took the third cup, the cup of blessing, and said, 'This is my blood, which is poured out for you and for the forgiveness of many. All of you, drink it.' They were forbidden to drink blood from any creature, let alone human blood. The disciples looked at Jesus, checking that he meant it. Then they drank. They were beginning to feel that events were spinning out of control. Bizarrely, they began to argue about which of them was more important. Jesus warned them that such thinking could lead only to disaster. He specifically warned Simon Peter not to trust in his own overweening self-confidence. Simon ignored him. However, in the days ahead, somehow the knowledge that Jesus had known all along that Simon would three times deny he knew Jesus was a thin line of grace holding him when despair would have swept him away.

As far as we can tell, the date was Thursday 2 April AD 33. The moon was full as they walked through the narrow streets of Jerusalem, crowded with pilgrims for Passover. Out through the Dung Gate into the Hinnom Valley, where rubbish fires burned all the time and piles of human refuse were brought to be burned. Crossing the Kidron Brook, they went up the other side to a place known as *Gatsemani*, the oil press. The oil press was located in a cave, surrounded by olive trees. The garden of Gethsemane. Jesus looked at the disciples. He loved them more than they would ever know.

'Sit here,' he said, 'while I go to pray.' He beckoned Peter, James and John: 'Come with me.' As he moved to a place of solitude under the olive trees, he said to them, 'Stay awake, would you? Pray for me. My soul is heavy with sorrow. It's unbearable. I don't know if I can live through this. Watch for me.' The prayer they heard was agonising, someone groaning in an extremity of pain such as they had never heard before. And never wanted to hear again. He used the most intimate word possible for his Father: 'Abba, you can do anything. Can't you take this awful cup from me?' He paused. As the silence stretched the disciples trembled. God was asking something terrible of their master. Would he truly turn away? Then they heard it.

'But not what I want; your will be done.' The vision held him true.

It was no good. They were fishermen, used to being out all night. But they could not stay awake. Something powerful, demonic, in the darkness was lulling them into sleep. He came back an hour later.

'Stay awake and pray. I know you are willing but you are very weak in spirit. You will fail if you only trust your natural abilities.' He went away and prayed the same prayer. When he came back they were asleep again. Again he went away, praying the same prayer for a third time. They knew he was struggling. They understood the process. But they could not help him. He was utterly alone. He returned for the third time. Then they heard a sudden clamour in the trees. They saw the light of blazing torches reflecting off armour and spears, saw the glint of the fire on helmets. It was a platoon of temple guards, led by Judas. Jesus was right – their good intentions were no use. Simon grabbed a sword, rushed out and hacked off the ear of an unarmed servant. Jesus whirled around and looked at him.

'What are you doing? Don't you know that those who save their lives by the sword will die by the sword?' Simon, renamed by Jesus 'Peter', 'the rock', dropped the sword. Panic seized him and he ran. Shame filled him as he ran and ran. They all ran.

For the temple servants it was disappointingly easy. They had expected resistance. So they slapped Jesus around a bit just for fun to pay him back for making them feel afraid. Jesus was alone and unsupported as they dragged him in manacles towards the Temple Mount, to the house of the High Priest. In the olive grove the real battle had already been fought and won. He had settled the inner argument and made up his mind. He had chosen with his will, not to do his own will but to do the will of his Father. Because he knew that his own human will was just not good enough. So he had said 'Yes' to his Father. And now he knew, as the soldiers dragged him along, that his Father walked with him. He remembered Abraham and Isaac – the father and the son going together to the place of sacrifice. He had taken the twelve aside and privately told them, 'We are going up to Jerusalem. Be prepared for this. Everything written by the prophets about me will be fulfilled. I'll be taken by the Gentiles, mocked, insulted, spat on, flogged. I will be killed. On the third day I will rise again.' At that time he had spoken in the third person, talked about himself as the Son of Man.

In his humanity, Jesus was like us. We may know something is going to happen. We may know how bad it's going to be. But we can always distance ourselves a little from it. That is the way our minds work. But then the reality of what we're facing hits us. For Jesus, that happened under the olive trees. As he is dragged along in chains, he is at peace with himself. He knows what is coming and has determined that he will face it. *All* of it.

Crossing the Kidron Valley, they took the route that would lead them as quickly as possible to the upper city. First to the house of Annas, not High Priest at the time but founder of a dynasty of high priests; a consummate politician, a wheeler and dealer, expert at exercising power through his sons and sons-in-law even when not High Priest himself. His son-in-law, Caiaphas, was now High Priest, but Annas still held the reins of power. He wanted to meet Jesus first, so he did. He questioned him.

Jesus answered honestly, 'I have always taught openly in the temple. You are asking me about my teaching. You must have people who've heard me.' Annas' officials slapped him full in the face for this apparent 'disrespect'.

'Why did you do that?' Jesus asked. 'If I said something wrong, point it out. If I spoke the truth, why hit me?'

Trial before Caiaphas followed. Annas was watching. It added to the pressure on Caiaphas. Lots of witnesses were produced. None of them agreed with each other. Jesus stayed silent. It was frustrating for Caiaphas and his staff of senior priests. Two men said Jesus had boasted he would be able to destroy the temple and build it again in three days. Still Jesus said nothing. Driven beyond legal restraint, Caiaphas leapt up.

'Aren't you going to answer? What is the testimony these people are bringing against you?' Still Jesus said nothing. Caiaphas knew the High Priest was not supposed to play such an active part but he was driven to confront Jesus.

'I charge you under oath by the living God. Tell us if you are the Christ, the Son of God.' The courtroom fell totally silent. None of those present had ever heard that oath of abjuration invoked. Never.

Jesus broke his silence. He regarded Caiaphas steadily. He saw the anger and fear in his eyes. Even now he felt for him. But he had no choice. He had to answer. In that magnificent courtroom, it echoed around the pillars: 'Yes, it is as you say. I say to all of you, in the future you will see me, the Son of Man, sitting at the right hand of the Mighty One and coming on the clouds of heaven.' Confident of who he was, gloriously, utterly convinced of his Father's presence, he spoke with calm assurance and a clear ringing voice. It is a magnificent moment and, for those who love him, it is utterly heroic. Spittle flying from his mouth, the High Priest whirled around and faced the rest of the court. Blazing with righteous anger, he signalled his verdict by ripping his robe. Jesus was to be torn out of Israel.

'He has spoken blasphemy. Do we need any more witnesses? What do you think?'

They began to shout, 'He should die.' They gathered around Jesus, spitting in his face and punching him, showing contempt by open-handed slaps, mocking. 'Come on prophet, tell us who hit you.'

Nothing. He was not there to perform. He had no need to prove anything. He knew who he was and what he had come to do. He knew where he was going. The cross was always before his eyes. But he knew that was not his final destination. He could see beyond it.

It has been said many times, 'Tough times don't last. Tough people do.' What makes it possible for them to last is that they see beyond the tough times and know that better times will come, if they hang on.

What I learn from David and his mightier descendant gives me courage to face difficult times and the strength to endure them. In them, I learn the power and vitality that is released when God's dreams become ours. Then, we release the awesome power of dreams.

Chapter 8

Go Right Through the Pain Barrier

HITTING ROCK BOTTOM

Philistine Border, Judea 1015–1010 BC

From his horse, David surveyed his men as they mustered, waiting for the baggage train to catch up. It stretched into the distance: donkeys and carts, children carrying large loads of supplies. A small army on the move – too small. He had finally admitted defeat. Saul's pursuit was relentless. Harried from pillar to post, there had been no rest. Nowhere was safe. There was no alternative but to leave Israel. And the only practical way was to go to the Philistines. He contacted Achish, King of Gath. Of course he remembered David's previous visit. But he was too smart to turn down the offer of allegiance from a warrior chief who had 600 men. Besides, he welcomed the chance to undermine the upstart King of Israel. So he gladly received David and his troops.

Topping the ridge, they made their way down into Philistine territory. Philistine territory meant Philistine gods. This was a failure. Had God's promise failed? He wondered, could he have done better? Repeatedly he had searched for a home but, wherever he settled, Saul, driven by his obsession, hunted him down. Repeatedly, David and his men left: Saul and his expeditionary force turned back. David was once more in the wilderness.

Day after day Saul had searched for him. He moved from one stronghold to another, sometimes even camping at Masada, later famous as the site of the final resistance by Jewish freedom fighters against the Romans. More and more men joined him, many skilled soldiers, even some from Saul's own tribe. But the larger the group of men, the harder it was to hide them from Saul's spies and troops.

In an area called the Crags of the Wild Goats, David and his men hid in a cave. They heard Israeli troops marching up the valley, then shouted orders to halt. The army was making a rest stop right outside. David and his men retreated deep into the cave and waited silently. Then, unbelievably, in the mouth of the cave he saw the silhouette of the man he still loved like a father. Saul. He walked into the cave and crouched down, spreading the flaps of his royal robes. Seeking privacy, the King had come to relieve himself in their cave.

Men whispered, 'This is it, the moment God promised. You can kill him right now; do what you like.' Silent as a cat, David crept towards Saul. His knife blade was sharp enough to cut a man's throat at a stroke. He reached out his hand, took a corner of Saul's robe. The King grunted as he relieved himself. David saw the white hairs. Saul was getting old. A single stroke with his knife cut the corner of the robe. Then David retreated to his men.

'Why didn't you kill him?' they asked.

'God forbid I should do such a thing. He is God's King.'

Saul completed his business and went on his way. David waited and then walked to the mouth of the cave.

He shouted, 'My Lord, the King!' Saul whirled around. David prostrated himself, then lifted his face.

'Why do you listen to those who tell you David wants to kill you? I could have killed you just now. Look, I have the corner of your robe in my hand. My father, I will never lift a weapon against you, for you are anointed by God.'

Saul's emotions could change in a flash, as they did now. Tears ran down his face.

'Is that you, my son, David? You could have killed me and you didn't. I know now you will be King of Israel. When you are, protect my family.' David swore he would. Saul returned to Gibeah. Unable to trust him, David took his men back to Masada. There he heard Samuel had died. It was almost as if the last link to God's promise had gone.

Saul returned to the hunt with a fresh raiding party, special forces – 3000 men, the best in Israel's army.

Once again, David had the chance to kill him. He and Abishai crept into the camp and took Saul's spear and water bottle. The subsequent conversation went as before. Saul wept and swore that he would never again seek to harm David. But it was the last straw. Though Saul withdrew, David, wearied beyond belief, decided to move out of Judah, to Gath.

Saul gave up searching when he heard. After a while Achish gave them the town of Ziklag. Then he summoned David and informed him that he and his men would march with Achish's army to fight with the Philistines against Israel. He invited him to be commander of his bodyguard. David agreed.

'Now you'll see what I can do,' he said. But he felt dead. The compromises he had made to stay alive and keep his men with him had eroded him on the inside.

The heroic young man, the idol of the young women of Israel, had discovered he too had a dark side, and the nobility he so prized, and which in early years he seemed to possess in abundance, was not limitless. It's the same for all of *us*.

When they got to the muster point, David saw Achish in fierce debate with the Philistine commanders. They needed only one look.

'What are these Israelites doing here? That's David. The girls of Israel sing "He's killed tens of thousands" . . . *of us*!'

Achish said, 'He's a good man. You can trust him.'

'Trust him to do what?' they said. 'What better way for him to get back into Saul's good books than turn on us in the middle of battle. Send them away.'

Achish came back. 'I'm sorry, David, they don't want you.'

David said, 'What's the matter? What have I done?'

Achish replied, 'To me, you're like an angel of God, but they don't want you. Go back to Ziklag.' So they did.

On the third day, as they crested a hill, they saw smoke rising. David had torched enough towns to know what it meant. Ziklag was utterly destroyed. The only consolation was that there were no dead bodies. But their wives, children and cattle had gone. Men weary after a long march looked at the devastation and wept. But tears soon turned to anger. He saw them in small groups, muttering, 'It's his fault. He led us into alliance with Israel's enemies. Now God is judging us. Stone him!' David knew the law: 'Those who lead men to serve other gods should be put to death without pity.' It was his darkest moment. 'They are right. I have led them to disaster. I deserve to die.' The guilt was crushing, the darkness suffocating.

He had no other refuge, no other place to go.

'O God, I've turned my face away from you, refused to listen to you, run from you, hardened my heart against you because the path was so hard. I repent of my stupidity. Hear my voice. Let your Holy Spirit fill me again.' Before he finished, he could feel it: a river, bubbling and sparkling, bringing freshness to a long-dry desert. He felt the strength flooding into his spirit and engaged with it, strengthening himself in the flow of life from God. He looked around, saw Abiathar, the priest.

'Bring me the holy robe. We're seeking God's guidance.' When David asked the question, God's reply was unequivocal: 'You will overtake them, and you will succeed in the rescue.' David looked at his men. There was a glint in his eyes and life in his face they had not seen for years. David was back!

'I'm going after my wives and children. Who's coming with me?' The exultant roar said it all.

Six hundred men set off on a march so fast that 200 could not keep up. David put them in charge of the supplies and the rest continued the pursuit. They found a young Egyptian, disorientated, dehydrated and starving, a servant of one of the Amalekite chiefs.

'Show us which way they've gone,' said David.

'Only if I don't have to go back to my master,' replied the slave. The Amalekites were spread across the countryside, having the biggest party, eating, drinking and celebrating. David held off until dusk, then swept in and fought the Amalekites through the night and into the evening of the next day. They killed them all, except for 400 who escaped on camels. Better than that, they got back every one of the hostages and an amazing amount of plunder. When they arrived back in Ziklag, David divided the plunder fairly among the men. He also sent presents to every town in Judah that had offered them hospitality in the last few years.

What David did not know was that the Philistines had inflicted a massive defeat on Israel. It was a total military disaster.

The night before the battle, lacking spiritual counsel and without the voice of God, Saul had gone to see a witch and called up the ghost of Samuel. Samuel rebuked him for even engaging in such a practice, and then informed him that he and his sons would be sleeping in death the next day. Bereft of direction, Saul and his sons lost many of their men, and became separated from their own command. On the slopes of Mount Gilboa, Saul saw his sons killed one by one, including Jonathan. Pierced by arrows, he fell on his own sword. So died Israel's first warrior king. The bodies of Saul and his three sons were stripped of their armour and nailed to the wall of the town of Bethshan – a warning to all Israel.

In the end, it was not the Philistines that had defeated him but his jealousy of David and his refusal to allow God first place. His fall coincided with David's rediscovery of his destiny.

HITTING THE WALL

Every runner knows about it – the moment we hit a wall of pain situated just beyond our energy limit. Right there we have to dig deep to find resources coming from way outside our normal comfort zone. Our problem is that nothing worthwhile comes without pain. And we hate pain. Most of us will do almost anything to avoid it, so we take the easy way out. In twenty-first-century culture, numerous strategies are available to enable us to avoid the difficulties of life. But in the end it does no good. All life has moments when we must press through the pain barrier. Every successful marriage/partnership has several times hit the wall. The people concerned have agreed explicitly or implicitly, 'We are not giving up. We are pushing through this difficult time because we believe in our marriage.' In family life, each child will test its parents in different ways. But one of them will push them to their limit or beyond. Every great project faces this issue. Those who are to succeed in any way have to know there will be moments when it hurts so badly they will want to give up. But at those moments they are going to press on through.

No area of life is exempt from testing. So, settle for it. Painful tests will come. Don't be surprised. It is inevitable. Physical, mental and emotional pain, disappointment, rejection and betrayal – these things happen to everyone. Intentional living means you don't allow them to rule or to define you.

Pain barriers come in different forms. The pain of David's failure at Ziklag could have been avoided, but only by opting for the pain of continual testing in Israel. The development of good character depends entirely on our facing the pain of testing with integrity.

WHEN NO ONE IS LOOKING

Character has been defined as who you are when no one is looking. It is the key to lasting effectiveness and reputation. Central to character is integrity, being the same person in public and in private. Inevitably, this will mean making painful choices. Being true to my marriage vows will mean saying no to the seductive beauty of romance outside marriage. Most marriages that last have faced this threat. Opportunities to stray creep up on us almost unawares. What begins as a seemingly innocent friendship can suddenly reveal itself as a deep attraction. Saying no to it can feel like ripping out your guts. You may feel, 'I'll never get over this.' But you can and you will.

Integrity in marriage also means saying no to the fierce pleasure of adulterous lust. No matter how tempting the offer may be, it really is best to run for it! The sudden opportunity at a party or on an overnight business trip may seem uncomplicated, simple and problem-free. No one will know. But they will. You will know, and it will change your interaction with your marriage partner. And it may precipitate disaster. The insidious temptation of pornography on the Web or late-night TV presents us with computer-enhanced images of perfection and impossibly compliant people whose only aim in life is to fulfil our wildest fantasies. It's a lie, of course. The question enters our minds, 'What's the harm? No one will ever know.' But they will. You will know. That will change the way you see yourself. It's hard to sustain self-respect when you are sucked in by something so despicable. The apparent anonymity of the Web adds to the power of the attraction. Turning away can be the toughest step of your life but it is worth it. Integrity is one of the rarest and most precious commodities in the world.

Being true to my business principles will mean saying no to the dodgy deal offered 'because you're a friend' and rejecting the exploitation of the vulnerable, adverts that lie and the glib re-assurance of quality that deep in my heart I know to be untrue. And it will mean saying no to petty pilfering and the hand in the till or even in the offering plate. Being true to myself will mean saying no to the white lie and yes to the truth. Truth-telling is vital to integrity. It does not have to be brutal, though it may be painful. But at the end of the day a lie will always be found out and will create more pain than if the truth had been told in the first place.

Jesus said this sort of integrity hurts, like cutting off your own hand or plucking out your own eye, but is gloriously worth it. Richard Nixon dreamed of going down in history as one of America's greatest presidents. But his memory is soiled by the lies of Watergate. Bill Clinton had a similar dream but his public effectiveness was compromised by private immorality. He is known as a masterful politician but an untrustworthy person. The truth is, you will never achieve your greatest ambition without an integrity that stays true to your values **even when it breaks your heart**.

STABBED IN THE BACK?

Disloyalty and dishonesty are the most painful trials we ever face. Jesus set his face to go to Jerusalem knowing that there he would be betrayed, abandoned and crucified. Almost certainly you will never have to face something like that, but some things may *feel* like it. Judas betrayed Jesus from a position of intimacy and enormously privileged trust. The pain he caused was in direct proportion to his closeness. It is difficult to know which is more painful, the treachery of a deliberate traitor like Judas or the failure of the weak. Simon Peter promised Jesus that no matter what happened he would *never* let him down. Jesus knew better. He knew Peter could not keep his wild promises. So when he heard him he looked at him with love in his heart, understanding and faith. I am glad Jesus is like that because I've let him down on more than a few occasions. His friendship never gives up. Just as well!

David, on the other hand, did not know how to deal with betrayal, even – or perhaps especially – by his own children. Jesus dealt with it gently but honestly and bravely. David was never properly fathered himself, so he had no idea how to be a father to his own sons. His favourite son, Absalom, killed his half brother Amnon in revenge for Amnon's rape of his sister, Tamar. David knew about the rape, but did nothing about it. His spiritual authority was fatally weakened by his own adultery with someone else's wife and his murder of the husband – as we will see in Chapter 10. David could not confront Amnon because of his own sexual sin. Then, because he loved him, and yearned for his love in return, he was unable to rebuke Absalom for killing his brother. Later on, Absalom set up a coup and took over the country. After a huge battle, Joab, David's Commander-in-Chief, killed him. It broke David's heart. Towards the end of David's life, Adonijah thought David was too old to reign, and conspired to take the throne. He was outrageously spoilt. The Bible says, 'His father had never interfered with him by asking him "Why do you behave as you do?"' Indulged sons became rebels and traitors. They would not have done that if David had confronted them. He tried to avoid the pain barrier, yet only made it all worse. Whoever we are, we will one day live through the pain of betrayal. Even if we manage lovingly to confront the situation and recover the relationship, it will still hurt. But the pain does not have to dominate. We can take authority over the memory and press on. We *can* let go of bitterness and grasp the joy of God instead. It is a choice.

TOUGH LOVE

Confrontation is painful. It is tough to go to someone and say, 'I believe we have a problem we need to talk about,' but it is necessary. First, you need to ask yourself, 'What is it about?

What is the real issue here? Is this person responding to hurts in the past which have nothing to do with me? Are they acting out old scenarios, repeating old scripts in their heads?' Whatever the answers may be, confrontation will have to be faced. It is a kind of dying, because whatever you do the relationship will never be the same. We avoid confrontation because it is painful. But if you get it right, the relationship can be reborn, stronger. Avoidance only makes matters worse and in the end creates more pain.

Though confrontation is vital if relationships are to be healthy, it must be done constructively. It is essential that we deal with our anger when it first erupts. It's so tempting to press 'send' on that email that says exactly what I feel, or to pick up the phone and give them an earful. But once it's said it can't be unsaid. Once it's sent it can't be pulled back, and the destruction caused may never be repaired. Those destructive responses usually have deep roots. Many of us were raised as emotional cripples by parents or step-parents who were themselves emotionally crippled. This inward disability will be expressed in different ways.

In some homes, a day never goes by without some enormous explosion of feelings. Emotional blackmail proliferates. Hurts from years past are dragged out time and again, with all the pride of old soldiers showing their war wounds. Extreme statements abound: You've *never* cared about me. You *always* say that. *Every time* I start to speak you put me down. You *never* listen to me! The battles rage on and the children of such homes learn nothing but psychological warfare and emotional pain.

Then there is the other extreme. Lots of us were brought up believing 'big boys don't cry', and not just the men! The days of 'keeping a stiff upper lip' may have gone but the attitudes linger on. There are houses where the slightest expression of feeling is regarded as the worst of bad taste. Clearing the throat can become the most devastating social comment. People stalk in silence through houses fuelled with venom and animosity, each inwardly blaming the other, with barely a word being said.

I have a problem with anger, and I've seen the pain caused by wrong reactions. So I've had to learn to deal with these things wisely. First, we *can* learn to express anger in a healthy way. We need a process that will neither rip others apart nor tear through us, leaving us exhausted, damaged and exposed to those who wish to harm us. For me, the most important element in the process is what I call 'taking my anger for a walk'. I ask God to keep me company while I walk. Then, in my imagination, I summon the one who has angered me. While they stand in front of me I tell them *exactly* what I think of them (alternatively, I write a letter to them in my head). When I have totally exhausted my fury, I review what I said. I invite God to comment. Then I have to admit: I was over the top! Eventually I come to a point of balance at which my rage has been fully expressed in the presence of my creator alone. Now I am ready to deal with the issues *without* my judgement being distorted. 'Taking my anger for a walk' has become a truly valuable tool in my collection – the start of controlling anger's destructive power, and perhaps of harnessing its energy for constructive purposes.

Second, we need to cultivate the ability to stand back from our own feelings and say to others, 'Can I tell you how that makes me feel?' Expressing my feelings as if they belonged to someone else enables me to treat them with some objectivity. It means I am taking further control of them, rather than allowing them to overcome me.

BEARING THE SCARS

There is no way round it: life hurts. Facing its painful tests in the short term will hurt more than if I run away. But if I run away from the pain it will catch me at some other time and place and be worse in the long term. The Bible says of Jesus that he was made *perfect* through his suffering. This is not implying that he was morally imperfect. However, before Jesus could truly represent us he had to endure life in a fallen world governed by greed, cruelty, selfishness, lust, pride and violence. Only by personal experience of what it costs to say yes to God's will in a broken world could Jesus become a representative for ever able to pray for us. He's been there and lived it. He knows suffering from the inside. Now he is perfect for us.

Jesus suffered more pain from temptation than any other human being, simply because he never gave in. We all chuckle when we read Oscar Wilde's little saying, 'Temptation is no problem to me. I always give in.' And of course he's reflecting the truth. Temptation is a problem only when we don't give in. And we want to. There is a bias inside us dragging us into the wrong course of action. I know nobody without that bias.

People tell me Christianity is escapism. All I can say is: you try it! Try following the man who said, 'Love your enemies, do good to those who hate you, bless those who curse you, pray for those who are spiteful to you.' Try it. Try loving your enemies. Think of ways to do good to those who hate you or to speak blessing over somebody who curses you. Think of the most spiteful person you know and then pray for them, intensely, passionately and sincerely. See how hard that is! There is nothing escapist about these demands. They make me face up to stuff in myself that I really don't want to see. I'd like to escape the reality of who I am and what I am like. But I can't. The only way I know to deal with it is to face it in partnership with Jesus himself. He is the key to my transformation. If it's going to happen, I must be willing to bear the scars like he does. He reminds me – no trouble lasts for ever. There is light beyond the darkness. It is vitally important that we press on through. It's the only way to be a winner.

WINNING WITHOUT COMING FIRST

Los Angeles, Summer 1984

The first-ever women's marathon in an Olympic Games. British commentators knew all about it! They assured us the winner would definitely be one of the European runners, who had demonstrated their pedigree and grasp of running strategy. They gave little hope to America's own Joan Benoit. Fortunately for her, Joan Benoit was not listening to them. Fourteen minutes after the start she pulled away from the rest of the field. Commentators said, 'Well, of course she will blow up. The rest of the field will haul her in like she is on a fishing line.' But she wasn't listening. She kept running through the heat and humidity. At one point she was about half a mile clear of the rest of the field. By the time she got to the stadium the people of Los Angeles, having seen her on television, were out on the streets cheering home their own girl. Inside, the crowd were mesmerised, watching on the big screen. The chasing pack was getting nearer and nearer. As she emerged into the sunlit bowl of the Los Angeles Coliseum, the place erupted with cheers. She ran that last lap bathed in their applause. She came home one minute ahead of the nearest challenger, who was followed closely by most of the field. It was a magnificent achievement and the cheers she received were well deserved.

About twenty minutes after she finished, a Swiss runner literally staggered out of the tunnel, entering the stadium in a fashion reminiscent of Dorando Pietri in 1908. She was almost unable to walk, her torso twisted, left arm limp, right leg mostly seized up, barely aware of her whereabouts and on the point of total collapse from heat exhaustion. She had run the race of her life, but now faced the final 400m, the longest and most excruciating single lap of an athletics track she would ever face.

Trackside officials desperately tried to persuade her not to continue, but she plodded on, wandering all over the track, determined to finish, drawing on her final reserves of strength. Eventually after 300m – which took about four minutes – she entered the home straight. By now team officials, doctors and a few fellow athletes were keeping alongside her while the 80,000-strong crowd was on its feet, all encouraging her to cover every last remaining and agonising centimetre to the finishing line, as it drew slowly closer. Taking steps shorter than her own feet, she shuffled, crooked and exhausted, to the most welcome white line she would ever see. She reached it and collapsed in a senseless heap. She had taken five minutes and forty-four seconds for that last lap. Then she was whisked rapidly away to hospital. She had finished thirty-seventh.

As she slumped over the line that told her, 'It's finished. Your fight is over. You've come home,' the crowd that had shouted itself hoarse as she completed that final circuit of the Los Angeles Coliseum mustered one final almighty roar. It was louder even than the one with which they had acknowledged their home-grown golden girl twenty-five minutes earlier. It was probably the loudest cheer afforded any competitor in all events of the entire Olympiad.

Gabriela Andersen-Schiess had won a great victory. She had not come first, but she had faced her own pain barrier and beaten it. She had won – and provided everyone present with a powerful reminder of the Olympic ideal and, even more importantly, an inspirational object lesson in courage and perseverance

KIDNAPPED!

For even the Son of Man did not come to be served, but to serve, and to give his life as a ransom for many.

(Mark 10:45 *NIV*)

Why was Jesus willing to go through the pain of giving up his life? Because he sees us as kidnapped and wants to set us free. In thinking about a kidnap scenario, we have to ask ourselves what it is kidnappers want. Are they ever really interested in their victims? No. The victims are merely pawns in a much bigger game. The kidnapper wants to extract payment of some kind from somebody (or some entity) that has a vested interest in the well-being and safe return of the kidnapped victim. If Jesus came to ransom the multitudes of the world, we have to ask who the kidnapper is, and what is the nature of the bondage in which he holds his victims? What does he want? What price is he willing to accept in order for his victims to be released? And who is he trying to extract a ransom from? Just who is his target?

The first answer is simple. At the very beginning of the Bible's narrative, we are introduced to someone who opposes God's plans on every level – Satan, whose name means 'the accuser'. The Bible depicts him as a kind of demonic lawyer, using every trick in the book to get the judge to bring in a verdict of guilty against anybody and everybody. In fact, even this is a ploy, since his primary accusation has always been against God. It appears to be based on the idea that 'might is right'.

The premise is that there is no such thing as moral authority, right or wrong. Authority is a matter of power. The entire creation, therefore, is in the possession of the one who has the power. Satan's accusation is that God is really God only because he has the power. But he pretends to be good, and so to have moral authority. This means God is a liar. Satan is the honest one, and therefore ought to be God. Satan's initial try for the throne having failed, he has now turned into a fiendishly clever counsel for the prosecution. He is truly going for 'The Big One'. He wants nothing less than to be master of all creation, to take God's position. It is a neat accusation. God cannot reach out and kill Satan because, if he were to do that, his action would appear to support the very accusation that has been brought against him. Therefore, he can win this battle only by establishing the triumphant superiority of who he is. Plus, because Satan is a creature made by the creator, the defence for God can be put forward only by another part of God's creation.

As we saw earlier, God's prime purpose in making human beings was that they should reflect his glory as creator. So the only one who can answer Satan's accusation is a human being. But the human being has to be perfect. There must not be any place inside that human being where evil rules or Satan has already won.

As for the kind of bondage in which we are held, for me it is best illustrated by the original *Matrix* film. The state of human beings in the *Matrix* world – living their 'lives' in a virtual reality while their bodies are maintained in womblike cells with no real awareness of their situation – is a parable of our own. Their bondage is unconscious, like ours. They are fed lies, presented with an illusionary reality in order to persuade them all is well, as we are. In truth, we are bereft of the contact with God that makes us truly alive. So we live a kind of shadow life, only dimly aware that somewhere there is a sunlit reality where we truly belong.

When it comes to answering the questions 'What does he want? What price is the accuser willing to accept in order for his victims to be released?', the answer there is simple. He wants God to become subject to his rule. So when God steps into our world in the person of Jesus, he enters the arena of death. Either he dies to redeem all those who are currently in slavery or else he refuses to die and saves his own life – but yields authority over all creation to Satan. That is why the story of the cross, the darkest hour of Jesus, is a story that vitally concerns every human being, whether they are a 'Christian' or not.

THE LONGEST DAY

The trials had been skilfully stage-managed so Caiaphas could be sure the right people from the Sanhedrin would be there. Having agreed that Jesus must die, they had to find a reason for the Roman governor to execute him. Charges of blasphemy would not cut it. By the time they got Jesus from Caiaphas' house to Pilate's quarters in Herod's old palace, the charges had changed to subversion, proclaiming himself an alternative king and forbidding the payment of taxes to Caesar. Dramatic stuff! Jesus is leader of an insurrection. But he doesn't actually look like a threat to the Empire. He has had no sleep for over twenty-four hours and been knocked around by the temple guards, and is just standing there, quiet and self-contained.

Pilate must have been irritated by the chief priests' insistence that he go out to them just to avoid their being contaminated by entering his quarters. He listened to the charges, went into the palace and summoned Jesus.

'Are you the King of the Jews?'

'Is that your idea?' asked Jesus. 'Or someone else's?'

'Do I look like a Jew?' Pilate replied. 'Your own people handed you over to me. What are you supposed to have done?'

'My kingdom is not of this world. Or I would fight. But my kingship is from another realm.'

It was a curiously enigmatic statement. As he said it Jesus was not being bombastic but tentative, as if inviting Pilate to join him in a different conversation. His eyes were still alert in his battered face and they sought out Pilate's eyes, almost interrogating him. Pilate shook himself. This would not do. He returned to the accusation against the prisoner.

'So, you *are* a king?' Pilate finally responded.

'You're right,' said Jesus, 'I am a king. I was born to be a testimony to the truth. All who recognise truth listen to me.'

'What is truth?' Pilate asked bitterly. He went out to the Jewish leaders. 'I can't find any reason to execute this prisoner. It is customary to release a prisoner at Passover. Do you want the "King of the Jews" freed?'

'NO!' they shouted. 'Not him!' So Pilate gave orders for Jesus to be flogged. A Roman flogging was severe. Flogged men died 'by accident'. The soldiers in this legion were from Samaria. Samaritans hated Jews and Jews despised Samaritans. Now they had the 'King of the Jews' in their hands. They could not have been more delighted. This flogging would not be gentle. It wasn't.

Stripped naked, he was manacled to the top of a pillar, his legs strapped around the base. The scourge was made of nine leather thongs studded with little lead balls; often, at the end of each thong, there was a piece of copper or bone sharpened to a point. The first strokes cut long lines through the skin, the next tore off strips of skin. By the time they were exhausted his back resembled a ploughed field made of living flesh. The thorns on a Jerusalem thorn tree are three-pointed, about 5–8 cm long, hard as iron, sharp as nails. Someone found a branch of it. They twisted it into a crown and stuck it on his head, hammering it home with a Roman officer's stick. They draped an old purple robe over his shoulders. It soaked up the blood. They struck him on the face, spat at him and mocked him: 'Hail, King of the Jews!' It was the most fun they had had in a long time. But the prisoner was disappointing. He would not retaliate. He was silent.

Pilate brought Jesus out in front of the chief priests and the mob they had summoned from the slums of Jerusalem. He shouted,

'Behold the man!' unconscious of any mystical significance – 'The Man', come to show us what God meant humans to be like.

The chief priests and their staff shouted, 'Crucify! Crucify!' and the ranting mob behind them joined in. Pilate was concerned. Clearly Jesus was innocent, but the chief priests wanted him dead. He hated being manipulated into using Roman power for their schemes.

But Annas and Caiaphas knew Pilate had been fatally weakened. His patron Sejanus, second to the Emperor Tiberius, had been toppled and killed. In the brutal world of Roman politics, Pilate was a mere step from disaster. Pilate talked again with Jesus, tried to release him.

'If you set this man free, you are no friend of Caesar,' the mob shouted.

He brought him out before them. 'Here is your king.'

'Crucify him!' they said.

'Crucify your king?'

'We have no king but Caesar,' they replied. Pilate was defeated. He knew it. If he let Jesus live he would be saying that Caesar wasn't king. If that got back to Rome, and they would ensure it did, he was dead. So he gave the orders.

THE DARKEST HOUR

They ripped the cloth off his back, replacing it with the splintered wood of the cross. On it was a notice: 'Jesus of Nazareth, King of the Jews.' People spat; soldiers hit him with their spear butts as he staggered through the narrow streets. The flogging he had already endured was more than enough to kill a man. He stumbled down through the city, out of the gates and so to Skull Hill, where he collapsed. It was an amazing feat of endurance. He could go no further. So the centurion forced a man from Africa to carry the cross. Was he black? Maybe. Whatever, that high privilege went to a North African. At the top of the hill, they laid the cross on the ground, laid the man on the cross, took a Roman nail, probably an eight-inch spike, and hammered it through the wrist bones or between the radius and the ulna. Not the hand – it has no structure that would hold the weight of a body. Always the right hand first, then pull the left arm out tight until the arms are almost popping out of the shoulders. Then a nail into the left wrist.

At last he broke his silence, saying over and over again, 'Father, forgive them, they don't know what they're doing.' Because of Passover, this man had to die fast. There is every chance they looped rope round his legs, pulled hard then hammered a nail through the ankles. They lifted the cross high, dropped it into its hole in the ground. The weight of the body plucked the arms out of their sockets. Inexorably, he began to die. The arteries in the arms were pulling at the heart. Eventually they would tear the fibrous sac that holds the heart. But it was a long and painful process. He couldn't breathe except by pushing up on his nailed feet. It was agonising.

Jesus looked down. Among some women from his discipleship team, he could see his mother and the faithful young man, John. Gathering a painful breath, he knew he must let his mother know. There would be no angelic rescue. Angels had come at his birth. But not now. He nodded towards John, his eyes on his mother: 'Dear lady, this is your son.' And to John, 'Here is your mother.' It was a stab to the heart. She knew he was saying. 'No rescue. I'm not coming home. I'm going to die.' John led her away, to his home.

Then it was just him and the other women; and the priests, mocking, laughing and jeering. Either side of him the thieves were a bit more pointed: 'Oy, you so-called miracle-worker. You may want to die, but we don't. You can do miracles; get us off these crosses!' Three hours of swear-words, curses and blasphemy. He said nothing.

Then one of them stopped. The other kept going, his bitterness rising to a poisonous crescendo. The quiet one shouted, 'Shut up! Leave him alone. He's not like us. I can tell.' Then he said, 'Jesus, I reckon you'll get your kingdom. When you do, think of me, won't you?'

'I give you my word. I won't just think of you. Today, you will be with me in paradise.'

Every time I look at that part of the story, I want to shout, 'What a man! What a glorious man!' I am so glad he isn't like me. I know the answer that man would have got from me. It would have been very different. Each part of it was a test: unjustly accused and found guilty, abused, nailed to a cross, stretched between heaven and earth. He went on loving them. Then his mother, tugging at the heartstrings of a loving son, but he didn't lose it as I would. Gently and courteously, knowing he was breaking her heart, he let her know, 'I'm not coming home with you.' Finally, the abuse of someone suffering alongside him hour after hour – vicious, unending. Then, when he says, 'Can I join the party?' Jesus says, 'Welcome.'

LIGHT IN THE DARKNESS

He passed all the tests. I think Satan began to realise what he had done. He had stretched out his hand to take an innocent victim, believing he could break him, make him respond with hatred, anger and bitterness. But he had failed – utterly. All he had done was expose God's true nature. Stripped of power, subjected to the ultimate test, the nature of Jesus the man – God in flesh – was proved to be pure love. Disaster yawned. There was nothing Satan could do to stop it. Suddenly, at twelve noon, after three hours, darkness swept over the face of the countryside. It was spoken of in cities across the Empire. It lasted three hours. In the darkness, the Father came, but not to rescue his Son. He came to charge him with the lust, hate, violence, envy, pride and greed of the broken world. As he hung there on that cross, the Father down-loaded to his consciousness the name and the sins, shame and suffering of every single human being that ever lived. He filled his own Son up with all the hellish filth and pain of our polluted human souls until the mighty soul of Jesus was saturated with it all. When he had finished, the Father turned his back on his own Son, walked into heaven and shut the door.

Jesus screamed, 'My God, my God, why have you abandoned me?' There was no answer. Such is the nature of hell. There is no answer from God. Then he gave a great cry of triumph. It echoed round the hills. 'Completed.' When they translated it into Greek they used the word *Tetelestai*. It means 'the final account has been paid'. Surely all heaven erupted at that moment, angels cheering from deepest to highest heaven. Onlookers thought Jesus was dead. But he lifted his head one more time, took in a last breath, then whispered, 'Father, into your hands I commit my spirit.' He was saying, 'Dad, I've done the job. I'm coming home.' Then he bowed his head, released his spirit and died.

Now the innocent victim went to the place of his tormentor. He entered hell, no longer as victim but as conqueror, and offered release to any who wanted to be free. Then he burst out of hell, leaving a hole torn in its roof so that no one need ever again be held captive who wants to be truly free.

That is the story of the cross – as best I can tell it. It is the story of a cosmic adventure greater than anything this world has ever known. One ordinary human being, tested beyond endurance, revealed to be pure and flawless. He marched alone into hell, defeating all the gathered powers of darkness, not by some mighty blast of power but by the radiance of limitless love, truth and purity. He is the ultimate hero – the greatest warrior the world has ever known. It is the reason why my life is devoted utterly to Jesus. I will follow him anywhere, in life or in death. And I know I shall see him when I die, because he died my death first. He got there before I did. So the first thing I shall see at the moment of my death will be his face. Then begins the adventure for which he paid – the adventure of eternity.

I once introduced a young man in the inner city to this Jesus and it revolutionised his life. When I went back to visit him at the church he was attending, he saw me and delightedly shouted from the front to me at the back of the church, ''ere Eric! This Christianity, it's bloody marvellous!' And it is just that. It's a bloody story – but marvellous.

But of course that's not the end of the story.

Chapter 9

Beyond Success to Significance

FROM EXILE TO THE THRONE

Hebron, Territory of Judah, 1010–998 BC

The mercenary cautiously raised his head. He had been feigning death for several minutes. The noise of battle had moved away. He thanked his lucky stars that none of the arrows had found him. They had certainly found many of those around him. The groans of the dying formed the soundtrack to his calculations. He looked again towards the hilltop. Saul and his sons still lay where they had fallen. Remarkably, their identity seemed to have remained undiscovered by the Philistine commanders. He saw the glint of gold on Saul's arm and was astounded no one else had spotted it.

Cautiously he began to move. No one responded. He had watched the last moments of Saul and his sons. Now it was time to move. He had no illusions about himself. He was a soldier for what he could get. From his perspective, only fools lived for a cause or died a hero. 'Better a living dog than a dead lion,' he whispered to himself. He had joined Israel's army for the possibility of loot. He was a scavenger. He had seen men die for honour and loyalty and thought them deluded. He had just a few minutes. He pulled the armband off the dead king and wrenched his crown off his helmet, then tucked them into the bag that always rested over his shoulders. You never knew when you were going to find something useful. This time he had hit the jackpot. He knew just where to go. David was at Ziklag and he would amply reward the man who brought him the crown of Israel. He slipped away from the battlefield as dusk fell.

He made good progress. It was important for his purposes that he be first to give the news to David. He had minimal rest and ate on the move. As he neared Ziklag, he realised that he needed to look suitably battle-worn and sombre. So he tore his robe and threw dust on his head. As he neared Ziklag, sentries challenged him, took him and marched him through the town. Clearly it had been burnt, but tents had been erected and order restored. Then he was standing before David. He knew the right way to behave and prostrated himself before him.

'Get up,' said David. 'Tell me where you've come from.'

'I escaped from the Israeli battlefield, just got away.'

'What happened? Tell me.'

'It was a rout, men were fleeing the battle; many fell and died. Saul and his son Jonathan are dead.'

David eyed the man. He knew his sort. 'How do you know – that Saul and Jonathan are dead?'

The mercenary had been thinking about this and he had got his story just right: 'I was right there on Mount Gilboa in the middle of the battle. Saul was leaning on his spear, the chariots and their riders almost upon him. He turned and saw me. He said "Who are you?" So I told him, "An Amalekite, serving Israel." So he said, "I've been hit by many arrows. I'm very near death. Help me. Stand over me and kill me." So I killed him; I knew he could not survive. Then I took the crown from his head and the band from his arm and brought them to you, my lord.'

He was not prepared for the response. David and his men tore their own clothes and wept. He was offered no food. The entire camp fasted. It lasted until evening. Then he smelt the welcome aroma of food cooking. He was looking forward to this meal; he'd waited long enough. David recovered his composure and sat on his chair with his platoon leaders around him. He was ready to deal with this man now. He knew his kind. He had already spotted the well-worn shoulder bag that he'd somehow kept through the heat of battle, the absence of any wounds on a man who'd seen almost all of Israel's army killed. His voice was expressionless as he asked, 'Where did you say you are from?' The mercenary felt uneasy, suddenly reluctant to answer the question directly.

'I'm the son of an Amalekite,' he answered. David's eyes narrowed. He doubted this man had truly killed Saul. But he had testified that he had, so he would take him at his word.

His voice was suddenly bitter. 'Why were you not afraid to take your sword and destroy the king anointed by God?' With a rising sense of panic, the Amalekite realised this was not going as planned. He was still trying to think of an answer when David turned to one of his platoon commanders: 'Kill him! Kill him now!'

After that, David wrote his lament for Saul and Jonathan. In the complexity of his relationship with them both, he had loved one as a father and the other as more than a brother.

After a few weeks, David asked God for guidance. He was told to go to Hebron in Judah. He and his men took over Hebron and many surrounding villages too. The elders of Judah, left without a king, appointed David as king over their tribal area. Meanwhile Abner, Saul's Commander-in-Chief, had made Saul's son Ish-Bosheth king over the rest of Israel. But he was a puppet; Abner was the real power. For the next seven years there was a struggle between David and his kingdom and the rest of Israel. As always, civil war produced tragic outcomes, engendering bitter feuds. In one battle Abner was reluctantly forced into killing one of David's nephews, Asahel. Eventually, Abner lost patience with his puppet. He came quietly to see David, offering to turn the rest of Israel over to him. After years of war it was a chance for the nation to be healed, an offer of peace and unity. As part of the negotiation David promised him a prominent role in the new united kingdom. Abner left in peace.

David was tired of civil war. Once Abner left, he could not stop smiling. He leaned back in his chair: peace at last, Israel united. It was a dream come true. But when Joab, Asahel's brother, heard, he was furious. Unknown to David, he sent a message calling Abner back to Hebron. He drew him aside into a gateway for a quiet word, stabbed him in the stomach and left him to die. He and his brother Abishai were well satisfied but David was utterly ashamed. His reign was dishonoured and his dream of a united Israel shattered because of their treachery. He gave Abner a state funeral and forced them to walk in mourning in front of his body, but refused to eat the usual substantial funeral supper.

Ish-Bosheth, meanwhile, lost all his courage. He had never had much, but now it was completely gone. He was a peaceable man, not much interested in war. One hot day, he retired for the usual midday siesta. Two of his own captains had decided that David represented the main chance. They entered his house in the quiet of that summer's day, stabbed Ish-Bosheth while he lay asleep, cut his head off, wrapped it in a bundle and ran to David at Hebron. They got the same reward as the Amalekite. David's judgement was clear. Wicked men had murdered an innocent man in his own house, on his own bed. This time he didn't just have them killed. Their hands and feet were cut off and they were hanged.

It took time for the pain of Ish-Bosheth's death to pass from Israel. But eventually the elders of Israel came and asked David to be king over the whole nation. He was forty. It was nearly twenty-five years since Samuel had anointed him king and seven and a half years since he had been crowned at Hebron. Hundreds of thousands of men had flocked to his banner by that time, determined to make him king of the whole country. The next two years were amazing. Zion, the great fortress of Jebus, at the old city of Jerusalem, was taken by a small group of commanders climbing up the water shaft into the city. David set up residence in the fortress, renamed it 'the City of David' and claimed the city as Jerusalem, 'foundation of peace'. Now, everywhere he went, victory came. His kingdom stretched from the border of Egypt to the Euphrates. No army could stand before him; no city could defy him.

One day, he revealed the desire of his heart to build a temple for God in Jerusalem. Nathan the prophet gave him God's reply: 'You're a man whose hands are stained with the blood of conquest. Such hands should not build my house of stone. But do not be disappointed, because your son will build my temple. More than that, I am going to make your family line, David, into a house that will last for ever.' David sat before God in the tabernacle, reviewing the journey of his life, from shepherd boy to king of a huge territory. He was overwhelmed with gratitude, and worshipped with wonder at the promise that someone descended from him would reign for ever.

In many ways, although he did not know it, this was the spiritual pinnacle of his kingdom and of his life.

FROM SURVIVAL TO STABILITY

Thinking back to the moment when David, the most famous soldier in Israel, was forced to flee from Saul's court alone and almost friendless, then to his life in Adullam's cave and the desperate fugitives who joined him, it is clear that this was a man in survival mode. I think he felt sustained at first by his destiny. He knew Samuel had anointed him and believed he would be king of Israel. In his early twenties, he probably felt that all he had to do was wait a while for God to bring it about. But it didn't happen like that. Saul's continuous pursuit of him wore away at his sense of destiny, and almost destroyed the most precious commodity any of us has – his sense of identity. As the weeks became months and then years, he became familiar with the pattern that most of us know from desperate and hard experience. God's promises are great. But waiting on their timing – that's the tough one.

In survival mode, we struggle to get through. Each day is a hard-won victory. Every weekend commences with another TGI Friday moment. Each month brings another financial crisis, too much month at the end of the money! When Pat and I first married we were romantically confident that we would make our way through every difficulty. That was quickly eroded. Life with a young family was a continual struggle. At one point I was working at the ICI sales office during the day and temping from 8 p.m. to 3 a.m. most nights as a driver for emergency doctors called to patients all over South London. For months, I survived on about three and a half hours' sleep a night. It wasn't a good way to live. But I felt I had no alternative. We needed the money for a growing family. It took years for that survival mentality to change to one that was at least on the way to stability. There were periods when, for years, I forgot who I was and what I was called to do – like lots of us.

So many of us seem to be sleep-walking through an existence

in which we never make contact with the reason for our existence. Lulled into soul-sleep by the chatter of entertainment and the 'white noise' of technology, we fearfully evade stillness that would enable us to know that God is, and more, is truly God. Somehow we fear the quiet, the silence in which God might reveal his presence. So we invent ever more effective ways in which the noise of our world can be omnipresent, enabling us to evade the voice of the eternal. In David's darkest moment at Ziklag he recognised that, no matter how hard he tried, he could not bring about his promised destiny. At that moment when he strengthened himself in God, he recognised, 'Only God can get me through this and into the place I am destined to go.'

For David, those years culminated in the sixteen months he spent in Ziklag. He had moved into financial survival and a measure of stability. But in order to achieve it he had compromised, lost his moral compass. Like many of us, he did what he had to do to get by. He lied and conned people, including Achish, who in turn used him. He lost any illusions he might have had about himself. But at Ziklag he was shocked when he realised how far he had fallen from his high ideals. Like any other young Israeli, he had memorised the five books of Moses – at least. He knew the law. Deuteronomy commanded of the man who caused people to serve other gods, 'Stone him to death.' It would have been easy to despair. But David turned to the Lord his God. He discovered what a friend of mine once called 'heart-stopping deliverance'. In just a moment a man in darkest bondage was set free, rose from a state of spiritual death and reconnected with the God who breathed life into him. For a while his outward circumstances did not change. He remained in Ziklag. But he was transformed, and everyone working with him was changed as a result. The transformation from a leader his men wanted to stone to death to one who could lead them in a magnificent victory was amazing. One of the things I love about Jesus is that he encourages me to believe in the possibility of astounding transformation. Because of what happened inside him, David moved from survival to stability. When he received the command from God to move to Hebron after Saul's death, he was ready.

STABILITY TO SUCCESS

Not long after David reached Hebron, the leaders of his own tribe, Judah, proposed that he should become king. The destiny prophesied by Samuel about eighteen years before had at last come true. The next seven years were a time of learning. He was king over only one tribe, albeit the most powerful tribe in Israel. He learned the art of wise governance. At first a trickle from other tribes came to join him, but as the years passed the trickle become a flood. At the end of those seven years, he had over 340,000 men, described as 'fully determined to make David king over *all* Israel' (emphasis mine). The astounding transformation that had taken place in his life at Ziklag was demonstrated in Hebron by a success beyond the wildest dreams of many who walked with him through the years of difficulty. But somehow David was able to accept the success he was given without losing touch with the truth about himself. He had not forgotten his abject failure in Gath and at the Philistine muster. He knew God had saved him from the disgrace of facing Saul in battle, of being there when Israel's anointed king was killed.

When after seven and a half years the elders of Israel came to ask him to be king over the entire country, there were three days of feasting and celebration in which much fruit, bread, meat and wine was consumed. The celebration is summarised by these simple words: 'There was joy in Israel.' Anybody looking at David from outside would have thought he had now achieved his dream, succeeded beyond anybody else's expectations, and should be able to enjoy what God had given him. But years of fleeing from Saul and the long, deadly months in the land of the Philistines had taught David something vital. They had taught him that no amount of material possessions or career success can adequately fill the void in the heart of a human being.

Many hundreds of years before St Augustine, David could have written the words, 'You have made us for yourself and our hearts are restless till they find their rest in you.' He had lost the relationship with God once and he was determined not to lose it again.

In fact, he was clearly determined to chase after God. He was passionate about encouraging the whole nation to do the same thing, not just to win wars and battles but to know God and enjoy his presence. He wanted more. In our increasingly shallow society so many have settled for worldly success, believing this is what they've been looking for all their lives. Others have been seduced by their affluence. For the latter, the years of recession have proved devastating indeed. It is time we all reassessed our lifestyle and learned to put first things first.

SUCCESS TO SIGNIFICANCE

Almost immediately after David had taken the fortress called Jebus, renamed it the City of David and reaffirmed the ancient name, Jerusalem, he revealed to Israel's national council the passion that had driven him through the years. His dream was to restore the ark of the covenant to its rightful position at the heart of Israel's life. The ark was the symbol of God's presence with his people. Throughout Saul's reign it had been almost completely ignored. But David knew that to thrive the nation needed a steady heartbeat of healthy, spiritual life. No one could create a life of any meaning whatever unless they flowed with the purposes of the great God who had made all things. Alone among the nations of the earth at that time, Israel proclaimed their God to be God of the heavens and the earth. He was no mere territorial deity, to be identified with some pathetic idol. He was the God of the skies, who had made the stars. He caused the sun and moon to rise. He was the great God of all the earth, the God of the seas and land, the forests and wheat fields, the wild animals and domestic stock. He was God over all the peoples of the earth. God of everything. David knew that many in Israel hankered after the fertility gods of Canaan. The ark would no longer be at the periphery of the nation's life. It was going to be central – a permanent reminder of Israel's true identity, and her destiny.

His new capital was wisely chosen, situated on the border between Judah and Benjamin. Benjamin was a small tribe, but highly influential in the nation. So his new city symbolised national unity. At the heart of it, he wanted the ark of God's covenant. David was determined not to simply settle for success. He wanted significance. His life aim was very clear to him. Even though he wouldn't get to build it, he knew the temple was to be the heart of God's holy city, and was determined to build towards that future.

If we are to live like we mean it, then surely we need to learn from this. It's overdue for some of us to sit down and ask what our own life aims are, write them all down, and then prioritise. What are the most and least important? Looking at our programmes, are our schedules organised according to our conscious life aims? Or are the most important given least time? If we are to be of any use at all, if we are to make a difference, we have to be willing to put our schedules and our diaries under this kind of personal microscope. I have to keep on reminding myself of the saying, 'Nobody on their death-bed ever wished they had spent more time at the office.'

THE STRATEGY FOR SIGNIFICANCE – LEARNING FROM JESUS

We should look at the world around us and ask, what can I contribute that will make a positive difference? What will leave others glad that I lived? It was not original, but I still remember the electrifying moment when President John F. Kennedy said to the American people, 'Ask not what your country can do for you, but rather ask what you can do for your country.' However, that probably won't be enough. It's nice to do things, good things that help others. But alone it is simply not enough. We need to return to what Jesus said about the number-one principle of living. He said, 'Love the Lord your God with all your passion and prayer and intelligence' (Matthew 22:37, *The Message*). It was a practical strategy for living life 'to the max'; the secret of his astonishing energy, life and effectiveness as a leader. Loving God passionately as he did, his ultimate focus was on his Father. That released him from the constant strain of drawing from people. It energised him, releasing him to live with enthusiasm. And the second principle of living, he went on, is to love others as you love yourself (v. 39).

Basically, love God and people with everything you've got. Do that and it releases God's love to flow through you in a way that is astounding. You'll actually discover what the world is hungry for – the love that never dies.

THE COSMIC ROMANCE

So the first part of our strategy, if we are to learn from Jesus, is to love God passionately. Pursue a relationship with him, chase after him, enjoy his company, listen to his voice, luxuriate in his presence. Romance like this energises me for every other part of life. Focusing on God is healthy. If I succeed, it greatly reduces the risk that I will 'believe my own publicity'. Spotlighting the greatness of God and his achievements, I can never grow complacent. Dwelling on my own achievements, I am bound to grow stale. Concentrating on my failures is depressing.

So a vital key to life and energy is learning to forget what is behind. God is ahead of us. We look to him – Jesus' face is always before us. We are running towards encounter with him. Human psychology works best that way – looking ahead. If I am to fulfil the purpose for which I was made, to become somebody of true significance, I have to be formed more by what I see in the future than by what is in my past. David died still holding on to the dream of a temple in Jerusalem, built to the design God had given him. Jesus' principal message was, 'Turn around; change your life. The kingdom of heaven is near enough to touch.' The clear implication was that, as long as you're looking backwards, you're never going to get it. No matter how good or bad it is, we cannot change the past. We have to turn from it to God's purposes for the future. Listen to these famous words of Jesus: 'Seek first his kingdom and his righteousness, and all these things will be given to you as well' (Matthew 6:33 NIV).

THE ETERNAL REALM

The kingdom of heaven is not some mystical or celestial version of Washington, Westminster or even Brussels. It is the dream God has for us, individually and collectively. The kingdom of God in your life is like the dawn of a new day. It is the possibility of a life fulfilling its potential, at last achieving its destiny – a person made in the image of God, so like him in nature that they reflect *his* creativity, brightness, warmth and passion. Of course, it's vital to learn from the past. As the poet Steve Turner wrote in *History Lesson*:

> History repeats itself,
> has to,
> Nobody listens.
>
> History Lesson

But if we focus obsessively on the past, we will be imprisoned by it. The only way to be changed is to allow our Destiny to become more significant in our lives than our History. Then we will indeed truly become people of *significance*.

And here's the extraordinary thing: the stuff we long for, the essentials of life – financial security, food, shelter, clothing – all these things will be given once we learn to put God first. Simple, isn't it? That's all we have to do. Just one tiny problem: I am aware of a horrible tendency within myself to look for the payback whenever I set out to 'put God first'. So, of course, I am not really putting God first. I am putting me first. In spite of that, because I want to be like Jesus, I refuse to give up on the quest. I encourage you to make a similar refusal. There is not much else we can do. If we want to become people of true significance, we have to press on, push into relationship with God. That ultimately is the only way we will be truly transformed.

But if that really is the key, we have a problem! Surrounded as we are by all the evidence of our own ingenuity, it is easy to live as if there is no God. Yet our technological comfort blankets prove uncomfortably thin and ineffective when the cold winds of life blow upon our circumstances. At the end of the day, if we were made for relationship with God then nothing else will satisfy us. So, it's simple. Put God first, seek his purposes – follow hard after those two aims. If that sounds rather counter-cultural, we should not be surprised. After all, what would you expect from the God of all creation? An encouragement to buy into the 'because I'm worth it' culture?

THE GLORIOUS IMAGE

Only a fool dismisses even the possibility of a creator without proper consideration. All thinking people owe it to themselves to ask the big questions. Is there a God? What is the meaning of my existence if there is – and if there is not? How will I live in the light of my answer? If you have read this far, I am going to presume you are willing to admit God's existence as a real possibility. Once that is admitted we have to allow for the additional possibility of some kind of personal intervention. If that happens we must expect the un-expected. God coming as a human – incarnation – is at the very heart of the Christian faith. It is the wonderful, wild assertion that the creator of the entire universe became a human being, not just incarnated in all of us in some general way; but actually became a single specific human being in a specific historical time and location. If God is going to intervene to offer us real relationship, he *must* come as one of us. But if he does that, he won't come in the messed-up state we demonstrate so ably. He will first show us what he, as creator, had in mind for us as humans. If the 'image of God' is his design-purpose, we have to expect that his perfect take on the image will be really glorious. Second, he will deal with the brokenness of our world in the way that I tried to describe in the last chapter. If it is remotely possible that this is true, then it is ridiculous to suppose that the man who was God in flesh, having died, would stay dead. After all, all life flows from this person. Taken into this mighty river of life, like a dam bursting, death itself would be overwhelmed and ejected and the one who had died would rise again.

Why not? If God, the magnificent creator of all things, becomes a human being, this is a singularity, a one-off event. Logically we could not expect him to do otherwise than rise again. So he did. That is what the historic Christian faith asserts. And if that has happened then Jesus is able to deal with every circumstance and situation facing us. He is able to set us free from anything that would hold us back, and so release us into our significance. The resurrection becomes not just a wild assertion by Christian fanatics, but the completely logical outcome of the creator stepping into creation and becoming part of it. The author has joined the cast and become the lynchpin of the whole production. Not only does this make sober, cold, common sense with regard to the logic, it's the only thing that makes sense of history.

Nothing is more certain than this fact: the disciples, after the crucifixion, were reduced to a bunch of hopeless losers. Their hopes and dreams had gone. On a personal level, they had been revealed to be cowards, men who had broken their oaths of loyalty to the leader they professed to love, running away and leaving him to face the venomous accusations of the authorities alone. Yet six weeks later the most prominent failure of all, Peter, was standing on a balcony, assuring thousands that the leader he had denied had risen from the dead and held the key to all of life. Something happened to change that group from frightened losers into world-changers. Historically, the only explanation is the one they themselves gave, the single central fact that formed the basis of the message they took to the world: Jesus truly had risen from the dead.

Jerusalem, Friday 3 – Sunday 5 April AD 33

Only one of the men among Jesus' followers stayed by his side even at the cross – the one who had finally truly realised Jesus' love for him and faith in him only at the Last Supper. Young John took Mary, the mother of Jesus, back to his house, and returned to the cross. The other disciples there were all women. After all the macho posturing of the twelve, especially Simon Peter – 'These may let you down but I never will', the one man who had stayed true to his word was the youngest of them all. It was Passover night. The streets were buzzing with activity. Because of the immense number of pilgrims, ovens for roasting lambs were set up in the streets. The atmosphere was like one huge street party. The contrast between that and the way the disciples felt could not have been greater. Shame-faced, they slipped past the crowds and one by one made their way back to the upper room where, only twenty-four hours before, they had met with Jesus to celebrate Passover in advance. Now their hero was dead and they had been revealed as turncoats and oath-breakers. The atmosphere in the upper room was heavy with suspicion, fear and blame. Every knock on the door brought fresh fear. They were cowering behind shutters and locked doors, waiting for the authorities to come and arrest them too.

Their shame grew as the women drifted back and told of the end of their leader's life, and the courage of Nicodemus and Joseph of Arimathea, who up to now had followed Jesus in secret. They were members of the Jewish high council, which was also the supreme court. They had feared exposure. But somehow the death of Jesus had released them from fear. They went to Pilate and asked for the body to be released. They were both rich. Joseph owned a new tomb, in the old quarry just below the crucifixion site. Once Pilate gave permission, it was the work of minutes for their servants to get the body down to the burial chamber. There was no time for the usual washing of the body. It was wrapped in a long cloth. Dried spices were stacked around it and the entire thing bound with wide bandages from head to toe. The head had a bandanna wrapped around the jaw and skull to keep them together as the body deteriorated. As dusk fell they placed it in the tomb and rolled a huge stone disc in front of the entrance. The stone weighed about two tons.

The women made their way through streets filled with festivities. It was almost unbearable. Through that night and the following day, as they hid in that room, the usual human tensions and reproaches must have revealed themselves; men seeking someone to blame, women wiser, honestly grieving. I have often pondered it. The tensions must have been very strong. Otherwise, why did not one man volunteer to go back to the tomb with the women? It was five o'clock in the morning, the first day of the week. They wanted to complete the anointing of the body, and possibly the washing that was not done when he was hurriedly buried. Maybe the women were just glad to get away from the men. Perhaps that's why they never even asked the question, 'Who will move the stone?' until they were almost at the tomb.

In the meantime, they did not know that a further obstacle had been erected. The chief priests, hearing that Jesus had not been thrown into a communal grave, as was normal with a crucifixion victim, but had been buried in a proper tomb, were concerned. They asked Pilate for permission to place a military guard at the tomb, to prevent the disciples from raiding it and then proclaiming that Jesus had risen. After all, he had prophesied that he would do that. Strange that the priests took Jesus' words more seriously than his own disciples did. Pilate had given permission for a quaternion of soldiers to be on duty outside the tomb, sixteen soldiers rotating guard duty, at least four of them on duty at any time. He had also authorised the tomb to be secured with the seal of Imperial Rome placed across the entrance.

In spite of these precautions, when the women arrived at the tomb the guards had vanished and the stone had already been moved. When they looked inside, the body had gone. While they were looking, two messengers apparently clothed in lightning suddenly appeared in front of them: 'Why are you looking for the living in the place of the dead? He is not here. He has risen. Remember all that he told you while he was with you in Galilee. He had to be crucified and rise again on the third day.'

Now I understand that sceptics are going to say, 'Come on! Do they expect us to believe in angels? This is the twenty-first century!' My only reply is, 'Why not?' Just because the life forms we are familiar with have been carbon-based, does it mean there is no such thing as a light-based life form? After all, every atomic particle and every wave form in the universe is simply a function of energy in a state of change. String theory, quantum mechanics, dark matter: in the words of Hamlet, 'There are more things in heaven and earth, Horatio, than are dreamt of in your philosophy.' Einstein has assured us that there almost certainly are other dimensions. If there are, messengers from those dimensions would not necessarily be subject to the same laws of physics that we are. But that's enough speculation!

As they hurried from the tomb, the women were afraid, joyful, then astonished. Jesus stood in front of them. 'Good morning,' he said. They fell to their knees with shock, then grasped his ankles. Jesus said, 'You don't have to hold on to me like that. There is no reason for fear. Go and tell my brothers to go to Galilee and I will see them there.' When they got back to the upper room, the women were greeted, I am ashamed to say, with fairly typical male prejudice. The Bible makes it clear the men believed the women were simply telling 'the kind of stories women tell'.

Simon Peter and John rushed down the stairs from the upper room and ran through the streets to the tomb. John was younger and fitter than Simon and arrived first. When Simon arrived, John was standing there, bent over, peering into the tomb, but had not gone in. Simon Peter shoved him aside and went right in. To his amazement, all the cloths that had been wrapped around the body were lying on the stone platform where the body had been placed. They lay flat, in position – but empty. There was nothing inside them. The headband from around the head was neatly folded, almost as if waiting for the next user. Then they accepted that the tomb was empty.

But they were ordinary blokes. They did not believe Jesus had risen from the dead. People of the first century were far more familiar with death than we are. The dead were laid out in their homes. They saw people dying at execution sites and the dead were carried through the streets, close enough to touch as they were carried to burial sites. They knew that dead men don't rise. They were far more certain of it than any of us in the developed world of the twenty-first century would be.

They made their way back to the upper room, leaving Mary

Magdalene weeping at the tomb. Jesus had rescued her; now she had nowhere to go. So she stayed at the place where his body had last been. Behind her she heard a footstep in the gravel. Blinded by tears, she turned and saw a figure standing there. She thought he was the caretaker.

'Lady,' he said, 'Why are you crying? Who are you looking for?'

Still thinking he was the caretaker, she blurted out her request. 'Sir, if you have carried him away, tell me where you have put him and I will come and take care of the body.' She might not have been able to see very clearly but nothing was blocking her ears. When she heard the voice she knew so well simply say, 'Mary,' she almost screamed in delight, a single word in Aramaic: 'My teacher!'

As she held him tight, Jesus said, 'You can't keep me, I'm afraid; I've got rather a lot to do today. Go and tell my disciples you have seen me.'

So she ran back. Her story was received with sceptical but tolerant smiles by the disciples. It was too much for two of them. Cleopas, and maybe his son, Symeon, decided they were going back to their home village. All this talk from hysterical women about angels and people rising from the dead was just too much and probably seemed disrespectful to the dead. So they set off on the walk home; not far, about seven miles.

They were joined by a total stranger. 'You look miserable,' he said. 'What's the matter with you?'

They stopped, looked at him. 'What do you mean? What's the matter with *you*? Don't you know what's been going on the last few days?'

'Do tell me,' he said.

'Jesus of Nazareth, a prophet. We thought he was the Messiah. But the Jewish authorities conspired with the Romans and killed him. It's only three days since it happened and now women are having visions of angels and saying he's risen from the dead. We can't even mourn him properly.'

'You are foolish,' he said. 'You're slow-hearted, fearing to believe in case of disappointment. Understand. The Christ had to suffer, die – and rise again from the dead.' Then he gave them a lightning tour through their scriptures, which Christians call the Old Testament.

As they listened, the gloom lifted and depression was replaced by excitement. Maybe they began to think, 'Jesus should have met this man. He would have liked him. He talks like him.' They got to their home. He waved goodbye. They said, 'No, don't go. Come in and eat supper with us.' When they put supper on the table, they asked him, 'Take the bread and bless it for us.'

He uttered the ancient prayer, 'God of Israel, thank you for grain, the gift of your creation, bread the work of men's hands, we break this in your holy name.' He held the bread in front of them. Maybe as he held it up his sleeves fell back and they could see the marks of nails. An astounding revelation hit them – the women were right! As they looked him full in the face and recognised him, he vanished. All they could see was the bread he had broken, resting on the table, and the indentation in the cushion on the floor where he had been sitting. They jumped up, ran all the way back to Jerusalem and into the upper room, and burst in, crying, 'It's all true! Jesus is risen from the dead.'

The other disciples looked at them and said, 'We know. He has appeared to Simon Peter.'

While they were talking to each other, with the door still locked because they were afraid of the authorities, suddenly Jesus was standing there. 'Peace be with you,' he said.

Their mouths opened and shut like goldfish. No words came out. Maybe somebody squeezed out, 'Pardon?'

He said it again. 'Peace be with you.'

Somebody whispered to a friend, 'It's a ghost!'

He clapped his hands together. 'Pretty solid kind of ghost if I am. Not many ghosts have flesh and bones, as you see I have. Touch me and see.' How many rushed forward? Take a guess. Nobody moved. They still could not believe it – they were afraid to feel that happy. They were afraid of the joy it would bring, because maybe it would be mistaken and then their devastation would be all the greater. I think he was enjoying it. He grinned at them. 'Got anything to eat?'

'Um, er – fried fish?'

'I love fried fish, you know I do. Give me a piece.'

Somebody found the courage to give him the fish. He ate it and another huge revelation hit them. Ghosts do not eat fried fish. Suddenly they were all around him, clapping him on the back. 'We thought you were dead.'

'I was dead.'

'Yes, but *really* dead.'

'I was *really* dead and now I'm *really* alive. Didn't I tell you about this?'

'Yes, but we thought you were just preaching, not telling the truth!'

'From now on,' he said, 'you will know the truth, because the same Spirit that raised me from the dead will come to live in you. You will be able to go and tell this Good News to the whole world. But you must wait until you have received the same power that raised me from the dead. This is not a message of words only, but an encounter with the power that comes from God.' He looked at them, still standing there, open-mouthed and amazed. Suddenly, unexpectedly, he took in a big breath, then blew at them all: 'Receive the breath that comes from God, breath of life, of courage, faith and holiness. Wait until you've received it.'

A few minutes later, while they were still chattering excitedly to each other, he vanished. But he had left behind him a group of men and women no longer defeated, blaming themselves and each other. Instead, they were understanding for the very first time that God really does know what he's doing, and Jesus had just unveiled himself clearly as the pathway to eternal life. They could not have been more excited.

Part 4

Living His Dream – Passing on the Baton

Nobody lives for ever. A wise person is not simply committed to smart goals for themselves, but builds a legacy to be taken forward by others. Passing the baton to the next generation is God's dream and our destiny. It is the last and greatest reward in this life.

Chapter 10

Prepare for Your Departure

PRIDE GOES BEFORE A FALL

Jerusalem, 995 BC

David was bored. At first the idea of staying in Jerusalem and allowing Joab to lead the army in its latest war against the Ammonites had seemed a good idea. After all, why should he go to battle just because it was the time of the year when the kings went to war? And things were going well without him. They had utterly defeated the Ammonite army and were now besieging their capital, Rabbah. Sieges were tedious. Staying behind in Jerusalem to enjoy the fruits of ten years as king of the undivided nation of Israel seemed like the best idea he'd had all year. Write some new songs, concentrate on his harp-playing. What he had not expected was that he would be this bored. Walking restlessly from room to room, he wandered out onto the balcony that looked out over the whole city of Jerusalem. Just beneath him he could see the point at which he and a small group of prized warriors had emerged from the aqueduct to surprise the Jebusites and take Zion, the 'impregnable' fortress of Jerusalem; what a victory that had been.

His eyes wandered carelessly across the city: so many new buildings, new houses; honey-coloured stone glowing golden in the sun. Here in this immediate quarter were the houses of his generals and principal lieutenants. His eyes drifted aimlessly across the flat rooftops. Forty-five years old, a man in the prime of his life, at the pinnacle of success, and bored.

Bathsheba was bored. Had she had children, all that followed might have been different, but she was bored. She was the rich wife of a successful and powerful man: a hero and a warrior to his fingertips; a leader of Israel, even though he was a foreigner, and her husband. But life as a 'trophy wife' was not what she expected. Marriage to Uriah had seemed so exciting. But under his glamorous exterior, the shining armour, the gold braid and the swaying cloak, Uriah was not exactly the most exciting man in the world. He was military through and through. She had seen him on parade before the army marched off to war and it was then he seemed most alive. With her he was loving and attentive, but when he received the message from Joab the commanding general to call him to battle, something lit up in his eyes. Besides, he had been away so long. She pouted. She had tried her coquettish best to get him to stay in Jerusalem for the summer but not even the knowledge that David was remaining in the capital would persuade Uriah to stay.

She stepped from the bath on the rooftop into the towel held out by her maid. She felt the heat of the summer sun on her skin. Years later, many years, she realised she had known David could be watching, though that was not something she admitted to herself on this day.

When the summons came she could hardly believe it, but the messenger stood there in all the trappings of the royal household: 'His Majesty would be honoured if the wife of Uriah would join him for a meal.' She gave the polite response, informed her household where she was going – and walked out on Uriah, effectively for ever.

When the polite requirements and greetings of society had been satisfied and they were alone at last in the king's apartment, it did not take long for the bored, rich, pampered housewife to fall into the arms of the king. Ruthless, forceful, charming, David could have seduced her and thought nothing more of it, but what he saw in her eyes at that moment captivated his soul as no other woman ever had or ever would. Their lovemaking was more glorious than either of them had dreamed it could be. When at last he sent Bathsheba back to Uriah's house, both knew there would be another time, but they had no knowledge of the price they or the nation would pay.

In making the conquest of Uriah's wife, David had been conquered by his own drives, and would pay a terrible personal price. When the message came, 'I am pregnant', he knew he must act, and fast. The child conceived in her husband's absence could not be explained. He sent a message urgently requesting Joab to send Uriah 'to report on the war'. Joab was no fool. He had his network of spies. It didn't take him long to find out what was going on. In the meantime, Uriah reported to the king and answered his questions about the war, the men and how senior command saw things. And he wondered why it was him David wanted to see. Then David said, 'Go to your house and wash your feet.' It was a socially acceptable way of saying, 'Have sex with your wife.' Were Uriah's latent suspicions aroused? The next day David asked why he had not gone home. 'The ark of God and the whole army are at war. Should I eat and drink and sleep with my wife?' That night David made him drunk. But drunks are paranoid. He stayed at the palace again. Next morning, David gave Uriah a sealed message for Joab. It ordered him to abandon Uriah, one of his oldest and most loyal friends, on the battlefield. Uriah died before the walls of Rabbah.

Political cover-up is as old as the hills. The corruption that entered the life of the nation would be a constant stream of poison in the body politic. David's authority was weakened because Joab knew. Even worse, sexual immorality, rape and murder would flow through his family down the generations.

After a suitable period of mourning he married Bathsheba and, when her time came, she bore him a son. All seemed well. But God knew and was not pleased. So, Nathan, the prophet, told David a story of a rich and powerful landowner with many flocks and herds. But when a visitor came to stay, he took and killed the only lamb of a dirt-poor shepherd to feed his friend. David was enraged.

'The man who did this deserves to die! To act in such a way, without pity.'

Nathan looked up at the king, looked him in the eyes, waited, then: 'You are that man.' The moment he spoke, David knew. He saw the faces of the others in the room and he realised that everyone knew. They knew. His elaborate deceptions fell down around him. It was the saddest moment of his life. He burned with shame on his throne. Nathan told the story from God's perspective. The raw pain in his voice told David what he had done to the One who had done so much for him.

'Because you did it this way, your son will die.' David had a glimpse then of the future – others would pay, and go on paying.

At that moment, it would have been easy for David, in his power as king, to call any such talk treasonous, to command Nathan to be silent or face death. He could have claimed he alone would be his own moral judge. But, unlike many of us in the twenty-first century, David was not that stupid. He had sown the seeds of potential disaster. But he now demonstrated that he would aim to live beyond his natural capacity. His response to Nathan was immediate: 'I have sinned against the Lord.' He got it. In grabbing at Bathsheba and murdering Uriah, the person he had sinned against most was not either of them, but God. The God who had already provided for him the beautiful wife of a man whose death had come about naturally, without any help from David, could do it again. But David had refused to trust God's provision. He saw immediately, understood how much he had wounded God's heart. His prayer of repentance is one of the most beautiful pieces of poetry ever written, and a most powerful spiritual testament. Through the years that followed, his poetry demonstrates how he relied on God's power, grace and life. He didn't always get it right. But because he was getting hold of God's grace and power, he lived beyond his capacity. He screwed up, but he faced up and he finished well.

Over a thousand years later, the great apostle Paul summarised his life like this: 'After David had served his generation according to the will of God, he died and was buried.' It's not a bad epitaph. And it demonstrates that God is able to take our messed-up lives and make them shine. David could have given up when he failed. But he didn't, and that is part of his glory.

If we're to unpack this story for our own advantage, we have to understand that God had chosen to take David, with his complex mixture of insecurities, hurts, abilities and talents, using him for his purpose, making David the defender and expander of the nation of Israel. Success and affluence bred complacency and loss of direction. He was a king and was called to lead the nation in war – which is where he should have been that day. When he stepped out of his God-appointed role, the need for conquest was still within him. Deprived of its true purpose the drive to conquer found an illegitimate target, releasing consequences that would haunt David for ever. The creator is the best judge of how our talents and abilities should be used. When they are not used according to his purposes, they will continue to function, but being out of control they will create havoc in our lives and in the lives of those nearest to us.

It is worth remembering we are most at risk when success lifts us high; we begin to believe we're above the rules, not under them. We adopt a 'special-case' mentality. David did that. The rules did not apply to him. How many of us have thought the same? 'I have special needs. God understands. The rules for ordinary people don't apply to me.'

It's a seductive line, one we would all like to believe. Sadly, it is not true.

LEGACY

One way or another, one day you will be leaving! No matter how important you may be within your family, your circle of friends, your company, or even your nation, nothing you can do will stop the onward march of time. Each moment takes us nearer the point in human history when we will no longer be part of life here. Since there is nothing we can do to stop the process, it would be wise to give at least some thought to preparing for the event when it occurs.

It hit me with special power the day my father died. He broke his hip in a fall. After a long stay in hospital, he finally accepted he should go into a retirement home. We found him a really nice place. It was a bit of a relief not to have to care for the garden and the house, though he missed his independence. But he settled in and did what the wartime generation always did – he made the best of it. He still missed my mother, who had died ten years before. But he lived each day by faith. As I looked at him at his ninetieth birthday party, surrounded by his family, I felt he was glad to have reached this milestone. And I had a sense he was saying goodbye, giving himself permission to depart. About five months later, I was getting ready to visit him when I received a phone call saying he had died. They had got him ready for breakfast and sat him in the chair in his room with his Bible next to him. They promised to come back to escort him down to breakfast. When they returned he was still sitting there, but dead. Later on that day I did go, quite literally just to see him. I stood looking down at the physical frame of this tall, thin, wise man. I looked at the face smoothed of lines of concern, briefly touched his pale, cool skin. I had seen dead bodies before but not been given the chance to truly observe one. It was strange. He was my dad, but he wasn't. The life that made him 'Dad' had departed. I stood in that room and spoke over him the first part of the 'Proficiscere' from Elgar's *The Dream of Gerontius*:

> Go forth upon thy journey, Christian soul
> Go forth from this world
> Go in the name of God, the omnipotent Father who
> created thee!
> Go in the name of Jesus Christ our Lord,
> Son of the living God who bled for thee
> Go in the name of the Holy Spirit who has been poured
> out on thee!

Standing there, I blessed him, and thanked God for giving me someone who had modelled for me courage, endurance and, above all, faithfulness. My dad kept his commitments. He did not break promises, and he did not compromise his Christian faith. In my early childhood, during the Second World War, his secret work on cameras for the Royal Air Force meant I hardly ever saw him. I found him difficult to get on with. Perhaps I was not a very easy child! But as I grew older, I grew to admire him and love him, and I still miss his presence. That's legacy, something left behind that the next generation will treasure.

LIVE BEYOND YOUR CAPACITY

One thing we can be sure of, on the day David sent for Bathsheba he was not even thinking about what he might leave behind at the end of his life. Was he untrained in such matters, incapable of recognising the problems he would be creating by snatching this glorious moment of passion? I am not sure we can offer him that excuse. He had been mentored by one of the spiritual giants of his age – Samuel, the great prophet of Israel, whose function was to speak God's message to the nation and to function as a judge. He travelled a regular circuit round Judea and was well aware of the variety of human sinfulness. The truth is, if David, on that day, had remembered the lessons Samuel taught him, they would have seemed boring irrelevancies. The moment David saw her, he knew she was forbidden fruit, and had already made up his mind to possess her. When he found out she was the wife of Uriah, one of his oldest friends, it made no difference to him.

But if one of us were able to meet him and say, 'David, do you know what you're doing? Because of what you're contemplating right now, your baby son will die. Your favourite son will rise in rebellion against you, drive you out of your own palace, then publicly sleep with your wives. The king that replaces you, captivated by beautiful women from all over the world, will lose his way morally and spiritually. The murder of this woman's husband will unleash a spirit of violence and revenge that will scar the House of David through centuries. And the relationship God intended to give you will be soiled by the memory of adultery and murder. Do you still want to go ahead?' I think David would have sent a message to Bathsheba saying, 'The King greatly regrets he is unable to entertain Bathsheba at this time and wishes her and her husband blessings for the future!'

It did not happen. Because it's not the way God works. He wants us to trust him. Yet, driven by boredom and his hormones, David rode roughshod over what he knew God had said. 'Do not commit adultery. Do not even covet your neighbour's wife.' He lived for the moment, and pretended to himself there would be no consequences. He ignored 'the law of legacy'. Yet it remains true that you reap what you sow. If at that moment he could have sown honour and integrity, Solomon, who would succeed him as king, would have had a very different spiritual inheritance.

IT'S NEVER TOO LATE

One thing David's story tells us is that even after the most massive moral collapse and failure, it is still possible to finish in the winner's circle. When you're surrounded by the wreckage of relationships smashed by your own stupidity, a reputation that seems destroyed beyond redemption, it is worth remembering this – the reality that comes at a moment like this is a magnificent opportunity for us to access God's two great gifts:

First, his *mercy* – the practical application of his forgiveness. Mercy means he speaks absolution over us, completely free of charge. There is nothing we can give him, nothing we can do for him that will atone for our stupidity. But he forgives. It is what Jesus paid for in his lonely march into the heart of darkness at the cross. So the punishment we deserve we do not receive – that is mercy.

Second, God's great gift of *grace* – God giving us what we do not deserve. The Jewish Bible assures us again and again that God is good. It means God is unreasonably, crazily, madly, wildly good to those who do not deserve it. It is the very nature of his goodness that he gives to us stuff we cannot earn. Lives wrecked by our own irresponsibility, when handed over to him, can be rebuilt and made better than they were before.

However, to do us any good, these great gifts must be received by an act of faith from the nail-scarred hands of the one who paid for them. It's not complicated. A simple 'thank you' will do it.

The 1970s' cult TV classic *Six Million Dollar Man* had the opening line: 'We have the technology. We can rebuild him.' Well, God has something better – spiritual power that can rebuild us from the inside out. He puts a new power in us. It releases us to become what he dreamed of us being from the beginning. At the heart of this book is the conviction that God has dreams for us. Think of what it could mean to live God's dream. I have taken the funerals of too many people who lived utterly alone and isolated. They rowed with everybody and were too proud to apologise or seek reconciliation. Bit by bit their circle of acquaintances eroded until there was nobody left. In the end it really doesn't matter who was right or who should have apologised first. Reconciliation is a two-way street and someone has to walk down it, if we're not all to die in our lonely, solitary foxholes without a soul to care whether we ever existed.

NEVER SAY NEVER AGAIN

One of the marvellous things the Bible says is: through what Jesus did on the cross, God has become reconciled to every single member of the human race. If reconciliation is a two-way street, he has already walked down that street, offering the hand of friendship. All it takes is courage on our part to reach out and clasp his hand, aware of the marks of the nails showing the cost of that reconciliation. If God is willing to do that, surely we have to be willing to do the same thing for others. For the sake of our sanity, can we decide never to say 'never' when it comes to forgiveness or an apology?

Saying sorry is worth it. Even if others are clearly in the wrong, one thing you can be sure of is that, from their perspective, you are most definitely in the wrong! Someone has to be first, and it's the work of those who have encountered Jesus to say, 'I'm going to be like him, I'm going to offer the hand of friendship.' Some may say, 'But relationships hurt.' Yes they do. But relationships nourish us too. They provide the essential nutrients for our souls. That is why Jesus said the number-one principle of living was loving God with everything we've got and loving people the same way we love ourselves. So we should never say 'never' about apologising, or forgiveness.

I shudder when people say, 'I'll never forgive them for what they've done.' Maybe what's been done is horrendous and in a sense unforgivable. Yet forgiveness is an act of power and authority in which the offended person takes hold of the situation and refuses to be governed by what has been done. They refuse to be a victim. 'I will no longer be bound by what you did. Your actions will no longer control me. I am taking authority over what happened in the past. I declare that I forgive and I claim my freedom by doing it.' Unforgiveness chains me to the one who offended me with handcuffs stronger than carbon steel. When we forgive, we are taking away the power of the offender. If they say they are sorry, then we are completely free. If they refuse to say they're sorry, we are still completely free of them.

My friend Pastor Mike Murphy from Shirelive, Sydney says, 'Unforgiveness is like drinking poison and waiting for the other bloke to die.' We will gain nothing if we refuse to forgive, except fill our lives with a bitterness that may be poisonous to our health or even fatal. It can certainly increase the risk of a number of chronic diseases. No matter what the offence, it really is never too late. We can embark on a new way and start to live in a new day.

THE POISONED CHALICE

Bitterness is a horrendous emotion. It draws us in like a drug. It is even worse for us than heroin or cocaine. Once bitterness gets truly rooted in the human soul, it taints everything, destroys all happiness and robs us of the ability to see that anybody else truly matters. It becomes the focus of our life and spreads like an infection to everybody within the family or friendship circle. The Bible describes it as a poisonous root, digging down deep inside us, sending its tendrils into more and more of our spirit, soul and mind. For our soul's health we can and must let go of it. If we will allow God into the situation, if we will forgive, it can be drawn out of us. Almost invariably, our unforgiveness means that at some level we are blaming God. So we have to come to the point at which we forgive him for not seeing it our way. That's the real problem: we are like spoilt children stamping our feet in a supermarket, demanding our own way, screaming at Mum or Dad, 'You don't love me! I hate you!' The heavenly Father is wise. He just keeps on saying, 'But I love you.' If we listen, we can actually hear that still, quiet voice.

I once walked into the lounge of our house to discover my daughter, who was then two and a half, with a carving knife which she was inserting, for some unknown reason, into the electric fire. Fortunately, the electric fire was not switched on. I have no idea how she got the carving knife. Presumably she had seen it on the surface in the kitchen and being an agile and intelligent girl had climbed up to get it because she wanted it. I said, 'That's not a good idea, Becky. Please give it to me.'

She said, 'NO!'

I said, 'Becky, give it to me NOW!'

She said, 'No, I won't; it's mine!'

I said, 'It's not yours, it's Mummy's; please give it to me.'

That exchange continued just a little while longer. Then I took the knife, at which point she stood up to her full 2 foot 3 inch height and said, 'I hate you!'

I replied, 'I love you.'

'I hate you! I hate you! I hate you!'

'I love you, I love you, I love you.'

'I hate you! I hate you! I hate you! I hate you!'

So I said, 'I love you, I love you, I love you, love you, love you.'

At which point she said, 'You make me so angry! I'm leaving home!' She walked out of the door and slammed it behind her. It was disappointing. It caught on the thick carpet. So she opened it again and pulled it after her, hurling all her weight in order to make sure that it shut with a satisfactory bang.

Then she shouted through the keyhole, 'That was for you!' I heard her determined footsteps stomping down the hallway of our home. About half an hour later, the door edged open. I was standing looking at the TV. She edged up to me and said, 'I didn't mean it.'

I said, 'Yes you did.'

'No I didn't,' she said.

'Well, you did at the time, didn't you?'

And she said, 'Yes.'

I said, 'Well, are you sorry, then?'

'Yes.'

I said, 'Well, I love you.'

And she said, 'I love you too.' That was the day I began to understand that God is a dad, and if I, as dad, could cope with my beloved daughter's tantrums, he could more than cope with mine.

Bitterness and unforgiveness are a poisoned chalice which we definitely do not have to drink from. It is never too late to let go of all that stuff and begin to live in joy. The route to that is the simplest one: accept the mercy of God, be a forgiven person, give that forgiveness to others. Accept his goodness; extend that goodness to others. Do the radical thing. Go to the person you are most angry with and do something good for them. It will utterly transform the way you see them. It will begin to release within you a fountain of joy.

SUCCESSION

Ask yourself, 'How do I want to be remembered? And how do I want people to think of me right now?' If I want them to be glad I am alive, then I have to give them reasons. If, after I am gone, I want them to be grateful they knew me, then I have to leave behind something valuable, a memory of relationship that will be treasured long after I have departed. A crucial part of preparing for the end of my life has to be a determination that when I leave there will be no loose ends, no unfinished business, and nothing I've held on to that I should have given away.

How do *I* want to be remembered? As the kind of person who gives value to others, helping people who feel worthless understand they are in fact of immense intrinsic worth. I do not want to be remembered as somebody who acts like a total prat and treats others like it too. So I have to learn that listening matters more than talking. People don't need me to tell them what they need to know half as much as they need me to listen to them. Few people in this world genuinely know how to listen. It is a skill that needs to be learned. Most of us listen only in order to get our point across to others.

True listening starts only when we set out intentionally to *hear* the other person. Then they begin to feel they truly matter. Listening is something we do with our whole bodies. We listen with our eyes, because sometimes the clue to what something means is expressed more in a physical response than in words. It means we have to actively look at somebody in order to *see* them. The continual parade of images in the media encourages us to see people superficially. So we don't see them. We register their presence and pigeonhole them. We see a type and make assumptions based on appearances. Yet the only way even to begin to know somebody is to look beneath the surface.

To do that, I try to let my mind go still. Life is complicated and lived at such a pace that it feels like I'm in the centre of a whirlwind, with the debris of my life flying all around me. To actually *see* somebody clearly, I have to let all that fall to the ground, let my mind be still and quiet in the presence of God. He is never in a panic. Then I begin to see stuff I never saw before. In giving someone my full attention, I am simply giving them what they are worth as somebody made in the image of God. Everyone I meet can show me something special about the creator. That makes every encounter exciting. If I could treat everyone like that they would be truly glad they knew me and grateful to have had me in their lives. I *want* to be remembered like that. I think I've still got a long way to go.

NO KIDDING

Since the end of the Second World War, our culture has been increasingly dominated by the imagery of youth. It is one of our primary values. We long to be young, or at least to be seen as 'young for our age'. Alongside that we seem to have grown increasingly incapable of facing the reality of death. Perhaps we just don't want to admit its personal application to ourselves. Why not? Fear.

I am walking out of my territory into the reality of the heavenly realm. If I have not yet taken the hand of reconciliation offered by the Lord of this realm then I am entering as an intruder. But if I have accepted his offer of relationship, I enter as a friend. And if God truly is love then everything he does and all he creates is done in love for human beings. So I have to believe that death is still a Good. Though the process may be frightening to me, it is not evil, but a positive Good. If I make the journey with Jesus, it is a transition from the physical life of this world into another life, as infinitely superior to my existence here as my life walking on planet Earth has been superior to my time in the womb of my mother. This life does not make those nine months in the womb meaningless. It takes the promise of the womb and makes it real. So life here comes to a conclusion, which is actually a transition into a new level of existence containing the greatest adventure of all.

So not only is there no point in kidding myself that I'm not going to die, I'm actually robbing myself of seeing it as part of the adventure. I'm taking away the sense of anticipation with which I should approach every part of life – including its end. It is clear that that was one of the greatest gifts Jesus left us. It was his legacy. So here it is – I'm going to die, and it's not the worst thing that could happen. No kidding!

A THING OF WONDER

Most of us are only too aware of our faults and failings. Too easily we allow them to become limitations. But there is no need for it to be like that. The truly exciting message of Jesus is that my faults and failings do not have to define me. This was his good news:

Repent – turn around. Don't follow your own ideas. They have already got you into enough trouble. After all, insanity has been defined as doing the same thing that you've always done, and expecting different results. So turn around.

For the kingdom of heaven is at hand – the kingdom of God is not just tasks or roles. It's about who we become. As I've said before, it's about living the dream, God's dream, because his dreams are biggest and best. So it is possible in spite of everything for us to live the kind of life that will make our family, friends and colleagues amazed.

The first name given to the Messiah in the prophecy of Isaiah is *Wonderful*. Those who follow him should be like that – full of wonder, always amazed and creating wonder in others.

If we live with enthusiasm, maybe enthusiasm will rub off onto others. If we take God's grace and become gracious to others, perhaps they may become more generous. What about laughter? There is not enough laughter in the world. Not just the laughter produced by a comedian. I love to listen to *The Goon Show* when driving or to watch a Jackie Mason DVD, because I love comedians who make me laugh at myself and at the foibles of the human race. But the laughter I am thinking of comes from a person full of joy, the overflowing of a happy heart simply because life is good. And laughter *is* contagious. Funnily enough, the people who are best at laughter are often those most intimately acquainted with tragedy. The pains they have passed through set them free from the emotional paralysis that grips so many.

What about anticipation? Too many people believe the best is behind them. But if God is calling me into his glorious destiny, I cannot be leaning back into the past. I have to lean forward, into the future. Who knows what may be around the corner? If I can pass that on to people around me, maybe they will take what I've given, run with it and exceed my limits and their own. That is a dream worth having. If, at the moment of my death, Jesus will be waiting for me with arms open wide and the most brilliant smile on his face, then the best is yet to be. And why not?

Someone who believed it was one of the finest preachers of the nineteenth century, Henry Grattan Guinness. This is the story of his departure:

21 June 1910
Howard was alone with his father-in-law when he died. He said
that Henry had suddenly sat bolt upright in bed. With a
rapturous expression on his face, he raised his arms to heaven.
He kept them raised for some time. Given the fact that he had
been too weak to lift them at all the previous day, this was
little short of a miracle. Then he let them fall, lay back on the
pillow and was gone.

(Taken from *The Genius of Guinness* by Michele Guinness)

BOARDING PASSES, PLEASE

We simply settle for the idea that we have to pass through the
doorway of death at some point and this is not the worst thing
that could happen to us. It is an entrance into a relationship richer,
wilder and more wonderful than anything we've ever experienced.
Suppose every time we've ever fallen in love was only a preparation for encountering God face to face, for falling into Love! If
that is the case, as I believe it is, then the only thing to do is
embrace it with a simple aim; to die well, like Henry.

Preparing for my departure means, first, that I will leave no unfinished business – no one who has offended me unforgiven, no
apology I should have given unissued. I will die free of conflict.
Next, I will die free of stupid pride. No 'I did it my way' bravado
for me. I have done many stupid things in my life, but I am not
going to be that stupid. I have no intention of entering eternity
with a flag of independence fluttering over my head. God is God.
I am not, and that settles it. He is Love. So the flag of my heart
will be lowered to the ground before him. Last, I am going with
bold anticipation, believing eternity is a vast continent of infinite
possibilities and adventures.

There I will be released at last to discover all the potential of
the unique 'once-only' person, first dreamed up in the heart of
God and released into the womb when the seed from my father
met the egg from my mother and possibilities undreamt of by

anyone but God were unleashed. Finally, all those talents can be fulfilled, not in an end-of-story way but in the way that C.S. Lewis intimated with the last words of *The Last Battle*, the seventh of the Chronicles of Narnia: 'All their life in this world and all their adventures in Narnia had only been the cover and title page: now at last they were beginning Chapter One of The Great Story which no one on earth has read: which goes on forever: in which every Chapter is better than the one before.'

The story of Jesus at his resurrection and in his subsequent interaction with his disciples is filled with joy and excitement, but also with farcical moments that highlight the authenticity of these events as things that happened to real, down-to-earth, ordinary people at a specific moment in human history.

BREAKFAST AT GALILEE

Lake Galilee, Tuesday 9 April AD 33

For the disciples, the day of the resurrection was the best day of their lives – but not the funniest. Thomas was not with them when Jesus came. He turned up later and found people buzzing with excitement. He felt left out. He got really angry. He shouted, 'All right! I'll believe in your precious resurrection. I'll believe it when I can take this finger and push it into the scar on his hands and take this hand and shove it into the wound in his side. When I can do that, then I will believe.' Life in the upper room was rather uncomfortable after that. The disciples quietly confident, Thomas determined not to give in to what probably felt to him like hysteria.

A week later, they were gathered again in the upper room. Suddenly Jesus came, just like the first time. One second he wasn't there and the next moment he was.

'Peace be with you,' he said. The disciples greeted him but Thomas slid down into his seat, hoping Jesus wouldn't notice him. Who could blame him? But you never can get away with that sort of thing with Jesus.

'Hello, Thomas.'

Thomas looked up, tried to put a good face on it. 'Hello, Lord.'

'I heard what you said.' Everyone chuckled, able to see Thomas thinking, 'Oh no.' Jesus said, 'Give me your hand.' He took Thomas' hand in his right hand and with his left pulled his robe away from the scar in his chest. 'Which do you want first, Thomas? Put your hand in this wound here, or your finger in these scars in my wrists?'

Thomas understood how wrong he had got it. But he was a thinker, and immediately understood something the others had yet to realise. He knew what this meant. He went down on his knees, looked up and said, 'You are my Lord and my God.'

Jesus' face lit up the whole room like a proud father smiling at his son's bar mitzvah: 'Well done, Thomas, you've seen me and have believed. You're a happy man. I promise there will be multitudes who will never see me and yet believe, and will be just as happy as you are right now.' The look on Thomas' face when he saw Jesus coming towards him must have made the disciples laugh for weeks afterwards.

His appearances did not run to a timetable. He came and then he went. He told them to continue to wait. I would have wanted Jesus to tell everybody. I would have wanted to go and bang on Pilate's door and say, 'I've got somebody here I'd like to introduce you to,' or perhaps to the High Priest and say, 'There's a man here I'd like you to meet.' But Jesus hadn't come to play those kinds of games. He kept saying, 'The day will come when all will see me. But before that day you must be filled with power from on high.' He kept talking about this power from God, the promise of the Father. But they had no way of understanding. They were young and impatient. They wanted to tell the world, and Jesus wouldn't let them. It was frustrating.

Home began to feel very appealing. James, John, Nathaniel, Thomas Didymus and a couple of others went with Peter back to Galilee. Jesus seemed able to find them anywhere, so it didn't matter where they were. They were waiting for the power Jesus had promised, but the waiting was getting to them.

Simon said, 'I've had enough of sitting around. I'm going fishing.'

So they all got into the boat and went out. It felt good to do something. Simon Peter was a good fisherman. It was rare for him to work all night and catch nothing. But that night he caught nothing. Then, through the early morning mist, he saw a man standing on the shore next to a fire. He shouted, 'Hello lads, caught anything yet?'

Simon shouted back, 'Not a thing!'

The man said, 'You're casting the net on the wrong side of the boat; cast on the right side of the boat and you'll find plenty.' To an experienced fisherman that must have sounded a bit of a cheek. But maybe he could see something they couldn't. They threw the net and when they drew it in all of them together could not pull the net into the boat, there were so many fish.

Simon was a fisherman. All he could see was a net full of fish as he happily pronounced, 'We'll get a good price for this catch.' But John wasn't thinking about fish. He stood up, holding onto the mast, looking at the shore. 'You know who that is, don't you?'

Simon Peter, irritated, said, 'I don't care who it is; just look at all this fish he's helped us find.'

John looked at him pityingly. Sometimes Peter really could be rather thick. 'It's the Master.'

Simon slapped his head. 'Of course it's the Master! How could I not know that? How stupid can I be?' He grabbed his fisherman's jerkin and wrapped it around him. (They fished naked. It saved their clothes from getting wet.) He plunged over the side and swam to shore. When he arrived, there was Jesus grinning at him. The others brought the boat in, dragging the catch behind them.

Jesus said, 'You might want to bring some of that fish I sent you.'

'Yes, Lord, of course!' and he helped to pull the net in. Old habits die hard; he had to count − 153 big fish and the net not broken.

Jesus looked at them. 'Come and have breakfast.' He already had some fish cooking on his fire. Now they had plenty more.

They all ate till they were satisfied; then he said, 'Simon, walk with me.' It was a pretty miserable fisherman who walked along the lakeshore with Jesus, thinking, 'He's going to tell me I can't be part of this any more. Everybody knows I blew it. Now I can't help to lead what he started.'

But Jesus never mentioned that night in the courtyard; he just asked him, 'Simon, do you love me more than all these?'

In the old days Simon would have answered with overweening confidence, 'Lord, I love you more than anybody.' Now all he said was, 'Lord, you know I am your friend.'

Jesus said, 'Take care of the little ones and the young ones.' He looked at him again and said, 'Simon, son of Jonah, do you love me?'

Again Simon replied, 'Yes, Lord, you know I'm your friend.'

He said, 'Look after the older ones too.' Then he asked again, 'Simon, son of Jonah, are you really my friend?'

That third question was like a knife through Simon's heart. There were tears in his eyes. 'Lord, you know everything about me. You know I really am your friend.'

Jesus looked him in the eyes as he said, 'All right, then, take care of the older ones.' They stopped walking and Jesus said, 'I have a message especially for you. When you were younger you dressed yourself, strode about and did whatever you wanted. There will come a day, when you're old, when you will stretch out your hands.' As he said that he stretched out his own hands so the sleeves fell back from his wrists and Simon could see the marks of the nails. 'Someone else will clothe you with a garment you don't want to wear and will take you where you do not want to go.'

It was a moment of sober reality. Simon knew he was saying he would die as Jesus had died. But somehow Jesus' having already been there would help him endure it, and die in the way he had died. Maybe Simon looked forward and saw it happening. Then he was back in the present with Jesus looking him straight in the eye, saying, 'You follow me.' Everything was in that command. 'All you require, all the resources you need, all the strength, faith, hope, joy and grace you require will be yours if you just follow me.' Simon knew what that meant. When a rabbi said, 'Follow me,' he meant, 'Live as I do. Follow my instructions to the letter. Walk so close you're breathing the same air.' The burden of what happened in the courtyard left him at that moment. Three times he had denied. Three times Jesus asked, 'Do you love me?' and each time he was able to say, 'I am your friend.' Each time he had been recommissioned with the task.

So – Simon was back! Of course, being Simon, he promptly stepped from drama to farce. Looking behind, he saw John, the young disciple, following them, so he blurted out the first thought that came into his head: 'Lord, what about him? You've told me how I'm going to die. What about him?'

Jesus shook his head and with a little half-smile said, 'Mind your own business. If I want him to live until the day I return in glory, what has that got to do with you? You follow me.' It was best that Simon didn't say anything after that. They walked back to the charcoal fire in companionable silence. That day must have been marked by lots of laughter. But when Jesus finally left them, they were still waiting for what he had promised.

Chapter 11

Affirm, Equip and Release Others

NEVER UNDERESTIMATE THE OLD MAN

Jerusalem, 971 BC

Adonijah checked his reflection in the polished bronze mirror, the finest that money could buy. He slightly adjusted the gold circlet resting on his head. It designated him a son of the House of David, a prince and, he thought, the next king. In the adjoining room, Joab and Abiathar were waiting. He could hardly believe Joab had managed to get Abiathar on board. It was over forty-five years since Abiathar had joined his father, David, as a fugitive in the wilderness. Since that time he had been his loyal friend and priest. He adjusted his robe, looked again in the mirror. He was the best-looking man in Israel, at least since Absalom had died. He looked every part the king.

In the adjoining room Joab whispered, 'You understand, this is not disloyalty. We must safeguard the legacy of the king. If we don't make arrangements now, there will be chaos when he dies. If we make it clear now that we are backing Adonijah, the other sons will fall into line.'

Abiathar looked at him. 'What about Solomon?'

'Solomon? He's too clever by half. If he becomes king, that will be a disaster. Adonijah is one of us. He is bright enough for the job but not clever enough to be a problem – agreed?'

'Yes, I see all that,' said Abiathar, 'but what about the King?'

'The King? I think he's forgotten who he is. Besotted with that serving maid they got to keep him warm at night.' He sneered. 'I hear she's still a virgin. Listen, the King is finished. I'll square it with him; no problem.'

In the room next door Adonijah was also thinking about the young virgin whom they had searched Israel to find, the most beautiful girl in the kingdom. Now she really did get the juices flowing. Nothing had convinced him more clearly that the time was right than the fact that his father had been unable to make Abishag his own. If he could no longer raise an interest in someone so beautiful then clearly he was as good as dead. What a queen she would make! And once he produced an heir through her all Israel would know he truly had succeeded his father. After all, most people knew already. Everywhere he went these days fifty men ran ahead of him with horses and chariots. It was time to go.

When he joined the others, he enquired, 'Everything ready at En Rogel?'

'Of course, sire,' said Joab, flattering the young king-to-be with the use of a title not yet quite his. He smiled to himself as he saw how the young popinjay preened himself. He might be in his mid-thirties but he was still a lad. When they arrived at the spring of En Rogel, all his brothers and the royal officials from Judah were there. But, he noticed with relief, not Nathan the prophet, Benaiah or any members of his father's bodyguard. There would be no objections or interruptions. The sacrifices and the ceremony of king-making went well. And the banquet that followed was magnificent. But no course was as sweet as the words 'Long live King Adonijah!' shouted by all present.

Nathan the prophet moved around the palace, aware that it was unusually quiet. Where were the king's sons and all the senior army commanders? For months, the palace had been a hotbed of conspiracy. It did not take long to find out what had happened already at En Rogel. Nathan was under no illusion about his likely fate if this coup succeeded. It was many years since he had stood before the King and accused him of his adultery with Bathsheba. Their first son had died, as the Lord had said. But their next son, Solomon, had become everything an heir to the throne should be. Nathan loved him as if he were his own son. He recognised that David had, as men so often do, reached out and grasped something God would in time have given him anyway.

Because of it, the relationship with Bathsheba had been overshadowed by the darkness of its beginning. Solomon was clearly God's plan. He knew he must move fast.

He found Bathsheba in her room, still beautiful, her eyes full of intelligence. He asked, 'Have you heard? Adonijah has proclaimed himself king.' She understood immediately, he saw. She and Adonijah's mother had never got on. 'If you want to save your life, go and see King David now; tell him what's happening. I will come and confirm it.' When Bathsheba arrived, the young woman Abishag was tending to the King's needs. Bathsheba bowed low. How frail David looked in his bed.

'What is it you want?' he said, his voice quavering, uncertain.

'My Lord,' she said, 'did you not promise me before God that Solomon, my son, would be king after you? But Adonijah has become king and you don't know it. He has sacrificed cattle and has the support of Joab and Abiathar the priest. I'm afraid that when you die, my son and I will be treated like criminals.'

While she was speaking there was a discreet knock at the door. 'Who is it?' asked the King, more alert now.

The servant entered. 'My Lord, it's Nathan the prophet.'

'Send him in,' said David, waving his hand at Bathsheba. She left. Nathan would need David's undivided attention.

Nathan bowed low, then asked, 'Have you heard, my Lord the King, that Adonijah has been declared king and after you he will sit upon your throne? Today he has made enormous numbers of sacrifices, inviting the King's sons, Joab, the commander of the army and Abiathar the priest. Right now, they are acclaiming, "Long live King Adonijah!" However, they did not invite me, Zadok the priest, Benaiah or his brother Solomon. Is this a decision you have made without informing us?'

The transformation in David was astounding. From a quavering old man, he was restored before Nathan's eyes to the man of decision he had always been. He sat up straight in his bed and demanded that Bathsheba come back in. 'Listen to me – as surely as God lives, this day I will carry out what I swore to you both before God. Solomon, our son, shall be king after me and he will sit on my throne.' Bathsheba bowed low. David said, 'Call in Zadok the priest, Nathan the prophet and Benaiah, son of Jehoiada.'

When they came he snapped out orders: 'Take all the senior staff from the palace, my own bodyguards, put Solomon my son on my own ceremonial mule and take him down to the royal spring at Gihon. Zadok, Nathan. You anoint him king over Israel. Then let the trumpets be blown and shout, "Long live King Solomon!"'

Benaiah, commander of David's personal bodyguard and second-in-command to Joab, recognised the truth immediately. 'This is the right thing,' he said. 'May God make it clear by prospering Solomon and making his throne even greater than that of my Lord the King.'

When the people of Jerusalem saw David's personal bodyguard escorting the young Prince Solomon, Zadok and Nathan down through the streets to the spring at Gihon, they knew something was happening. They brought musical instruments. It became a rolling party. Hundreds were there by the time they arrived at the spring. When the trumpet blew, the sound of their shouting was enormous. It echoed down the valley to En Rogel. Joab, alert to the slightest change in atmosphere, asked, 'What is the meaning of all the noise in the city?' At that moment Abiathar's son arrived to give them the news: Solomon had been crowned king at the royal spring of Gihon and escorted by David's own bodyguard up to the palace and into the throne room. David's bed had been carried in there, his eyes sparkling with a mixture of pride and mischief as Solomon took his throne and the palace resounded with cheers: 'Long live King Solomon!'

Adonijah looked around him in disbelief. Panic-stricken, his guests were leaving. Surely Joab and Abiathar would do something? But they had already left. Adonijah knew exactly what he would have done to Solomon had his coup succeeded, and he expected the same. So he claimed sanctuary. He ran to the altar of God, the place of sacrifice and forgiveness, and clung to the horns by which sacrifices were fastened to the altar. When they told Solomon he said, 'If he is worthy and loyal, he will not suffer the loss of a single hair on his head. Bring him to me.' Adonijah bowed before King Solomon. Solomon knew that at this moment it was important he should act in a way that would demonstrate the assurance of someone who had nothing to prove, and who wished to make peace with his enemies. As Adonijah trembled before him he thought how easy it would be to order his death. 'Brother,' he said, 'go peacefully to your home and stay there.'

As David watched, tears filled his old eyes. 'I praise you, my Lord and my God, that you let me live long enough to see the right person sitting on my throne.' Then, 'Take me back to my room. The kingdom is in good hands.'

INVESTMENT

David's most obvious and public failure was his affair with Bathsheba and the murder of Uriah. But there was a consistent fault line that ran all the way through his later life, and that was the fathering of his children. He seems to have been helpless before them. They were indulged but never disciplined, loved but never questioned about their activities, nor held to account in any way. Maybe he was compensating for his own experience as a child, feeling unloved and harshly used. If that was the mechanism driving him, then clearly he overcompensated. By the end of his life, though, he recognised that Solomon needed more than emotional overindulgence. He needed guidance and advice. He needed investment.

He had always understood this in the area of his life where he excelled – as a leader of men. David knew other men needed investment, and he was good at it. By the time he died, the priests, who were a vital component of the life of Israel, had been turned from a disorganised and demoralised group, often disaffected and disunited, into a coherent body with a vision for the nation. The army had been transformed from an undisciplined, ragtag bunch of freedom fighters into a high-morale, tightly organised fighting force that was man for man by far the most effective military force in the Middle East.

In each of those areas, David brought forward individuals who were great leaders, men of talent, vision, heroism and ability whose aptitudes he had schooled till they reached their highest possible level. The same had happened in government and the economy. The shepherd boy from Bethlehem demonstrated a genius for organisation not always evident in a front-line warrior. Yet, when it came to his family, he seemed unable to apply those principles to his own children.

This is not unusual. In some ways I find this the most difficult section of the book to write. I am aware of how little I seem to have truly invested in my own children. It was my privilege to know a man called David Pickford. He was an outstanding businessman who built up a large property empire without, it seems, ever making a real enemy. He was described at his funeral as 'gentlemanly, gracious, generous, godly and of good humour'. But the most powerful testimony to the quality of his life came from his children. They talked about a man who called each of them on the phone every day. Whether he was in the country or not, he was always in contact, investing in them, giving them time, telling them how much he loved them and believed in them. I have to admit, when I compare my rather sad efforts at fathering to those of my friend, I feel wholly inadequate. But he inspires me. I am not dead yet and my children are still just that – my children. There is nothing to stop me from encouraging them to find out who they are and what God has in mind for each of them.

David's investment in Solomon came late. But it was not too late. He encouraged him to understand that the God of his father was utterly committed to him but was looking for Solomon to respond to him with his mind, his will and his heart. He encouraged him to be strong, especially when he felt afraid, to be courageous, and not to allow himself to be discouraged. He put before him the enormous task of building the temple according to the blueprint that God had already given to David. He was investing in Solomon and attempting to give him the solid foundation he needed for his role as king. Better late than never! But I am sure that, at this moment in his life, David looked back and wished he had spent much more time encouraging his sons and daughters to fulfil the purposes for which God had made them, and, in the words of this book, to *'live like they meant it'*.

If there is one thing that marks Jesus out, it is his astonishing capacity for investment in others. He gave so much to people, especially to those who would have been regarded by many rabbis as quite simply not good enough to be disciples. Jesus deliberately called the 'unsuitable' to be his disciples; those who were not sufficiently talented, gifted or clever even to be considered as disciples by other rabbis. He invited them to walk with him, to live so close to him that the dust kicked up by his own sandals would rest on their robes and they would breathe the same air that he did. That was why it was so powerful when he blew on them in the upper room after the resurrection.

CELEBRATION

One of the traits in David that most endeared him to his men and made them so intensely loyal was his celebration of them. Forty years after men had joined him at Ziklag, he was still writing the history and celebrating their triumphs, naming them as architects of his own victory. I have already mentioned the amazing elegy that he wrote for Saul and Jonathan. Although Saul, whom he had loved like a father, set himself up as David's enemy, nonetheless David paid him full and generous tribute when he died. There is a big heart here, and it creates a culture of celebration. We begin to recognise in each other those very qualities that have already been picked out and celebrated by the wise father, leader or company director. It builds a champions culture in which nobody is a loser because we are all part of a winning team.

That is something families need to build. Sometimes it is completely unconscious. I remember sitting down at dinner with our family around us, thinking God had been so good to us, then saying to my new son-in-law, 'When you joined this family, you joined a family blessed by God.' His response was immediate: 'You're telling me!' he said. 'Since I joined you my life has changed totally.' We're not perfect as a family, but we do try to celebrate the good things. We know mean-minded people tear others down. But big people build others up. Jesus was good at this. At one point he said to the disciples, 'Little flock, do not be afraid.' He knew how they saw themselves – a small group of people, not apparently very dangerous or effective. What he said next was big enough to blow them away: 'It gives your heavenly Father great happiness to give you the kingdom of heaven.' When you consider who he was talking to, what an incredibly varied group they were, and how not one of them had been chosen to be a disciple by any other rabbi, this was an astounding statement. It expanded their understanding of who they were and of the possibilities inherent in their lives.

Earlier on we saw how Jesus humbled himself by washing the feet of the disciples. He was their leader, yet he was serving them. He was emphasising to them the high privilege of the power and authority he had already passed to them by calling them to help with his mission.

IDENTITY

One of the most powerful moments in modern film is the point in the Coliseum at Rome when the *Gladiator* declares his identity:

> My name is Maximus Decimus Meridius;
> Commander of the Armies of the North;
> General of the Felix Legions;
> loyal servant to the true emperor, Marcus Aurelius;
> father to a murdered son;
> husband to a murdered wife;
> and I will have my vengeance, in this life or in the next.

It resonates with us because so many of us are unsure of who we are, don't understand our history and have not grasped any destiny or purpose. We long to have the kind of clarity Maximus possesses.

David knew who he was. Others joined him and found themselves. He loved generously. He had a huge capacity for friendship. His friendship homed in on the able and the gifted: those he instinctively understood would become part of his team, and help to build the kingdom of Israel. But it would not have been recognised that way by anybody else. He saw potential. That is exactly what marks the ministry of Jesus. He saw potential in the disciples when no one else would see it. He made Simon Peter first among his disciples. That had nothing to do with his leadership abilities at the time, but everything to do with potential. James was a brilliant administrator, the kind of person who becomes Director of Operations. Without such a person, no leader can hope to be effective. But John, his younger brother, was sensitive, insecure, intense, poetic. Who would have picked him? Jesus did – because he saw potential. As he picked these men and all the others who were in the group, he gave them an identity they did not have before. He even changed names. We have seen that Simon the Reed became Peter the Rock. It was a prophetic change: the one who was like a piece of grass blowing in the wind of his emotions and his circumstances became a rock and part of the foundation of the New Testament Church.

Someone asked the other day, 'What is your attitude when you enter a room? Is it "Here I am", or "There you are"?' I have a feeling that when Jesus entered a room it was the second that applied. From his story, he was so secure in who he was, so at home in his own skin, that he loved to help others discover who they were. The only people he would not be able to help would be those so fixed in a false identity that Jesus' invitation to truth felt like the biggest possible threat. It's fear that keeps us hiding behind those shadow identities.

Some of us live like the wizard in *The Wizard of Oz*, hiding behind a huge booming façade. And behind it is a frightened little person, hoping nobody will ever find out our secret. But Jesus comes to unveil who we really are, so that we can be free at last. And no one will rejoice in that freedom more than God himself, since he is the one who has invested a seed of his own life in us so that a new creation can be born. That was the good news the apostle Paul celebrated when he wrote these words: 'If anyone is in Christ, he is a new creation; the old has gone, the new has come!' (2 Corinthians 5:17, NIV). It's no wonder he got so excited about it and wrote, 'The whole creation is on tip-toe to see the wonderful sight of the sons of God coming into their own' (Romans 8:19, J.B. Phillips).

GENEROSITY

Real generosity is fairly rare. We're all familiar with the kind of giving that is actually all about drawing attention to the giver. It's not really giving at all. It's just paying for attention. God's generosity is of an entirely different nature. He gives to those who love him and those who hate him. He gives whether we say thank you or not. He is good to all whether they deserve it or not. That can be very irritating. There are people to whom God is very good and we find it extremely annoying, because we know they don't deserve it! In such moments we easily forget that, from the perspective of others, we probably do not deserve his goodness either. But if we can let go of our mean streak, and start to be glad when other people get helped or do well, perhaps we will begin to grow larger in soul.

Somebody once said to me:

> It takes a big person to *Affirm* someone else, especially before others.
> It takes a bigger person to pass on skills that will *Equip* someone else.
> It takes a great person to *Release* the one trained to go and excel – to exceed my own limits.

That is what we are called to do. We are called to act generously, like the God who made us. The truth is, most of us don't mind being fairly generous, especially if those to whom we have given something freely acknowledge we have been good to them, and if they are suitably grateful. But what if somebody has taken the affirmation, the equipping and the release we have given, used it, claimed it as their own, trampled on it and betrayed the one who gave it to them in the first place? The temptation is to say, 'I won't do that again.' Why not? Will you let one bad apple spoil the whole harvest? Besides, it is better to help people than not to. It makes us feel better. In affirming somebody else I am actually giving something away that eventually will come back to me. If I'm passing on skills to equip somebody it may be that, in years to come, I will see them do what I do – but doing it so much better. I can only feel satisfaction: 'Well, he got that little bit from me.' Once we have trained them, what else can we do but let someone go? It's far better if we actually have the guts to release them gladly.

Of course there can be moments of meanness in our spirits, when we may resent someone we trained who is now doing so much better than we are. We can nurture that resentment until it spoils the relationship and robs us of our joy in the achievements of the person we trained. If there is a betrayal then we must forgive them. We cannot allow the wounds caused by betrayal to dominate us. We have a choice: we can refuse to give it a home, let go of it, forgive, *then move on*! It is far better to engage in thankfulness. It's far more fun, as well, to thank God that he used you to train somebody who is now doing something bigger and better than you could ever have achieved on your own. In 1980, a friend called Roger Simpson introduced me to a 20-year-old Greek Cypriot who proved to be a brilliantly talented communicator. He worked full-time as my assistant for two years, then on and off for another three. He was a passionate learner, naturally creative in sharing his faith. J.John has far outstripped my own achievements. Sharing his adventure has been one of the most rewarding experiences of my life, and definitely fun!

Passing on our expertise freely, gladly and gratefully is more than worth it. We may think what we did was original to us, but actually it was his in the first place. So we might as well enjoy receiving his gift, then giving it away, because that way it is more truly ours than it ever was. There are enough miserable people in the world – don't let's add to their number.

DEVELOPMENT

So let's take that a bit further. Developing and helping others is great, because people are the greatest resource in this world. As the great poet John Donne wrote, 'No man is an island entire of itself; every man is a piece of the continent, a part of the main . . . any man's death diminishes me because I am involved in mankind.' Similarly any man's life enhances me. So when I help others I simply cannot lose. When people do something wrong, it is so easy to blame them. Pastor Steve Kelly of Wave Church, Virginia Beach says, 'Don't blame them – train them.' It is so easy to grumble. Yet I could take the same energy and use it to try to make a difference. In the family, the community, the workplace and the local church there is a great need for people who will take up the task of leadership. Not for people who will 'big themselves up', but for those who will aim at the growth of others. The great thing is, those who commit themselves to develop others are, in the process, transformed themselves. It may not be what they aim at, but it is what God is aiming at. So it's worth making it a part of our life strategy to help others reach their goals. The effort we put in, the investment we make, will not be lost. At some point, what we have done to help others will come back to reflect on us.

Developing and helping others extends our influence far beyond what we can accomplish alone. For instance, if you're a skilled athlete, it is worth taking time to develop younger athletes. If you're not that skilled an athlete but you have the capacity to coach, then what better thing could you do than see others fulfil the dream of becoming a champion and know you had a part in it? Tom Landry was one of the greatest coaches in the history of the National Football League. He was a legendary coach of the Dallas Cowboys in their greatest years. He said, 'My job as a coach is to make men to do what they don't want to do in order to enable them to become what they dream of being.' He knew he was never going to get the glorious touchdown that would win the Superbowl. But he knew he could contribute to it. And he was willing to give everything he had in order to enable others to achieve. If he had been small-minded and selfish, he would never have achieved the pre-eminence he did. His funeral thanksgiving was attended by players and managers from all over the NFL and the AFL (American Football League). He was remembered as a gentleman, a tough but fair manager, and above all an investor in others. He was also someone who said his life did not make sense until he started reading the Bible. It gave him a foundation of peace and the essential focus for his life. It made everything make sense. And why not? He was drawing on the wisdom of Jesus himself.

As he drew near the end of his earthly ministry, Jesus devoted much of his time to teaching his disciples, sometimes in large groups. At other times he concentrated on the apostles, just twelve, in whom he invested himself completely. He followed a classic pattern: first, he did it in front of them. Then he did it with them helping. Then he let them do it with him; and finally he sent them off to do it without him. He did that so they would understand that what they were able to do was derived from contact with him. This was a deliberate strategy. He wanted them to know that when he departed they needed somebody else. No matter how hard they tried, they could not do it alone. He was preparing them to realise their need of the Holy Spirit. It is a lesson the Church keeps forgetting, which is why it is not exciting, fervent and pulsating with life like Jesus but so often deadly dull, predictable and boring. Maybe one day we will learn the lesson!

TRIUMPH

In a letter to his son in 1935, American banker and diplomat Dwight Morrow (1873–1931) wrote, 'The world is divided into people who do things and people who get the credit. Try, if you can, to belong to the first class. There is far less competition.' Ronald Reagan was quoting Morrow when he said to the American people, 'You can achieve an enormous amount in this world if you don't mind who gets the credit.' Rejoicing in the victory of others is a real art. Not many of us seem keen to be good at it. Yet it adds enormously to the pleasure of living.

As Jesus neared the moment when he would say goodbye to the disciples, he reminded them that things that once applied to him now applied to them. Early in his time with them he had turned water into wine, healed a dead child at a distance and released a man from thirty-eight years of paralysis. Then he said, 'To your amazement, the Father will show the Son even greater things than these.' As he approached the time of leaving, he said what he had shown them at the beginning was what they would be doing in the future. 'Anyone who has faith in me will do what I have been doing. He will do even greater things than these because I am going to the Father.' He was expecting the disciples to exceed even what he could do. Though he was God, he was localised in one human body, to demonstrate to them what God can do with a human being fully yielded to his purposes and filled with his power. So Jesus was confidently expecting that these men who had been with him, listened to him, loved him, failed him and returned to him, would now multiply his ministry many times over. And eventually there would be millions across the world doing the same. That was his expectation. It is the vision for which he came, died and rose again. It is still the vision he has for ordinary screwed-up people like you and me. So, every time something brilliant happens in the Church worldwide, I rejoice – even if I happen to disagree with some of the things those people believe.

C.S. Lewis reportedly said, 'The problem with God is, he insists on using people I do not much like and methods of which I do not approve.' As in most things, he was right. I can't help being glad he is right, because I don't always like myself, or approve of the way in which I've operated. But the amazing thing is, God has used me to touch people with the reality of his presence. I don't understand it. It usually happens when I feel most unfitted for the task. But then what should I expect? As Paul wrote, 'When I am weak, then I am strong.' I guess it is at such moments that my burgeoning self-confidence, being defeated for a moment, lies down, gets out of the way – and God is able to pour his power through this often-foolish servant. To be honest, that is what makes it such fun. It is why laughter and tears are so near to us at all times. Triumph is what we do, not because we are great, but because he is. In our weakness he gets to win, then we win, because he gives us all the credit. It is completely crazy – but then God is the most wonderfully wild and crazily generous person I know.

WEIRDLY LOGICAL OR LOGICALLY WEIRD?

I suppose we have already been to some pretty strange territory. The idea of a man's physical body actually being raised from the dead and walking out of a tomb is already weird enough. And yet, things now get truly weird. There is a special problem with this, but not simply because it's weird. The weirdness is not being reported by John, the mystic, the writer of the book of Revelation, from whom we might well expect 'weird and wonderful'. Nor is it coming from Matthew, steeped in the legends of his Jewish past and seeking at every stage to demonstrate Jesus fulfilling the prophecies of old. No! This report comes from the most dispassionate writer of the Gospels, Luke, who wrote to a friend called Theophilus, 'loving friend of God', promising he would give him a carefully researched account of everything handed down about Jesus, by those who were eye-witnesses. He was almost certainly Gentile, most likely Greek. He was certainly well trained in a Greek understanding of logic and the rational Western European approach to history and historical truth. Against this background we have to put his repeated and, as he said, carefully researched assertion that Jesus, having completed his time with the disciples, ascended from the earth, was received by a cloud, vanished and never returned again.

This story became part of one of the earliest-ever worship songs of the Church, in circulation by AD 66. Having acknowledged that to secular twenty-first-century ears this story is weird, I have to declare that, for me, it seems entirely logical, and not just because I love a bit of sci-fi! If God really did set aside everything in being God that is incompatible with being human, in order to enter our world in human flesh, it's the sort of thing we could expect. Given the premise that he died and rose from the dead, he is not going to die again. Neither is he going to decay. The Bible says his post-resurrection body was made of glory – quite literally 'the weight of God'. Certainly it was an extremely unusual body. It was definitely physical. He was able to eat; he was able to touch others. Yet without the benefit of a 'transporter room' (much loved by followers of *Star Trek*) he could move effortlessly from a locked room without the door being opened. He was able to walk out of a cave without the stone that sealed it being moved. All this was carefully researched by interviewing eye-witnesses. So if we adopt the premise, there is really only one thing that makes sense. Jesus must take this body with which the disciples have now become familiar and remove it publicly from planet Earth by taking it out of this universe into another dimension entirely. It's not illogical, just highly unusual.

Jerusalem, May AD 33

It was not illogical to the disciples. For Simon Peter, in particular, it made perfect sense. From early on he had never doubted. Once he said, 'You're the Christ; you're the Son of the living God,' he had never doubted Jesus' identity. For him, it was obvious. Jesus was the Son of God. His divinity was not something Simon found difficult to believe. It was his humanity that needed explaining. How could the Son of God be an ordinary bloke as well – and yet *not* ordinary? Clearly there was a power within him, an authority that rested on him, unlike the kings that occasionally passed through Jerusalem, or the high priests in their processions around the temple precincts. Simon never doubted Jesus, though he often doubted himself.

At some point after his appearance at the lakeside in Galilee, Jesus called the disciples back to Jerusalem. He told them to wait there and not leave until they had received the power God was going to send them. Through almost six weeks, he appeared repeatedly to them, speaking about the kingdom of God. On one occasion, while he was eating with them, he commanded, 'Do not leave Jerusalem. But wait for the gift which my Father has promised to give you. You've heard me speak about it. The truth is, John the Baptist baptised with water and people were soaked in it. But in a few days you will be utterly soaked, baptised in the Holy Spirit.'

This made very little sense to them. Once again they were being asked to believe in something they could not see and wait for something they'd never experienced, when everything in them wanted something to happen. So the next time they met him a group decided they must ask the question. 'Lord,' they said. 'We are all waiting. Are you going to restore to Israel the kingdom God promised?' It was the big question, beating inside them. They were waiting. As far as they were concerned, it was the logical next step. Jesus was the Messiah, the Son of God, and he had defeated death itself. He could not be beaten. Therefore the logical thing was to lead the nation of Israel into its rightful position as head over all the nations of the world. Caesar himself would have to come and bow the knee to Jesus. The Roman Empire would be subservient to the land of Israel. They could see great new roles for themselves in this new kingdom. Jesus looked at them, perhaps with a twinkle in his eyes: 'I can't tell you the answer to your question because it's not for you to know. The Father has set the dates for those kinds of events by his own authority. You do not need to know about it. But what you will get is the Holy Spirit and when the Holy Spirit comes on you, you will receive power to live as my witnesses, here in Jerusalem, throughout this country and Samaria. It will take you to the very ends of the earth.' Then he said, 'Let's go for a walk.'

He led them out of Jerusalem, across the Kidron Valley for the last time and up the road that leads to Bethany. When they reached the top of the hill, he turned again to them, lifting his hands in the sign of blessing – as the high priest would do. He spoke over them the familiar words of the blessing Aaron had been given by Moses:

> God bless you and keep you,
> God smile on you and gift you,
> God look you full in the face and make you prosper.

The strangest thing is that while he was speaking his feet left the top of the hill on which they were standing. He began to go upwards, and they knew this was different from the other appearances. He was actually departing before their eyes, not just vanishing to reappear later. He was going. They stood there watching long after he had vanished. His last command had been, 'Stay in the city until you have received the power from on high.' But they stayed there, reluctant to leave. Even after he vanished into a cloud and was hidden from them, they stayed gazing intently into the sky. The strange thing is, that definitely has the ring of authenticity. It's exactly what we would all do, just wait, to see whether he might come back again, and what would happen next.

Then suddenly there they were, two men apparently clothed in lightning, standing beside them asking the question that always puzzles angels, 'Why do human beings so rarely obey the last instruction given to them?' They said, 'You Galileans! Why do you just stand here looking up at an empty sky? This very Jesus who was taken up from among you to heaven will come as certainly – and mysteriously – as he left.'

So they went back to Jerusalem to the upper room to do what they found most difficult – to wait. Though perhaps somehow those next few days weren't quite as bad as they thought they would be. There were about 120 of them. They spent a lot of time praying and praising, and it was then that Jewish men discovered women could pray just as well as men. That was something Jesus had done. He had set them free – men and women. While they were waiting, they held a lottery. There were two candidates to replace Judas, who had killed himself. They couldn't work out which of them was more suitable, so they asked God to guide them while they drew straws. They chose a man called Matthias. It was the last time they ever had to go for that kind of guidance. They were still waiting for what Jesus had promised.

Chapter 12

Fulfil Your God-Ordained Destiny

THE ONCE AND FUTURE KING

Jerusalem, 980–959 BC

About twelve years before Adonijah's attempted coup, David had finally acknowledged he was too old to fight in Israel's wars. It left him restless – bored. That was when the idea came – to count all the fighting men in Israel's army. Joab opposed him, but David was determined. It proved calamitous.

After the count, the prophet Gad came. He told the king how much he had offended God by putting his trust in numbers of men and not in the Lord, who had watched over him through so many years. He gave him three equally disastrous alternatives. David chose the shortest and most severe option – a plague. For three days it raged. All Israel cowered under the threat of death. Seventy thousand died. David was devastated. He knew it was his stupid pride, his sin, that had brought this disaster upon the nation. Clothed in sackcloth, he led the elders of Israel out of the palace to stand before God in repentance. Then they saw a gigantic figure standing between heaven and earth, to the north of Jerusalem, with a drawn sword extended over the city. They fell face down and David pleaded with God, 'This is all my fault, Lord. I ordered the numbering of the fighting men. These people are my flock. I should protect them. But they are being judged because of my sin. Let your judgement fall on my family, but not on them. Have mercy; remove the plague.'

Then Gad gave David God's instructions: 'Go to the land on which the angel is standing. Sacrifice there to the Lord and he will forgive you.' It was Araunah's threshing floor. He offered David the site, the oxen for the sacrifice, and his farming equipment as fuel for the fire. But David refused to make a burnt offering without paying for it, in full. The plague stopped. At that moment, David was certain this was to be the site of the altar of burnt offering for the whole of Israel – the place where the new temple would be built.

Now he began extensive preparations for the building of the temple. He knew Solomon was God's choice to replace him. A few years later, David sent for his young son, realising what an enormous task he was bequeathing to him. He took him to the window, looking north over what had been Araunah's threshing floor. A large area had been cleared and, in the quarries, huge stone blocks were being cut. Immense piles of cedar logs were stored nearby. As they surveyed the site, David said, 'Son, you know how desperately I wanted to build a house for the Lord my God, but he told me, "You cannot do it, because you have spilt so much blood in establishing the kingdom. My house must be a house of peace. It will be built by your son, and I will give him peace throughout his reign. He will be my son and I will be his father and his throne will be established over Israel for ever."'

David's eyes glistened with passion as he looked at his son. 'You understand? He has said he will be with you as your father. That is a rare and wonderful promise. May you have success and build this house according to the design God gave me years ago.

'Just one thing – don't ever let building the temple be a substitute for being totally committed to the Lord. Keep him in the centre of your heart. Always love him. And don't be afraid: you will have all you need. During my reign, I have gathered much gold for this purpose, 100,000 talents in all.' The sum was gigantic (3750 tonnes, worth something like £85 billion pounds today, or $120 billion dollars). Solomon looked at him. He had heard rumours about an enormous sum set apart for the temple, but never knew it was so much. 'Keep this to yourself, my son. There will be many who would like to spend it in other ways. But I have set it aside for the temple of my God.'

Solomon looked again at the site and began to realise just how magnificent the temple could be. He would take his father's dream and make it his own. This temple would be one of the wonders of the world, worthy indeed of the great God of Israel, the God of his father.

After Adonijah's abortive coup, David gathered together all the leadership of Israel with the priests and their assistants, the Levites. Before them, he once again charged Solomon with building the temple. He commanded them to be loyal to Solomon and serve him so the temple would be built. 'I have already provided gold sufficient to build the temple and to cover its interior in gold. But there is still much to be done. I am now donating my personal treasures of gold and silver, 110 tonnes of gold.' The leaders themselves pledged another 190 tonnes (together worth about £7 billion, or $9.5 billion dollars). The people were amazed at this level of generosity, overwhelmed with gratitude that God had given so much to them and astounded they could give so much to the building of a house for him, providing for worship throughout centuries to come.

After David's death and burial, Solomon threw himself into the work and construction began in earnest. The huge blocks of stone that had already been carved were dragged to the site and put in place. Because this was to be a place of peace, all carving was done in the quarries. Only wooden mallets, levers, pulleys and ropes were to be used in bringing the parts of the temple to their places. All three main sections – the porch, the holy place and the holy of holies – were panelled in cedar carved with intricate designs of palm trees and chains. Pine planks formed the floor. But everything, including the floor, ceiling beams and doors, was overlaid with gold. Inside the holy of holies two enormous carved angelic beings covered in gold had wings that stretched from one wall to another and touched in the centre. The incense altars and ten huge lamp stands were all made of gold. When the lamps were lit the interior scintillated, the gold reflecting the light back and forwards, irradiating everything with a constantly moving golden glow. Even the great altar in the courtyard outside was made of solid bronze, as was the large pool for the washing of the priests.

Finally, all was completed. The day was set. Excitement in Jerusalem and the countryside was at fever pitch. Hundreds of thousands came. For the first time people understood the true extent of David's enormous achievements, seeing the obvious evidence that he had made Israel one of the most prosperous nations on earth. Finally, a great procession led by Solomon carried the ark of God to its new home, stopping every few feet to sacrifice to the Lord – because this was a holy journey. Only 600 yards, but it signified so much. The ark of the covenant of the God of the whole earth was coming home, to the heart of the City of Peace. That was the dream. For one brief, shining moment that dream was to be fulfilled.

Solomon thought back to his visit to the tent of meeting at Gibeon. Deeply mindful of his father's urging that he should be fervent in love towards the Lord, he offered a thousand cattle in burnt offering on the great bronze altar that Uri, son of Hur, had made for Israel in the wilderness. That night he had a dream unlike any he had ever had. God appeared and asked him, 'What would you like me to give you?' On that night his heart had been as generous as his father's.

'The nation you've given me to govern is more numerous than anybody could count, and the task is bigger than I could possibly accomplish. Therefore, please give me discernment, so I may lead this people wisely.'

Incredibly, God smiled with delight, and said, 'You've asked for wisdom, not for the lives of your enemies or for riches. Therefore you will have riches and honour such as no king ever had before or ever will have again. I will grant you what you've asked and more.' He was reminded of that dream right now as he looked at uncountable thousands before him, as far as the eye could see. Still he felt inadequate. Alongside his mighty father, how could he possibly compare?

At last the ark was placed in the holy of holies. The musicians began to sing and the temple was filled with a cloud so dense that the priests could not continue with their service. Solomon prayed a prayer of dedication, committing himself and the people to walk in relationship with God; to return to him whenever they sinned. Then the glory of the Lord came, and everyone knew God had come to his temple.

Solomon knew David's dream was realised. For the first time he felt like a worthy descendant of an awesome father. The ark of God was in its holy temple. The presence of God now rested upon the ark. Israel had moved into a new time of covenant with her God. It was the dawn of a new age.

THE GOLDEN AGE

So, for a glorious moment in the vast sweep of human history, there really was a Golden Age. A wise and compassionate king ruled over a peaceful people in a nation where spiritual values formed the very foundation of national life. Affluence grew as the nation prospered through trade. Yet, as always with our flawed race, the problem was the people themselves. The king began to believe his own publicity. He lost contact with the God who had promised him unparalleled wisdom. He lost sight of his God-given purpose. He began to believe it was all about him. His voracious sexual appetite led him astray. He lost his spiritual footing. For the sake of his wives, he participated in the worship of cruel gods whom he once despised, gods who demanded human sacrifice in their rituals – even babies. We become what we worship. So this formerly compassionate king became cruel and vindictive.

In all this God was grieved. But he was also training his people to understand that even a perfect environment will not produce perfect people. The problem is not, in the end, our social setting. The problem is in ourselves. Solomon forgot that the gifts he had received were given to enable him to fulfil his purpose. The major calling was to develop a passionate relationship with God. And in that he fell way behind the example of his father. In the end, Solomon lost his way. He forgot that destiny was not a position, but a pathway.

It is not only your destiny to *be* something but also to *become* something greater even further down the track. You have a destiny. I have a destiny. God has dreamed it and called us to it. It is bigger than our career, our families or any other achievement that we might value or strive for. Our destiny begins here in time and ends in eternity. It begins on planet Earth but it expands into the ultimate purpose for which the maker of the entire creation made us.

At the end of it all, there is no quest bigger than the quest that takes us into the heart of the creator: to know the love of the Father, to walk in the generous brotherhood of the Son and to be filled continuously with the all-pervading breath of heaven. All this is a dream far, far bigger than anything we could accomplish in this world. The aim of God's strategy for human beings has always been to draw us into closer relationship. That is why Jesus, in the promises he gave his disciples, gave them a **purpose** to fulfil, sending them out into all the world to proclaim his good news – good news of forgiveness, healing and liberation. But it was not just a message to be proclaimed, it was a lifestyle to be shared, communicated through the process of discipleship. In walking with Jesus as their rabbi, the disciples were invited to learn how he worked, the way he constantly received power to go on. And that was the second part of his legacy to them – the *power* to go on. In that moment after the resurrection when he stood before them and blew on them, then said, 'Receive the holy breath,' he was prophetically encouraging them to be ready for the day when God would send the wind of heaven. He would pour into them the breath of his life, so that they would receive a new kind of dynamic, something to sustain them not just for a few days or weeks but for all the years to come, right to the end of their lives.

The third bequest Jesus made to the disciples was the promise of his **presence**. Having set them a purpose to fulfil and made available to them power to go on, he now told them that he would be with them, to the ends of the earth and to the end of time. There it is again – the same quest – God drawing us deeper into relationship with himself.

THE HEAVENLY INTERSTATE

So destiny is not a place or a position, but a pathway – and because it is drawing us into the heart of God, it goes beyond survival, stability or success, beyond any measure of significance we can achieve in this world. In this, as in everything else, Jesus is our model. Almost every time he spoke about himself, he referred to the 'Son of Man'. To us that seems enigmatic, even strange. But to Jews, both his disciples and his enemies, it was highly significant. He was proclaiming himself to be **the** representative human being, the ultimate illustration of what God had in mind when he first said, 'Let us make man in our image.' He is the 'demonstration model' of humanity, and as such he shows us the fullness of the way God deals with us. There were numerous prophecies about his ancestry, the place and the manner of his birth, the places where he would live, his entering into Jerusalem, his death and his resurrection. If you look at all those prophecies, you could say his destiny was mapped out before him, and it was – but it never precluded his choice, his freedom to say yes or no. The marvellous thing about him is that at each point he said yes to the purposes of God and no to his own fear, comfort or personal pleasure. It was his destiny to make the choice, and each time he made the right choice it put him on the pathway to another choice.

Too many people have the wrong idea about destiny. They think it's like a railway track – once you get on it, you can't get off. Actually it's much more like a highway, with many turnings and sometimes confusing direction signs, and at each junction you have a choice. God has arranged it like that so we will walk in relationship with him through every part of the journey. Every major choice you face is a choice God has destined you to face. The reason is simple – it is in our confusion that we begin to ask the question, 'What should I be doing?' We are nearer to God in those moments than at almost any other time. The need for his wisdom opens us up to him. If Jesus is the representative human being, and he had a clear pathway prophesied for his life, then that implies God has a pathway for our lives too. Ours is not written down in the Bible, but it is written in heaven. If God wrote it before we were born, then it stands. We can of course screw it up – and we do. The only person who can recover it when that happens is the one who screwed it up – that's you or me. The scary thing is that we can't avoid the issue. Even 'avoiding it' is making a choice. So we return to the theme of this book: Intentional Living. If we are faced with choices that have eternal consequences, we had better start making those choices as if we **mean** to do so. Not choosing is a choice – but a stupid one.

In Chapter 4, we looked at the power of The Big Story. In our

Judeo-Christian tradition, the author of that story is an active God who plans for each of us a good destiny. He invites us to participate in a plan that he has already prepared. The fiery young prophet Jeremiah heard this from God: 'I know what I'm doing. I have it all planned out – plans to take care of you, not abandon you, plans to give you the future you hope for' (Jeremiah 29:11, *The Message*). Because God is relational, his plans always involve relationship with him. They are not inevitable. He puts plans before us and asks for our active, enthusiastic participation. The problem is that in our consumerist, mechanised and computerised society we have become used to being passive. We are passengers. We talk about flying the Atlantic, but of course we are not flying at all. The plane is doing the flying, somebody else is flying the plane, and we are just sitting there, hopefully resting peacefully. Some, of course, spend the entire journey panicking, under the illusion that by their worrying they are contributing to the process! When we commute we often go by train – again, we are passengers. And even if driving on a commute involves us in some minimal level of physical activity, the real work is actually being done by the engine!

TRUSTING – EVEN IN THE DARK

Walking with God involves active participation, step by step. Staying on his pathway involves effort, and commitment to reaching the finishing line. The energy must come from inside us. That is why we need the energy that only Jesus can give. The power of his Holy Spirit is poured into us, on the basis that he paid for it, we need it, it's free – but it requires our active reception and use of its power. God puts his plan before us, knowing it will stretch us beyond our abilities. He plans that, needing resources greater than we possess, we will come to him to receive the energy of his Spirit. Each time we do that we recreate a vital connection with him that is, at the end of the day, what we were created for and which waits for us in eternity. He is building us up in relationship, teaching us how to know him, how to draw on him. He is encouraging us into intimacy with him. In every situation and circumstance, he waits for us to discover that things actually work better when we walk with him, drawing on his power, allowing him to be sovereign. We really do have a choice. We can go with the flow of God's plan. When we do we will discover, time after time, that God's plans are always better.

My friend John applied for a job with a Christian organisation for which he seemed to be perfectly suited. Nobody looking at qualifications on paper would have chosen any other candidate. His professional experience fitted exactly. When the advertisement appeared, he had prayed passionately and become certain this job was for him. He even disregarded another opening when it came, because he and his wife were convinced this job was God's provision. Another man, inferior in experience and less qualified, was appointed to the post he had rejected. Still he trusted God. Then he discovered he had not even been invited for interview to the 'ideal' job. He was completely thrown. He asked God, 'What are you playing at? Why are you messing around with my life like this? Don't you know that we were sure this was your guidance that I should apply for this job?' He received no answer other than the quiet whisper, 'Trust me.' This was not much help! He became angry, and for the first time in his Christian discipleship, mistrusted God's love. I asked, 'John, has God been faithful to you in the past?' He agreed he had. 'Has his guidance before this been helpful, healthy and good for your family?' Again, he agreed that it had. Then I said, 'Now you're in the dark, you don't understand and God is saying, "Will you trust me even though you don't understand, because I am trustworthy? And you know I have never let you down in the past?"'

John looked at me. 'I understand. Yes, I will trust him even though I'm in the dark.' He came away from that conversation a different man, with a different perspective. A few days later, he learnt that a colleague who had been so impossible to work with that John had moved jobs, was himself moving. If John had been given the job for which he had applied, his nightmare colleague would have become his new boss. God really did know what he was doing!

That is a perfect illustration of the choice God asks us to make – to trust him when we are confused, and even more, to obey him when we do not understand.

GOD'S GUIDANCE SYSTEM

God's guidance of the Israeli people took them into Egypt to save their lives in the middle of a famine. It brought them out of Egypt 400 years later when they had become slaves. Forty years after that it took them into the land God had promised them. Approximately 300 years later Solomon became king and built the temple. Through all that period the people were relying on the promise that they would live in the land God had shown to Abraham and there they would experience freedom, peace and plenty. It all seemed very simple when Joshua first brought them across the Jordan and into the land they had been promised. God's promise to him laid down the conditions of service: 'Obey the law I gave to Moses and do not deviate from my instructions. Speak out the words of scripture and make sure you do all I command – you will be successful everywhere you go, prosperous and successful.'

First, the dream was, 'When we get into the promised land, everything will be all right.' Then the dream became, 'When we get a king, everything will be all right.' Then it was, 'When we get a temple, everything will be great.'

Throughout those hundreds of years God was training his people to understand that although a good environment is better than a bad environment, it will not automatically breed good people. He also wanted them to grasp that although it's good to have his words written in a book, even intimate knowledge of those words will not guarantee good human behaviour or spiritual life. After the death of Solomon, the kingdom fell into discord and disunity. Israel was divided into two kingdoms – Judah and Israel. In the ensuing chaos, prophets arose, calling God's people to something more effective and fundamental than anything a simple change of circumstances or ever tighter and tighter religious restrictions could achieve.

So, as Jeremiah wrote: '[God says,] "This is the brand-new covenant that I will make with Israel when the time comes. I will put my law within them – write it on their hearts! – and be their God. And they will be my people. They will no longer go around setting up schools to teach each other about God. They'll know me firsthand, the dull and the bright, the smart and the slow. I'll wipe the slate clean for each of them. I'll forget they ever sinned!" ' (Jeremiah 31:33–34, *The Message*). Even later, when Israel had been dispersed and Judah taken into captivity in modern-day Iraq, the mighty prophet Ezekiel rose up to say, '[The Lord says,] "I'll give you a new heart, put a new spirit in you. I'll remove the stone heart from your body and replace it with a heart that's God-willed, not self-willed. I'll put my Spirit in you and make it possible for you to do what I tell you and live by my commands"' (Ezekiel 36:26–27, *The Message*). The prophets were indicating that something new was required – a new internal dynamic. The finest religion in the world was simply not enough to change the hearts of human beings.

That is as true now as it was then. If God's dream for you or me is to be fulfilled, there must be the kind of change that can come about only when the power of God's own purpose is inside us. The astonishing thing about God is that he never gives up on us. One way or another he will ensure that his purposes triumph in the end.

DON'T GIVE UP ON YOUR DESTINY

As the nation of Judah fell increasingly into spiritual decline, God sent one of his greatest messengers ever. Isaiah was a magnificent poet, and a composer of symphonies in prose. Through the reigns of four different kings, he brought God's message to the people. He always held their failures in tension with God's power and purpose. Late in his life he spoke about the inevitability of rain, snow and eventual harvest. Speaking for God, he said, '. . . so is my word that goes out from my mouth: It will not return to me empty, but will accomplish what I desire and achieve the purpose for which I sent it' (Isaiah 55:10–11, NIV).

If God wrote a destiny for you before you were born, then he has not rescinded that. He will keep it in his heart; hold it in his heavenly memory bank. He will never let go of that dream, because he will never stop loving you. It is possible for you to reject the dream, or to screw it up. No one else can do that. But you can if you choose to. However, and here is the amazing thing about God, the moment we give him a chance to rewrite that dream so as to incorporate our screw-ups, our mistakes, even our rebellions, he is able to do that, and he will. That is his glory. But he will not intervene until you ask him to. He will not invade your space. He will not involve himself in relationship with you unless you open the door to him and say, 'I need to talk.' I'm aware that many of us have screwed up spectacularly in the past, and we may feel we're disqualified from discovering God's redrawn dream. But we should never give up on it. Because he won't.

What about your dream? Perhaps you have already bought into the lie that says, 'People like me never get to do things like that.' Are you allowing circumstances, your background, a difficult upbringing or lack of education to hold you back? Maybe a marriage breakdown, personal weakness or previous financial failure has left you feeling paralysed? You still have the power to choose. The best first choice to make is to reconnect with your creator, to acknowledge, 'I'm in the wrong place, and it was my choices that got me here. But I don't want my own stupidity to be the epitaph for my life. God, forgive me, and give me grace to start again and this time to walk close to you.'

No one can take that choice from you. We all have a wounded and defiled history. The only thing we can do with that is give it to the God who is outside time and Lord of history. Once we give our history to him, he can start to work on it, like a master craftsman remaking what is broken, carefully reshaping it into something of beauty, as seems best to him. As we do that, we begin to reign over our lives, instead of letting our lives rule us.

It is vital that you understand that your destiny runs clear from here into the glory of eternity, and it is never too late to get back on that pathway. Maybe you will have to begin the journey with more burdens than you would have had. But God is so good. He has a way of dealing with the burdens and making them light. It really is worth getting back on track. Remember, too, you have an enemy. His principal strategic aim is to bring you to a place of despair so that you lose all hope. He brings up lots of evidence to suggest that we are pretty useless. It is such a temptation to give up.

One of my great heroes is Winston Churchill. He was invited to speak at his alma mater, Harrow School, on 29 October 1941. It was one of the darkest moments of the Second World War. Here is part of what he said: 'This is the lesson: never give in, never give in, never, never, never, never – in nothing, great or small, large or petty – never give in except to convictions of honour and good sense. Never yield to force; never yield to the apparently overwhelming might of the enemy.' I like that. Remember: the might of the enemy is never overwhelming until you allow yourself to be overwhelmed.

Never give in – whatever has happened, you still have a destiny. It still extends before you, a bright and shining pathway, though it may seem beset by darkness, danger and difficulty. It stretches from here to eternity. No one and nothing can take that away from you. Right now you can ask: What matters most to God? What are his dreams? What steps should I take to recover what I've lost? How will I see those dreams fulfilled? However, you can settle for a smaller dream, a sub-standard destiny. Here – slightly updated – is the story Jesus told of one such man:

EAT, DRINK AND BE MERRY!

A wealthy landowner had invested wisely and was growing more crops than he could deal with. His factories, processing the food, were at full stretch and his storage facilities were packed out. He pulled in his accountant, his director of operations, the production engineer and a leading industrial architect. They made magnificent plans for an entirely new plant and storage facilities that would ensure them complete dominance of the market for years to come. It was a long meeting, but a productive one. To celebrate, he finished the day by treating them to an excellent dinner.

After they had gone, he sat by the fire, poured himself a large whisky and said to himself, 'George, you've done well, better than anybody ever expected you to, and you've done it all yourself. You don't owe anybody anything and after today you've got it made for years to come. It's time to sit back and enjoy yourself. You've been working all these years towards this moment. So, tomorrow, book yourself a state room on a world cruise. But, before that, make sure you do a tour of the French vineyards, buy a good stock of the finest wine for the years to come.'

But while he was talking to himself, congratulating himself on how smart he was, his creator was watching and listening, seeing something very different – a man without God, isolated from himself and others. God's response was very different: 'You idiot! This very night while you are asleep, death will come for you. Then who will get all that you have built up for yourself?' As this man takes his large tumbler of whisky to bed with him, dreaming about what else he can do for himself in the future, what he doesn't know is that tonight, a massive heart attack will kill him. Jesus said, 'That's the way it is for anyone whose focus is on storing up stuff for himself but is not rich in God.'

The landowner had forgotten that although all his land was free-hold, it was actually only leased from the creator. As the principal investor, the creator was calling him to account for his use of the resources that had been given to him.

That is a scary thought. If God is indeed God, then he is not just a major shareholder, he is the *only* shareholder, and surely he is entitled to look at the accounts and ask for a return on his investment. Jesus was making it clear that unless we bear his interests in mind, we're stupid – truly, and maybe even terminally, stupid. The Bible says it is God who gives us the power to make wealth. Therefore, whether we acknowledge his presence or not, it is not only his resources we are using on planet Earth, but also the talents and abilities he gave us. He is entitled to ask us why we have used them in the way we have. Our prolific use of planet Earth's resources contributes to global warming and the destruction of so much that is beautiful. Consumerism has turned us into monsters engaged in devouring the delicately balanced network of resources that sustain us. What we are doing to the environment is mirrored by what we're doing to each other. The world is filled with need – the starving, the homeless, the oppressed and the abused are all on stage with us as part of the cast in God's vast production. But we ignore them, act as if they are not there. One day God will show them to us and ask whether we ever understood that the most precious resource on planet Earth was not gold, oil or uranium, but people.

In his promise to Joshua, God said that if we followed his way it would make us prosperous and successful. God's definition of success is very different from ours, because it includes a healthy balance of relationships, and emotional and spiritual health. Prosperity in God's terms is never just about money and possessions. It is always about the person you are becoming. The greatest truth is that it is never too late to grasp God's goodness and run with it, to begin to become the person God has called you to be. He still has a magnificent dream for us. It is the reason Jesus came, taught, died and rose again. And God's dream for us is the reason that Jesus, having risen from the dead, did not stay on planet Earth, but departed. The dream of God was that the victory of Jesus would be invested in us so that we would live lives of resurrection power, drawing on the same resource that made Jesus so irresistible. In taking himself out of the earth, out of this physical reality, Jesus was clearing the way for an even more powerful dynamic to be released in us, the power of his Holy Spirit.

PENTECOST

Jerusalem, 24 May AD 33

Early on in the ministry of Jesus, the men he later called apostles realised Jesus was the Messiah, the anointed one of God. He was their rabbi and their master. They loved him, not just because he was an amazing man, but because he first loved them, and gave them a value they had never had before. They began to see themselves through his eyes. They began to change, to believe that they, though very ordinary men, could yet be people of significance. Then, as the evidence of his miracles mounted before their eyes, some of them quite extraordinary, they found themselves grappling with the question of his identity. He called himself the Son of Man – the man who shows what human beings are meant to be.

When they gathered together, they discussed it. As so often, it was Simon Peter who first said what some of them were thinking. Jesus asked, 'What are people saying about the Son of Man? Who do they think he is?'

They replied, 'Some say John the Baptist or Elijah come back from the dead, Jeremiah or one of the other prophets.'

He looked at them. 'And you? What about you? Who do you say I am?' There was a moment of silence. No one knew quite how to say what they were thinking.

So Simon Peter blurted it out: 'You're the Christ! You're the Messiah, the Son of the living God.'

There was a smile in his eyes and an infectious joy as Jesus responded, 'God bless you, Simon, son of Jonah! You didn't get that answer out of books or from teachers. My Father in heaven, God himself, let you in on this secret of who I really am. And now I'm going to tell you who you are, *really* are. You are Peter, a rock. This is the rock on which I will put together my church, a church so expansive with energy that not even the gates of hell will be able to keep it out. And that's not all. You will have complete and free access to God's kingdom, keys to open any and every door: no more barriers between heaven and earth, earth and heaven. A yes on earth is yes in heaven. A no on earth is no in heaven' (Matthew 16:17–19, *The Message*).

Then, knowing how much they would want to tell everybody what they had just heard, he swore them to secrecy. They kept those words with them all through the dark days leading up to the darkest day of all – the Friday of his death, Passover, AD 33. Those words must have haunted Peter as he wept in a dark corner of Jerusalem's streets. When Jesus reappeared after the resurrection, those words came back, no longer to haunt him but to be celebrated and savoured. Then after his ascension, they went back to Jerusalem to do what many of them found so difficult, perhaps especially Simon Peter – to wait.

Pentecost was the feast of harvest and the day of the first fruits. On that day devout Israelites expressed gratitude for the harvest and thanks to God for his deliverance. Many used it as a celebration of the giving of the law at Sinai. So it was a really significant festival. Jesus' followers had gathered early in the morning, men and women praying and praising as usual. At the third hour of the day, nine o'clock in the morning, they started to hear a noise. It sounded as if a gale was blowing through the place. But the curtains weren't moving and people's clothes remained still; the flames of the lamps did not flicker. But the sound of a wind increased. As Simon looked at the group, their faces were different and it seemed to him that dancing over each of their heads was a single tongue of flame – 120 men and women on fire.

They began to feel fuller and fuller. The image that came to Simon was a wineskin filled with grape juice fermented to the point of bursting. The pressure built inside them all until none of them knew how to relieve it except by opening their mouths. Once they began to speak, each one realised the language they were using was not Aramaic, Hebrew, Greek or Latin, but something they had never heard before. It flowed out of them like a river. As they looked around the room, they discovered that everybody else was doing the same. It went on for hours. Nobody realised it could be heard outside. Then it was as if the pressure was building inside the room itself. A sense of God filling up everything and everybody became almost impossible to bear.

Somebody walked across to the doors that opened onto the balcony, just to get some air to release the sense of pressure. They walked back in and said, 'Simon, I think you'd better come and see this.' Nobody wanted to leave that room. But he walked out to see thousands of people jammed into the square below the balcony, all looking up. As the disciples crowded out onto the balcony, it turned out that what they were saying could be heard in the languages of all those in the square, people groups from all over the ancient world. Luke kindly listed a good number of them for us: people from Parthia, Persia, Elam, Mesopotamia, Cappadocia, Pontus and Asia, Romans, Arabs, Greeks and Cretans could all understand.

I think it was at that moment that the solution to the quandary, the riddle that had been puzzling them, came. Now they understood how it was that Jesus had been what he was. He was Son of God; and he was an ordinary bloke. He had become an ordinary bloke so that he, as God, could show them what ordinary people were supposed to look like. But, as an ordinary man, he had become filled with the Spirit of God. Therefore when he did miracles it was God doing miracles, through him *as a man*. Simon understood: the Son of God had become the prototype God-filled man, in order to show them all what human beings were meant to be like. As he looked at the crowd, he wanted them all to understand. He remembered the first time Jesus ever met him, and said, 'You will be a fisher of men.' Now he realised why he had been picked, why those words had been spoken to him. It was for this moment.

He moved to the front of the balcony, opened his mouth, and scriptures came pouring into his mind as words flowed from his mouth in a way he had never known before. With every word he spoke, he could see the power of God hitting the people in front of him. While he was speaking, is it possible he remembered the charcoal fire and Jesus saying, 'Do you love me?' Was he responding,

'Lord, you know the truth; I love you with all my heart'? As he continued to explain who Jesus was and what he had done, people began to shout from the crowd: 'What are we going to do?' They were desperate. Simon could see it and he knew exactly what to say: 'Repent, be baptised in the name of Jesus Christ for the cleansing of your sins, and you will receive the Holy Spirit.' At last, he understood that he, having received forgiveness of his own sins, could promise that same forgiveness to others and, having received the gift of the Holy Spirit, could guarantee that others would also receive the same gift. *Now* he understood why Jesus had said he had come to build 'a church so expansive with energy that not even the gates of hell would be able to keep it out'.

From that balcony in Jerusalem until today, the same Holy Spirit has been poured out on ordinary human beings. Because the real bearers of the Church's power are not necessarily those wearing the robes of ministers, bishops, cardinals or whatever, but the people who have discovered that God's power can be joined to their human spirits, so they become something completely inexplicable, different and radiant. These are the people who have discovered their God-ordained destiny. They don't always get it right. In fact, they are perhaps more conscious than anybody else of so often getting it wrong. Yet God makes available to them a power that will keep them going all the way through their lives until they reach the very end, and then through the doorway of death into the bright shining land of the eternal. After all, if you *Live Like You Mean It*, then dying as you are intended makes the best possible sense.

But, however attractive and glorious that prospect is, not one of them wants to get there sooner than God calls them, because they are acutely, wonderfully aware that they have a destiny to fulfil here on earth. And those who have fallen in love with this man Jesus, much as they long to see him, do not want to rush into his presence with their task incomplete. They would much rather wait until they can see the smile on his face as he says to them, 'Well done, good and faithful servant. Now enter into the joy of your Lord.'

What a prospect!

Afterword

The speeches of Martin Luther King were always personal and powerful. His last speech, he was shot by James Earl Ray the following day, concluded with this poignant passage:

'Well, I don't know what will happen now. We've got some difficult days ahead. But it doesn't matter with me now. Because I've been to the mountaintop. And I don't mind. Like anybody, I would like to live a long life. Longevity has its place. But I'm not concerned about that now. I just want to do God's will. And he's allowed me to go up to the mountain. And I've looked over. And I've seen the promised land. I may not get there with you. But I want you to know tonight, that we, as a people will get to the promised land. And I'm happy, tonight. I'm not worried about anything. I'm not fearing any man. Mine eyes have seen the glory of the coming of the Lord'

Martin Luther King, 3rd April 1968

Bibliography

Start from Who You Are
Viktor Frankl *Man's Search for Meaning* (1984 Washington Square
   Press)
Malcolm Muggeridge *Chronicles of a Wasted Time* (Regent College
   Publishing 2006)

Being a Human among Humans
C. S. Lewis *The Four Loves* (HarperCollins Publishers Ltd; New
   edition 2002)

Live in Balance with the Rhythm of Life
C. S. Lewis *Surprised by Joy* (HarperCollins Publishers Ltd; New
   edition 1998)

Be an Obedient (Hard-Working) Servant
Andrew Marvell *An Horatian Ode Upon Cromwell's Return From
   Ireland*
(A Miscellaneous Poems 1681)
Carl Beech *The Twelve Codes* (copyright Carl Beech CVM used
   with permission)

Follow Your Vision
Stephen Covey *Seven Habits of Highly Effective People* (Free Press;
   Revised edition 2004)
L. P. Hartley *The Go-Between* (Penguin Classics; New edition
   2004)

Beyond Success to Significance
Steve Turner *History Lesson* (*Tonight we will fake love* ,Charisma
   Books, London in 1974)

Prepare for Your Departure
Michele Guinness *The Genius of Guinness* (Ambassador
   Publications 2005)

Acknowledgements

It would simply be impossible to list all those friends and colleagues whose advice, help and companionship has meant so much to me through the years. I have learnt from all of them and freely acknowledge that they may well spot themselves or ideas they have passed to me in these pages. No plagiarism is intended. It's just that what they have imparted to me has literally become part of me. I must acknowledge the invaluable aid I received from Nick Page's brilliant book about the last days of Jesus, *The Longest Week*. All mistakes and bloopers are of course mine and mine alone.

I am indebted to the people of St Lawrence, Kirkdale who taught me so much in the early 1990s. Since then, the people of St Luke's, Maidstone have trusted me to lead them through almost 15 years. It has been an enormous privilege and I am deeply grateful for their continuing loyalty and love, and their tolerance during the period of writing this book. Special thanks to the leaders who picked up so much of the slack – bless you.

I owe so much to the members of the Hippos for their fellowship and even more to the Rhinos for long years of covenant friendship.

Finally, the family; there is the priceless love and support of our children and grandchildren always encouraging and terrific fun.

And above all, my thanks to Pat, who has loved me and put up with me for nearly half a century. Endurance of that kind is very definitely beyond the call of duty!

Most of all, heartfelt gratitude to the three-in-one God; the Father who loves us, the Son who died for us and the Holy Spirit who transforms us.